CHARLES PÉGUY

The Decline of an Idealist

CHARLES PÉGUY

———◦∞◦———

The Decline of an Idealist

by
HANS A. SCHMITT

Louisiana State University Press

Library of Congress Catalog Card Number: 67–13894
Manufactured in the United States of America by
American Book–Stratford Press, Inc.
Designed by Jules B. McKee

To Florence

Preface

THE following pages reflect a good many years of reading and thinking about Charles Péguy. These have left the writer with the conclusion that the innumerable memoirs, biographies, and monographs on Péguy have been little more than variations on the same theme. The image of Péguy as a "study in integrity," to put it more explicitly, has been drawn and retouched continually, most recently in a very readable book by Marjorie Villiers, the first full-length biography in English.[1] Whether socialist or clerical, internationalist or chauvinist, Péguy has invariably emerged in all postures as morally flawless. His many chroniclers, almost without exception,[2] have begun by talking of a man and concluded by describing a saint.

There seemed to be room for a more critical assessment to which the following pages, it is hoped, will make a contribution. They offer no biography, for that task has been admirably discharged in French by Bernard Guyon[3] and in English by Mrs. Villiers. They provide the essential biographical information in

[1] *Charles Péguy: A Study in Integrity* (New York, 1965).

[2] René Johannet, *Vie et mort de Péguy* (Paris, 1950), questioned the disinterestedness of Péguy's philo-semitism, but without adducing any evidence that the editor of the *Cahiers de la Quinzaine* befriended Jews to obtain funds for his publication.

[3] *Péguy, l'homme et l'oeuvre* (Paris, 1960).

an introductory chapter and then proceed to trace what this writer believes to be a disturbing, but neglected process of moral decline. Subsequent chapters pursue this theme on the basis of Péguy's own texts, beginning with the dramatic trilogy *Jeanne d'Arc,* published in 1897 at the author's expense, and terminating with his last polemic on behalf of the philosopher Henri Bergson in 1914. Much of the trilogy may be negligible as literature, but it is essential to an understanding of Péguy's development. Thus, this early work, the seed from which the noble blooms and vicious weeds of later years emerged, has been emphasized.

The author owes a great debt to his teacher, S. William Halperin of the University of Chicago, in whose classroom he discovered Péguy. He salutes three reference librarians who aided in the pursuit and location of Péguyana: Miss Catherine Hall of the University of Chicago, Miss Opal Carr at the University of Oklahoma, and Mrs. Dorothy Whittemore at Tulane University. Mrs. Reba Herman typed the manuscript, and pretended to enjoy the chore.

My wife Florence Brandow Schmitt deserves credit for whatever literary merit may reside in these pages. She has more than deserved the dedication. All errors and conclusions which the reader may find in this volume are the writer's own.

New Orleans, 1966   H.A.S.

Contents

CHARLES PÉGUY

The Decline of an Idealist

I

$\mathcal{C}$he Preparation of a Hero

CHARLES-PIERRE PÉGUY was born at Orléans on January 7, 1873, the only son of only children. His father Désiré, in turn the offspring of small vintners and farmers, had been considered too sickly to till the soil, and followed the trade of a cabinetmaker until the Franco-Prussian War. The winter campaign of 1870–71 broke his health and forced him to become a *petit fonctionnaire* in the customs service. He survived the birth of his son by less than a year and died on November 18, 1873. Cécile Quère, the mother, seems to have been an illegitimate child. When she was only nine, her mother took her from Genetiennes-en-Bourbonnais, where she had been born in 1846, to Orléans; just why, no one remembers. Following the death of her husband, she vowed never to marry again and to devote her life to the rearing of her boy.

Two hardy and resourceful women brought up Charles: the young widow who provided income by mending chairs and the grandmother who kept house, dressed, fed, and disciplined the boy "whenever it was necessary." [1] Her grandson remembered her as a sociable rather than a devout churchgoer who loved of a

[1] Charles Péguy, "Pierre, commencement d'une vie bourgeoise," *Cahiers de la Quinzaine*, XXI, No. 7 (1931), 36–37. The magazine will hereinafter be cited as *Cahiers;* the author will be Péguy unless otherwise indicated.

Sunday to greet friends passing along the street, witness the doings of the socially prominent, and pick up a quick piece of gossip at the church door—in short, one who enjoyed to the fullest all those opportunities provided by a visit to the spiritual and social center of the community. Péguy spoke of his grandmother with affection and looked upon her with gratitude. Though she could neither read nor write, a fact he mentioned almost proudly, he credited her skill as a story teller with awakening his interest in history. For "the best historian is . . . he who loves a good story." [2] Of his mother Charles saw little enough. She "never, never once went for a walk with [her] son." When she had a few moments of leisure at home, she would read to him over and over again the few letters his father had written her during the war.[3]

It was a small and frugal household—poor, to be sure, but apparently not in need; simple, but not primitive; a bit dreary perhaps, but not without the hope that Désiré's son would one day justify every sacrifice by amounting to something. The future rested on the boy's shoulders, and in later years Péguy at times looked back upon his austere childhood with considerable bitterness. Only rarely did this resentment break out into print, for instance, when he wrote "that the people who raised me always did so for themselves," [4] or when he pondered parental selfishness as the cause of many divided families and singled out mothers as the worst offenders. A conversation in 1891 with a friend of his adolescence revealed the depth of these unhappy recollections. To his two mothers, he claimed, affection had been a sign of weakness and a waste of time. Friends he had had none. He was forbidden to play in the streets because he might have torn his clothes. As soon as he was strong enough, he was put to delivering chairs to his mother's customers or helping her flatten

[2] "Pour Moi," *Cahiers,* II, No. 5 (1900), 2; "Victor-Marie, Comte Hugo," *Cahiers,* XII, No. 1 (1910), 19.

[3] Daniel Halévy, *Péguy and the Cahiers de la Quinzaine* (New York, 1947), 4; Villiers, *Charles Péguy: A Study in Integrity,* 22.

[4] "Résponse brève à Jaurès," *Cahiers,* I, No. 11 (1900), 58.

with a small hammer the willow reeds she used as mending material.[5] The grey succession of work days was rarely brightened by diversion. The annual fair of the parish and an occasional hour purloined to watch a procession were the boy's only holidays. Then he might be seen walking among the stalls and the merry-go-rounds observing the gaiety of others. "There could be no question of tasting a sweet or climbing on a wooden horse. To be truthful, he did not even mind doing without; the mother's iron discipline had killed all desire." [6]

School was Charles-Pierre's first release. In 1880 he entered the training school attached to the École Normale of his department, only a few steps away from his home. Now his Spartan upbringing, which, it must be granted, was the fruit of necessity rather than caprice, was vindicated. His teachers marveled at the precocious and ambitious pupil. One lesson he had learned early and well: in a life devoid of laughter and ease one found happiness at work, if one found it at all.

Péguy's zeal won him friends who counted. His teachers were eager to help him. The parish priest is said to have offered to find him a place in a seminary. A neighbor lent him books, mostly histories, which no ordinary child of that age could have begun to comprehend but which Péguy read rapidly and with evident pleasure. At school he won prize after prize. "A model student," one instructor wrote on his report card. "May he continue," commented another when he was promoted in October, 1884, to a secondary school for the children of humbler citizens, the École Professionelle.[7]

---

[5] "Un nouveau théologien, M. Fernand Laudet," *Cahiers*, XIII, No. 2 (1911), 141. These and other references to Péguy's reflections on his own past are made in full consciousness that his recollections were not invariably accurate. It will become apparent that Péguy wrote a great deal about himself, not always consistently, nor accurately. Cf. Hans A. Schmitt, "Charles Péguy: Autobiographer," *Renascence*, VIII (1956), 69–77.

[6] Henri Roy, "Péguy que j'ai connu," *Amitié Charles Péguy, Feuillets Mensuels*, No. 17 (1950), 8–9. This publication will hereinafter be cited *ACPFM*.

[7] Halévy, *Péguy and the Cahiers de la Quinzaine*, 5–8; Gustave Fautras, "L'Enfance de Péguy," *Reforme Sociale*, LXX (1915), 385.

The year 1885 brought a greater reward for Charles Péguy when Théodore Naudy, the director of the Orléans Lycée, heard of the "model student" and helped him to a municipal scholarship at his institution. Péguy entered his new surroundings a year behind his fellows but soon caught up with and surpassed them, acquiring the reputation of a scholastic genius-in-residence as he did so.[8] When André Bourgeois, later Péguy's lifelong associate at the *Cahiers de la Quinzaine,* entered the Lycée in 1886, a small, poorly dressed boy with a big head, close-cropped hair, and a wart on the ridge of his left nostril was pointed out to him: "That is Péguy . . . the first in the fifth form." [9] Another *condisciple,* two years younger, recalled in his old age that the widow's son from Orléans' Faubourg Bourgogne had enjoyed at the lycée and in town "a great, an almost legendary reputation."[10]

As he quickly climbed the ladder of learning, Péguy's position in the matriarchal household seems to have changed. Now he had time to himself. He went out sketching and painting. More important, he sought and found a substitute for the father he had never known. The blacksmith Boitier, who had regaled him with tales of the Franco-Prussian War when he was a child, became the object of frequent visits. Instead of reliving with him past military exploits, Boitier awakened Péguy to the impending battles for a new society. Around them the socialist movement had recovered from the stunned paralysis that followed the defeat of the Paris Commune. Syndicalism and Marxism had furtively rebuilt the shattered cause. After the general amnesty accorded the survivors of the uprising of 1871 in 1880, socialism became legitimate once more, and with freedom came a period of expansion, experimentation, and unbridled factionalism. Every major socialist conclave seemed to add another mansion

[8] Marcel Abraham, "Charles Péguy au Lycée," *Revue Hebdomadaire,* XX, No. 9 (1926), 8.

[9] Charles Péguy, "Lettres à André Bourgeois," *ACPFM,* No. 8 (1950), 3; Jérôme and Jean Tharaud, "Le souvenir d'André Bourgeois," *ACPFM,* No. 43 (1955), 20.

[10] Henri Boivin, "Le Péguy de notre jeune temps," *ACPFM,* No. 24 (1951), 31.

to the jerry-built house of the French labor movement. Boitier, who became Péguy's first guide to this region, seems to have entertained no clear-cut allegiance to a particular group. Personally he stood on the socio-economic divide between artisan and worker, closer to the guild than to the union, more at home with Victor Hugo than Karl Marx, looking for inspiration to Robespierre rather than Louis Blanc, and stressing solidarity of nation rather than class. This man very likely planted the seeds of Péguy's hybrid socialism which would never submit to any political discipline. In the modest *bibliothèque populaire* which Boitier maintained with a group of like-minded associates, Péguy found a spiritual haven. He still went to his catechism as before; but when his religious mentor, the Abbé Bardet, asked him to consider the priesthood, young Charles countered with a firm though courteous refusal.[11]

After Péguy received his baccalaureate degree on June 21, 1891, he entered the Lycée Lakanal at Sceaux on a state scholarship which paid half his expenses to prepare for the entrance examination at the École Normale Supérieure, the academy whose alumni constituted so significant a portion of the Third Republic's political elite in the twentieth century. As was his custom by now, he shone among his classmates and received the *prix d'excellence* at the end of the year. But when the list of the twenty-four who were to be admitted in 1892 was posted, Péguy's name was missing. Placing twenty-sixth, he was high among the alternates; but since vacancies rarely occurred, he faced another year of cramming. Contrary to the view purveyed by most of Péguy's biographers, who have dutifully copied each other, this was not the tragedy it has been made to appear. To take the examination after only one year of preparation was foolhardy, and the fact that he had come so close to success constituted an impressive performance. Péguy certainly did not lose his scholarship to Lakanal because of his academic performance. His grades were outstanding, and the school would have been happy to welcome him back. Persistent rumors that he lost

[11] Roger Secrétain, *Péguy, Soldat de la liberté* (New York, 1944), 57–66.

his grant as a result of disciplinary difficulties can at least not be traced to any evidence in the school's records.

Péguy, having gambled and lost, simply decided to do his military service rather than "waste" another year in school. Knowing the difficulties under which his mother labored in order to contribute half the cost of his education away from home, he undoubtedly felt compelled to don the uniform. Undaunted in his youthful optimism, he fully expected to continue scholastic preparations in his leisure hours at the *caserne,* thus satisfying two obligations at the same time.[12]

This gamble failed, too. In 1893 Péguy placed twenty-fifth in the examination, and the gates of the formidable establishment in the Rue d'Ulm remained closed to him. What happened next is neither very clear, nor necessarily very important. Again there was no question of disgrace. The young scholar merely had to resign himself to a second year at a preparatory school. In October, he followed his friend Henri Roy, later the Radical-Socialist senator from Orléans, to the Lycée Ste. Barbe in Paris, this time on an all-expense scholarship. Several persons, including Roy and Édouard Herriot, have taken credit for intervening in his behalf after he returned to civilian life, but the difficulties which they have described as part of the transaction do not seem to have existed, except in the imaginings of their old age. As early as July, 1893, it was apparently settled that Péguy would transfer from the suburban Lakanal and be made welcome by his new teachers.[13]

All of Péguy's chroniclers, among whom his classmates are well represented, have described Péguy's arrival at Ste. Barbe as a kind of triumphal entry, which is hard to understand when one considers that most of the students had never met him. He was somewhat their elder, a veteran and a serious student, which might account for his quickly becoming "incontestably the first" in the circle he frequented. At the outset he knew only Henri Roy, but in time his friends at Ste. Barbe included Jérôme

---

[12] Jules Isaac, *Expériences de ma vie, Vol. I: Péguy* (Paris, 1959), 37–68, 295–98, has supplemented his recollections with a thorough review of the relevant school records.
[13] *Ibid.,* 74–85.

Tharaud, the elder of the two writing brothers; Léon Deshairs, the art historian; Paul Acker, the novelist; the engineer Charles Lucas de Peslouän, later an important link between Péguy and Maurice Barrès; Louis Baillet who became a Benedictine monk and who was to play a crucial part in Péguy's religious life; and—finally—Marcel Baudouin, *ce* Baudouin *lunaire,* whose sister became Péguy's wife in 1897.[14]

The Péguy of those days has been represented by some as a cheerful, lighthearted fellow with an irrepressible sense of humor; by others as a mature, serious, and at times compelling personality; and by one dissenter as an insufferable prig who posted on the bulletin board of the dining room "his thoughts on the private conduct of his fellow-students."[15] If the first was true, then the year at Ste. Barbe stands isolated between past and future. Péguy, industrious, poor, and ambitious, twice thwarted in his attempt to gain admission to the École Normale, had no good reason for lightheartedness. On the other hand, he had not missed by much and he now had a year ahead in which to close that small gap between failure and success. Though he undoubtedly looked upon it as his last chance, it is perhaps fair to say, in retrospect, that in an austere and frustrated existence, the year at Ste. Barbe was more joyous and carefree than any he had known. A declared enemy of the more conventional forms of student dissipation, he was nevertheless capable of deserting his books to attend concerts and the theater. In the controversy between the disciples of Wagner and Berlioz, he loyally took the part of his countryman, though the music of both invariably put him to sleep. More profound discoveries awaited him on the stage. At the Théâtre Français he discovered Sophocles, who always remained to him the greatest master of the drama. This discovery led to one of Péguy's few journeys beyond the Paris-Orléans-Chartres triangle, a trip to Orange in the summer of 1894 to see and hear the great Mounet-Sully in a performance of *Oedipus Rex.*

This unique excursion capped a successful year. On the third

14 Jérôme and Jean Tharaud, *Notre cher Péguy* (Paris, 1926), I, 5–9.
15 Jean Luchaire, *Confessions d'un français moyen, 1876–1914* (Marseille, 1943), 85–86.

try, Péguy was admitted to the École Normale. The doors were at last ready to swing open. Before the eager *normalien* from Orléans lay the prospect of several years at the feet of the finest teachers of France spent in the company of the choicest minds of his generation. At the end of the course was the near-certainty of a distinguished academic or public career.

Entry into the École Normale coincided with another turning point in Péguy's stormy life. To the surprise of some of his friends and the disappointment of his sponsors, it became the beginning of a long and painful process of moral orientation, rather than the overture to a conventional career. Péguy had fallen under the spell of socialism, "a movement as important as the French Revolution or the Christian Revolution." [16] He opted for "all progressive forces" against "the forces of repression" of the "ruling *bourgeoisie gouvernementale*." [17] In this respect his case was common enough; his two roommates shared his political convictions, as did many of his generation throughout France. But Péguy felt that socialism demanded more than a vote for a particular slate of candidates on election day. To him a meaningful commitment to social justice involved fighting for principles that were a long way from conquering France. It meant dedication to a new life with values different from those current in the sphere for which he had been destined by his intellectual preparation. After a year of successful study, much of which passed in the company of his two illustrious roommates, Albert Mathiez and Paul Mantoux, Péguy suddenly requested and received a year's leave. He needed time to think and—for the first time—time to write.

During his leave Péguy began to work on a dramatic trilogy, *Jeanne d'Arc,* which had grown into an impressively bulky manuscript by the time he returned to school. He kept it in a large satchel under his bed, sternly labeled "do not touch." His days as a star pupil were past. His conscience barred further progress toward his anticipated career. In February, 1897, his

[16] Quoted in Albert Beguin, "De la Jeanne d'Arc de 1897 au Mystère de 1909," *ACPFM*, No. 53 (1956), 12–13.

[17] Charles Péguy, "Lettre à Collier," *ACPFM*, No. 10 (1950), 1–3.

first article appeared in the *Revue Socialiste*.[18] Four months later *Jeanne d'Arc* went to the printer, to appear in the fall at the author's expense.

In October, 1897, Péguy married Charlotte Baudouin, the sister of one of his closest friends at Ste. Barbe. Inspired by Lucien Herr, the socialist librarian of the École Normale who led men like Jean Jaurès and Léon Blum to socialism, the young couple put the entire Baudouin dowry into a socialist publishing venture. Clearly Péguy had decided upon a socialist life first and relegated his professional ambitions to the uncertainties of a clouded future. His shop, near the Sorbonne at 17 Rue Cujas, was much frequented by friends and well-wishers. On the other hand, people intent on the purchase of books and magazines rarely entered it. By coincidence rather than by design it became the headquarters of the socialist champions of Captain Alfred Dreyfus, and prospective customers more and more avoided a book store that looked and sounded like a debater's meeting hall.

After the discovery of socialism, the Dreyfus Affair was the second hurdle interposed by fate between Péguy and an academic career. Coinciding with Péguy's first year at the École Normale, the original conviction of the Jewish general staff captain, allegedly for selling official secrets, evoked indignation and concern for France's security, but scarcely controversy. Treason was a serious matter, and everyone was relieved to see the traitor punished. But by 1897, the certainty of Dreyfus' guilt was no longer unanimous. Disturbing new evidence had been uncovered. The pens of Zola and Clemenceau joined to arouse the public to doubt. Following *J'accuse* and its author's trial, a few socialists led by the eloquent Jaurès, emerged from their a-plague-on-both-your-houses neutralism and joined the camp of Dreyfus.[19]

---

[18] Charles Péguy, "Un économiste socialiste, M. Léon Walras," *Revue Socialiste*, XXV (1897), 174–86.

[19] Daniel Ligou, *Histoire du socialisme en France, 1871–1961* (Paris, 1962), 134–36. Until 1890 many French socialists had been open anti-semites; cf. Robert F. Byrnes, *Anti-Semitism in France* (Rutgers, 1950), 176–77. On the divisions after 1897, see Aaron Noland, *The Founding of the French Socialist Party, 1893–1905* (Cambridge, Mass., 1956), 61–68.

In 1898, the quarrel moved into the streets. More than once the windows of Péguy's shop were smashed by opponents. More than once, too, the doughty socialist avant-garde, led by the young man from Orléans, scoured the streets of the Left Bank to find the vandals and repay their depredations with interest. Péguy seems to have relished reinforcing the cause of justice with well-aimed, vigorous blows. He never forgot those days when decisions were easy and the call to action irresistible. The cause of the court-martialed captain became the embodiment of public morality. His partisans had been on the side of justice, and to their student-leader it meant that they had signed in blood a pact to eschew wrong forever.[20]

Péguy had been a socialist before he became a Dreyfusard; but in the course of this battle, socialism and Dreyfusism to him became one. He soon realized, however, that the identity of these causes had not been accepted by all leaders of his party. Victory gave the Dreyfusards no ascendancy in socialist councils. This was particularly true during the prolonged and venomous debates which eventually resulted in a union of the many factions of the extreme Left.[21] Péguy's own involvement in these feuds was inevitable, although he had never taken any clear position on party dogma. The Marxist attacks on the defenders of Dreyfus, which persisted throughout most of 1899, aroused his wrath. Friendships, furthermore, prompted him to associate with the Independent Socialists led by Jaurès. But "independence" in Péguy's case was more than a label. His profound, though passing devotion to the great orator from the Carmaux district was neither uncritical nor complete. In the autumn of 1898, he refused to contribute to a new Dreyfusard daily *La Volonté* because the founder was a Radical and because "I have known few Radicals who have become good Socialists." [22] Neither Jaurès, who had himself been a Radical at the outset of his

---

[20] Hubert Bourgin, *De Jaurès à Léon Blum; L'École Normale et la politique* (Paris, 1938), 255–58.

[21] Noland, *The Founding of the French Socialist Party*, 71–80.

[22] Charles Péguy, "Péguy à Franklin-Bouillon," *ACPFM*, No. 60 (1957), 5.

political career, nor Lucien Herr succeeded in changing his mind.

A maverick socialist at most, Péguy nevertheless had acquired status and position within the party. He was its spokesman before the students on the Left Bank. The publications of the Librairie Georges Bellais, his book shop, promised to make of socialism an intellectual force among the postwar generation. In addition to his own *Jeanne d'Arc,* the stalls in front of his establishment displayed in 1898 *Marcel. Premier dialogue de la cité harmonieuse,* his own socialist confession. He published the first manuscripts of Romain Rolland and Jérôme and Jean Tharaud. His shop became the editorial office of the *Mouvement Socialiste* of Hubert Lagardelle and of a number of more specialized and ephemeral periodicals. For a while, Pierre Caron's *Revue d'Histoire Moderne* tried its wings at 17 Rue Cujas. The *Petite République* hailed Péguy's *librairie* as one of the most important manifestations of socialist growth.[23] Yet, for a young man on the way up, Péguy was too independent and, in truth, too unsuccessful. In August of 1898, he failed the examination for the *agrégation de philosophie* and abandoned his academic pursuits, his mother's outraged protests notwithstanding. Six months later he discovered that the Librairie Georges Bellais was facing bankruptcy. No one bought the books he stocked; no one read the authors he published. He appealed for help, and a consortium, headed by Herr and Blum, raised substantial sums with which the shop was reorganized into the Société Nouvelle de Librairie et d'Edition. Péguy continued as editorial director with a salary of about 3000 francs per year. The society acknowledged a debt to him of 20,000 francs, about half of his original investment, on which it agreed to pay 5 per cent interest.[24]

The next few months were unique in Péguy's life. For the first and last time he worked for someone else. Soon he and his board clashed on every conceivable policy question. While Péguy sought to discover literary talent, his employers preferred to

[23] André Boisserie, "Les Notes Politiques et Sociales de Péguy dans la 'Revue Blanche,' " *ACPFM,* No. 39 (1954), 5.

[24] Isaac, *Expériences de ma vie,* I, 319.

support scholarly publications like Brière and Caron's *Repertoire Méthodique de l'Histoire Moderne et Contemporaine de la France*. Since the editor had demonstrably failed once, the five-member board, though equally inexperienced, was not disposed to accept his proposals. On November 21, 1899, Péguy sent Herr his resignation. He was persuaded to withdraw it, and for the next few weeks the first General Congress of French Socialist Organizations (December 3–8) raised questions more momentous than editorial policy at 17 Rue Cujas. But it was a short armistice. The congress, in fact, contributed to make it so. To Péguy's alarm it did not commit Socialism to Dreyfusard justice. Instead it imposed serious restrictions on intraparty debate for the sake of unity.[25] This meant an end to his attacks on the Marxist wing led by Jules Guesde. When he nevertheless proposed the founding of yet another socialist fortnightly "on revolutionary action," the board lost its patience, and his second resignation went unopposed.

Péguy founded his own organ, the *Cahiers de la Quinzaine,* whose first issue appeared on January 5, 1900. But he did not resign from the employ of the Société Nouvelle until October. His break with the party was more gradual still. The *Mouvement Socialiste* handsomely complimented the new *Cahiers* and more than once during the next two years urged fellow socialists to support "the work pursued with such perseverance and success." [26]

This era of good feeling, and the publicity attending it, ended only in December of 1901. Péguy, whose *Cahiers* managed to achieve only a modest success, wanted to withdraw his share of the capital from the Société Nouvelle. It was none too soon, for his successors had managed no better than he and the firm became defunct in 1902! The editor of the *Cahiers de la Quinzaine* needed for his second venture every sou of capital he could

[25] Noland, *The Founding of the French Socialist Party,* 102–13; Isaac, *Expériences de ma vie,* I, 199–212.

[26] E.g. Paul Fauconnet, "Les Revues," *Mouvement Socialiste,* I (1900), 318–19; Hubert Lagardelle, "Les Revues socialistes," *Mouvement Socialiste,* II (1900), 573; Hubert Lagardelle, "Revues Socialistes," *Mouvement Socialiste,* III (1901), 704.

salvage from the first and finally enlisted the help of the courts. The verdict validated his claim, and after endless litigations that dragged on until 1906, the board of the Société Nouvelle met its obligations. From the personal point of view it was an expensive settlement, for the protagonists were never able to meet as friends thereafter and the reverberations of their differences coursed through endless polemics for years to come. Péguy's heated pursuit of money stood in odd contrast to his professed indifference to material success. But unlike his chief adversary Herr, who suffered and paid up in silence, he had no government salary to fall back on, only a growing family to support. The *Cahiers* stood between him and destitution.[27] He was not greedy, merely anxious to survive. His adversaries had not been dishonest, only inept. Péguy got his money and lost some friends; Herr and his consortium acquired another debt and an eloquent enemy.

After 1902, on the other hand, Péguy was free. If the *Cahiers* constituted all he possessed, he could also unreservedly claim them now as his own. They never became the organ of a party; instead, they expanded into a vigorous publication of independent views, never rich, but always viable, never famous, but respected among some of the liveliest intellects of the French capital.

II

The first editorial office of the *Cahiers* was at 19 Rue des Fossés-Saint Jacques "between the Pantheon and the Rue d'Ulm." Its tenant of record was Jean Tharaud, a candidate for the *licence de droit,* whose older brother Jérôme had been Péguy's classmate at Ste. Barbe and the École Normale. Every

[27] Péguy explained his actions in "Pour moi," *Cahiers,* II, No. 5 (1901), 14–17. Herr's case was presented much later by Charles Andler, *Vie de Lucien Herr* (Paris, 1932), 157–58, but was immediately challenged by Mme. Charles Péguy in "Correspondance et réponse [à] M. Charles Andler sur la vie de Lucien Herr," *Europe,* XL (1932), 122–29. For the most recent judgments rendered by what are probably the last surviving participants, see Isaac, *Expériences de ma vie,* I, 229–30, taking the side of Péguy, and Félicien Challaye, *Péguy socialiste* (Paris, 1954), 101–106, speaking for Herr.

Thursday Jean and his roommate André Poisson allowed Péguy the run of their modest apartment, retreating to a library or a park while he edited his texts and proofread his copy. Only after the growing bulk of unsold issues threatened to engulf Tharaud's and Poisson's bedsteads, did the young editor of the *Cahiers* seek more spacious quarters elsewhere. [28] For a short time he rented an office at 16 Rue de la Sorbonne, but in 1901 he moved down the street to number 8 which became his permanent business address. Here he also acquired his only associate, André Bourgeois, who relieved him of the routine tasks of correspondence and administration.

In the editorial back room Péguy reigned in autocratic solitude. He accepted no interference from subscribers, but claimed at the same time never to have changed a line on a manuscript once it had been accepted for publication. The opinions of his contributors were sacrosanct to him. No matter how much he might take issue with anyone in verbal or written debate, there was no editorial censorship at the *Cahiers*. The remarkable history of Péguy the editor contains no evidence of compromise with that principle.

Truth and freedom yielded only modest profits, but Péguy and his family subsisted on them. After a very precarious first year, the *Cahiers* ended their second series with 1,200 subscribers, a solid minimum seldom surpassed for any length of time, but a hard core that substantially held together until the war closed his shop in 1914. In November of 1900 the format changed from a periodical to a serial publication in which each issue was given over to one work.

In this guise the *Cahiers de la Quinzaine* came to include virtually everything Péguy published after the turn of the century, and that was a great deal; they also provided a forum for other young men who later managed well on their own. Romain Rolland followed Péguy from the Rue Cujas to the Rue de la Sorbonne. His first literary success, *Beethoven,* appeared in 1902; the first volume of the picaresque *Jean Christophe*

---

[28] Tharaud, *Notre cher Péguy,* I, 197–204; Jean Bonnerot, *Jérôme et Jean Tharaud* (Paris, 1927), 11.

emerged from Péguy's office two years later. The prolific and successful literary careers of Jean and Jérôme Tharaud hit their stride at the same address. On April 12, 1902, the *Cahiers* issued *Dingley, l'illustre écrivain,* to be followed in 1904 by *Les Hobereaux.* A number of young poets, such as René Salomé, André Suarès, François Porché, and Jean Schlumberger, found a berth at the *Cahiers* before they became part of the illustrious team that made the quality and the reputation of the *Nouvelle Revue Française.* Georges Sorel contributed two volumes to the third series of the *Cahiers,* the title of one of which—*Socialismes nationaux*—was in itself no less a landmark than his more famous later *Réflections sur la violence.*

Above all, however, the *Cahiers de la Quinzaine* were a monument to Péguy's own restless energy and to his growing fertility as poet and essayist. During the first two years as independent editor and publisher, Péguy tried to disentangle the forces and issues which had drawn him into mass politics and then driven him into the solitude of his dark office in the shadow of the Sorbonne. He analyzed them politically; he tried to come to terms with them morally. Before founding the *Cahiers,* Péguy had, in *Jeanne d'Arc,* outlined a searing vision of temporal and spiritual salvation. In his *Marcel. Premier dialogue de la cité harmonieuse,* he had attempted to describe the moral climate of socialism. As he reviewed his past associations and setbacks, the traumatic experience of the Librairie Georges Bellais became in his mind part of the universal conflict between good and evil.[29] Tracing the outlines of a socialist morality proved difficult, moreover, because concern for man's absolute duty again and again led Péguy away from politics into what he called metaphysics. Was salvation from temporal misery indeed the highest goal to which man could aspire? Was there nothing beyond it? In several early issues of the *Cahiers,* Péguy admitted that he did not know. He felt on uncharted ground, embarking on a journey whose end was beyond his range of vision.[30]

This dilemma, from which Péguy liked to escape into acri-

[29] W. B. Gallie, "Péguy the moralist," *French Studies,* II (1948), 70.
[30] "Entre deux trains," *Cahiers,* I, No. 9 (1900), 24–25.

monious recapitulations of his more mundane troubles with the board of the Société Nouvelle, led to his first great essay, "De Jean Coste," which ushered in the fourth year of the *Cahiers de la Quinzaine* on November 4, 1902.

Jean Coste, ou l'instituteur de village was a novel by Antonin Lavergne first submitted to Péguy when he was still in the service of the Société Nouvelle. It described the miserable existence and eventual suicide of a country school teacher and his family.[31] The author, a humble *instituteur* himself, incurred the ill will of the authorities for his frank portrayal of the heartrending difficulties of his profession, and in later years was only too anxious to make the world forget this literary indiscretion.[32] For the moment, however, its publication in the *Cahiers* symbolized the independence of author and editor. Péguy, his own master, was no longer constrained to ask a board's permission. "Jean Coste" marked his emancipation.

The year 1902 also coincided with the decisive Radical victory at the polls. Émile Combes succeeded René Waldeck-Rousseau as premier of France. An unprecedented alliance, between Jaurès' socialists and the bourgeois forces of the Left, assumed control of the Chamber of Deputies. The dormant resentments of the Dreyfus Affair were re-awakened to help enact the anticlerical legislative program of the new coalition. Péguy viewed the alliance as a betrayal of socialism and its use of the cause which had marked his entry on the stage of history as a desecration of justice. Estranged from Herr because of quarrels over money, he now turned against Jaurès on matters of principle.[33] He could not accept his former idol in the role of a persecutor. He refused to accept anticlericalism as an answer to bigotry. Above all, this change of front on the part of a man whom he had trusted so implicitly convinced him that politics invariably corrupted. He felt, therefore, that the pure in heart must remain above the parliamentary and electoral battle; that they must speak and preach, but never seek votes or offices.

[31] "De Jean Coste," *Cahiers,* IV, No. 3 (1902), 4–10.
[32] Halévy, *Péguy and the Cahiers de la Quinzaine,* 81 n.
[33] *Ibid.,* 80.

Politics and the militant new secularism of the majority in the chamber became now his most hated enemies.[34]

Péguy's first attack on the corrupters was launched with another preface, to the young English novelist Israel Zangwill's *Chad Gadya,* a French translation of which appeared in the *Cahiers* in 1904. He attacked the secularist's confidence in continuous and limitless progress. As he saw it, the bigotry of the Church was being superseded by an equally dangerous and bigoted faith in human omnipotence. The committed Dreyfusard Péguy who had defended freedom against Army and Church now issued a call-to-arms against the despotism inspired and led by his former friends.[35] This polemic battle intensified as the victory of anticlericalism was confirmed by successive acts of Parliament. On four separate occasions between 1906 and 1907, Péguy held a mirror to the new tyranny. His reasoning was simple. The anti-Dreyfusards had failed, and the country had been saved. Their adversaries, intoxicated by their victory, were now copying their methods. Who would save France from them? As long as no Dreyfusard volunteers appeared, Péguy undertook to wage the lonely battle of national salvation.[36]

Péguy was not fighting for moral and intellectual liberty alone. The year 1905 witnessed more than the disestablishment of the Church in France. At the same time, the first Moroccan crisis threatened to destroy the Third Republic as a power in international affairs; and Péguy's concern for his nation's greatness was as abiding as his solicitude for the freedom of his soul.

Never a practicing pacifist, Péguy had always taken his military obligations seriously. Though neither he nor his friends left

[34] Tharaud, *Notre cher Péguy,* II, 70–71; Marcel Péguy (ed.), *Lettres et Entretiens de Charles Péguy* (Paris, 1926), 43.

[35] "Zangwill," *Cahiers,* VI, No. 3 (1904), viii–xvi.

[36] These views constitute the *Leitmotiv* of the following four essays: "De la situation faite à l'histoire et à la sociologie dans les temps modernes," *Cahiers,* VIII, No. 3 (1906); "De la situation faite au parti intellectuel dans le monde moderne," *Cahiers,* VIII, No. 5 (1906); "De la situation faite à l'histoire et à la sociologie et de la situation faite au parti intellectuel dans le monde moderne," *Cahiers,* VIII, No. 11 (1907); "De la situation faite au parti intellectuel dans le monde moderne devant les accidents de la gloire temporelle," *Cahiers,* IX, No. 1 (1907).

a description of his year in the ranks, there is no doubt that he liked to wear the uniform; and on days immediately preceding and following summer encampments, he appeared at his office in full regalia. Since 1897 he had been a lieutenant in the reserves. His service record depicted him as an officer of unusual ability.[37] The Dreyfus Affair revealed his fighting heart in the face of civil war; the first Moroccan crisis and the prospect of invasion roused him no less. He concluded that the government had been so intent upon dividing France that the nation had become incapable of defending itself. On June 6, 1905, Foreign Minister Théophile Delcassé was forced to resign as a result of German pressure, and ten days later Péguy wrote a friend that he had bought all necessary equipment in preparation for the call to arms. He accepted a state of perpetual alert, and he urged that his countrymen adopt a stance of continuous mobilization.

These exhortations were addressed to the readers of the *Cahiers* in an essay whose title, "Notre Patrie," was an open challenge to socialist pacifism. Only a few months earlier its most radical exponent, Gustave Hervé, had restated that creed in the most uncompromising terms when he published his book *Leur Patrie*. He had attacked patriotism as a means of economic exploitation and had unmasked what he considered the patriotic myths with which historians indoctrinated Frenchmen from the cradle to the grave. He had ridiculed the French pretensions to soldierly prowess, reminding his countrymen of Waterloo and Sedan, and challenged France's revolutionary traditions, which he claimed to be English and American in origin. Hervé proposed that all socialists make clear their unconditional refusal to march if war were declared and expressed confidence that his "anti-patriotic propaganda"—to use his own words—would doom any future attempts to involve France in an international conflict.[38]

[37] For Péguy's service record, see *ACPFM*, No. 19 (1951), 14–18.

[38] Gustave Hervé, *Leur Patrie* (Paris, 1905), *passim*. When war broke out Hervé abandoned his views for an equally extreme chauvinism. He gained further notoriety in the 1930's for being among the first to call on Pétain to become dictator of France. See *C'est Pétain qu'il nous faut* (Paris, 1935).

Péguy offered no explicit rebuttal. To him, who was to become Bergson's most famous disciple, Hervé was merely one more traitor, one more example of what he had come to know and live with in the *durée française* which stretched from the Roman invasions to the present.[39] His answer to *Leur Patrie* was a forceful Bergsonian chronicle, an account of the threat from abroad in which he reproduced a history of the crisis through a cinematographic succession of seemingly identical yet subtly different images which suddenly confronted the viewer with the startling fact that he was looking at a changed scene without being able to fix the moment or place at which it had begun to present a new aspect.[40] "Like everyone else I had come to Paris at nine o'clock in the morning. Like everyone else, I knew at eleven-thirty that . . . a new period had begun in the history of my life, in the history of this country, and assuredly in the history of the world." [41]

"Notre Patrie" was therefore also a milestone in the evolution of Péguy's art. Up to now his essays, though often strongly subjective reactions to men and issues, had been compact in style and composition. "Notre Patrie," in comparison, read like the forerunner of a stream-of-consciousness meditation. Péguy attempted to recreate the events of those hectic days as they had successively impinged upon his mind. He let his readers follow him as he wandered through the streets that were festively decorated in honor of the visit of young Alfonso XIII of Spain. Thoughts followed each other on paper in the order in which they had presumably crossed his mind, regardless of their relevance to one another. He reproduced incidents in the authentic asymmetry of their sequence: first the unsuccessful attempt on

[39] Albert Thibaudet, "Bergson et Péguy," *Nouvelle Revue Française,* XXXVI (1931), 590–91.

[40] For Bergson's influence on Péguy see André Henry, *Bergson, maître de Péguy* (Melun, 1946), especially pp. 68–69 and Roméo Arbour, *Henri Bergson et les lettres françaises* (Paris, 1955), 288–313, neither of which, however, mentions "Notre Patrie" in this context. On "the parallelism between the notion of the stream of consciousness . . . and the Bergsonian concept of flux," consult the recent study by Shiv K. Kumar, *Bergson and the Stream of Consciousness Novel* (London and Glasgow, 1962).

[41] "Notre Patrie," *Cahiers,* VII, No. 3 (1905), 117–18.

the life of the king, then the successful German attempt on the honor of the Third Republic, and finally the abrupt realization that the world would never again be the same. In "Notre Patrie" there emerged Péguy, reconstructing life with self-conscious meticulousness, refusing to touch up his narrative in the manner of the historical artificer.

Throughout 1906 and 1907 Péguy continued his attacks on the rampant secularism whose crowning achievement was the separation of church and state. Then he suddenly fell silent and published nothing for more than two years. On June 20, 1909, the *Cahiers* observed the completion of their tenth series with an appeal from the editor to his "friends and subscribers" to help him achieve a less marginal existence. It appeared as if the author had wholly surrendered to the editor and publisher.

This barrenness camouflaged years of tumult and agony. In their course Péguy declared his return to Catholicism. The precise moment of conversion has been debated. Jacques and Raïssa Maritain have insisted that he greeted the news of theirs in 1906 with the exclamation: *"Moi aussi, j'en suis la."* [42] Maritain's mother, on the other hand, who was very distressed by this step, recorded that Péguy sympathized with her anguish.[43] An illness which kept Péguy bedfast for four weeks during August and September, 1908, forced the first clear admission from him, about which there is no doubt whatsoever. His friend Joseph Lotte, a teacher at the Lycée of Coutances, visited him in September; and as they chatted about nothing in particular, Péguy suddenly raised himself on his elbow and with tears in his eyes told the visitor that he had become a Catholic.[44]

This personal decision turned out to be the easiest part of the conversion. Neither Péguy's wife, who was agnostic, nor her family shared his new allegiance. There was so little confidence and unity in the household that Péguy actually asked Maritain to

[42] Raïssa Maritain, *Les grandes amitiés* (Paris, 1948), 194–95.
[43] Geneviève Favre, "Souvenirs sur Péguy," *Europe*, XLVI (1938), 157.
[44] Pierre Pacary, *Un compagnon de Péguy: Joseph Lotte, 1875–1914* (Paris, 1917), xvii.

tell Madame Péguy of his decision. This utterly inexplicable procedure naturally led to a row. Maritain, with the convert's self-righteousness, sought to force the wife to follow the husband's example. When she demurred, he informed her that she was living in sin and that her children would have to be considered illegitimate. It is a miracle that the marriage survived the activities of this maladroit ambassador. It took the intervention of Maritain's free-thinking mother to restore peace in the Péguy household.[45]

At the same time, Péguy sought to sell the *Cahiers*. He longed for a peace which he seems to have associated with the life of a provincial *professeur de lycée* and for a while appeared to have been quite determined to find a position commensurate with this dream. But he had no degree and could never decide to resume his quest for the *agrégation*. He did not want to abandon his work without finding a successor. Negotiations with the publishing house of Plon were complicated by his concern for the future of the faithful André Bourgeois. In the spring of 1908, he wrote to Daniel Halévy and offered him the editorship of the *Cahiers de la Quinzaine*. But Halévy, fearing that "quite soon after persuading me to take over the *Cahiers* he would accuse me of robbing him," declined. With this refusal in hand, Péguy resigned himself to a life term at No. 8 Rue de la Sorbonne.[46]

Unable to resolve the proliferating problems of his environment, Péguy escaped into the world of imagination. When he took up the pen again, after more than two years of virtual silence, he began the most fruitful and original period of his life. Pain, conflict, and frustration drove him to become, not a philosopher, but a poet. One day in December, 1909, Daniel Halévy met him at the door of his office. "Péguy unbuttoned his long greatcoat, and took out of the inner pocket the freshly

[45] Halevy, *Péguy and the Cahiers de la Quinzaine*, 173; Favre, "Souvenirs sur Péguy," 163–64; Tharaud, *Notre cher Péguy*, II, 101–102.

[46] Halevy, *Péguy and the Cahiers de la Quinzaine*, 103–104. That Péguy may have continued to think of an academic career even later is indicated by his registering a thesis topic at the Sorbonne in June of 1909. Cf. "Sur les thèses en Sorbonne de Péguy," *ACPFM*, No. 76 (1960), 29.

printed *Cahier* that had appeared that very day. I read the title: 'Le mystère de la charité de Jeanne d'Arc.' "[47]

The "Mystère" was intended as the first of twelve books describing the evolution of Joan of Arc from the shepherd girl to the national liberator. Only three volumes were actually completed: "Le Mystère de la charité de Jeanne d'Arc" in 1910, "Le Porche du mystère de la deuxième vertu" in 1911, and "Le Mystère des saints innocents" in 1912. Subject and form illustrated the mode and nature of Péguy's work. The topic constituted a return to the absorbing preoccupations of the middle 1890's. The "Mystère," for instance, included every word of the first ten pages of his *Jeanne d'Arc* of 1897, now expanded into a free-verse dialogue of 150 pages. The number of protagonists had been reduced to Joan, her friend Hauviette, and Madame Gervaise, the pious nun. The earlier, elaborate references to the siege of Orléans became now even more submerged in the soul-distress of the mystic shepherd girl in whom the observant reader could recognize the author himself.

It was interesting that Péguy should have chosen this precise moment to revive and expand the work of his youth. Since the appearance of Louis Quicherat's *Procès de condamnation et de réhabilitation de Jeanne d'Arc* in 1841, the Maid of Orléans had undergone successive rediscoveries by her countrymen. This interest increased in the years immediately preceding the 500th anniversary of her birth. In 1909 no less than seven works dealing with Joan made their appearance in France. Four more were published in 1910, three in 1911.[48] If the topic of the "Mystère" was in fashion, its style reflected also the author's sensitivity to currents of poetic experimentation. Péguy wrote his *mystères* in free verse, which was beginning to be no less in vogue.

This verse form had been introduced into French literature by writers of predominantly foreign origin, among whom the Amer-

---

[47] Halévy, *Péguy and the Cahiers de la Quinzaine,* 100. The *Cahier* was dated January, 1910.

[48] Wilhelm Grenzmann, *Die Jungfrau von Orleans in der Dichtung* (Berlin, 1929), 73.

ican Vielé-Griffin and the Greek Jean Moréas were the most illustrious.[49] A complete translation of Walt Whitman's *Leaves of Grass*, as well as the first full-scale French biography of the American bard, appeared in Paris in 1908.[50] Péguy's friend Halévy had been among the first to nurture this budding Whitman cult with an article that had appeared in the *Pages Libres* in 1901.[51] Whether these currents affected Péguy remains a matter of conjecture. His reading habits were not eclectic. Among contemporary poets his esteem was confined to Paul Claudel and Émile Verhaeren, who may have provided the connection between the author of the "Mystère" and the foreign originators of free verse. His knowledge of foreign literature, except for the authors of antiquity, rested on second-hand information or recollections from anthologies forced upon him in school. No one knows of whom he was thinking when he told Joseph Lotte in 1910: "All the attempts in free verse of the last twenty years have put into my hands an excellent instrument."[52] So much of his own rhythmic, repetitive prose placed him on the threshold of versification that one may well wonder whether he needed any examples at all. In fact, if one chose to regard the *mystères* as a way-station between Péguy's essays and the later quatrains and alexandrines, it may suffice to explain his entire career as a writer in terms of an evolution in which instinct and predilection were the only explicit and recognizable forces.

To the reader whom Péguy captivated, form became a minor concern. The importance of the three free verse epics on Joan of Arc rested on his gift to communicate his own agony of soul. Passages like the stirring narrative of the passion of Christ were lifted into the context of current conflicts by Joan's angry assertions that no good Frenchman would have deserted Him as did his disciples. Mme. Gervaise's rejoinder, that the Maiden was denigrating the Community of Saints with this charge, met the

---

[49] See the chauvinistic attack on this verse form in Henri Clouard, *Les Disciplines* (Paris, 1913), 164.

[50] Leon Bazalgette, *Whitman, l'homme et son oeuvre* (Paris, 1908).

[51] P. M. Jones, "Whitman in France," *Modern Language Review*, X (1915), 27.

[52] Quoted in Romain Rolland, *Péguy* (Paris, 1942–45) II, 276.

stubborn and irrelevant boast: "Our [i.e. France's] saints were not afraid of blows." Like the conflict in Péguy's own life, the dialogue quickly returned to the problem of salvation. Could his heroine achieve it on terms agreed upon with God and without clerical intercession? Péguy sought anxiously for an answer through Joan and at last found it in Hope, *la petite espérance*, the treasury of grace flowing eternally and inexhaustibly from the Creator's hand.

This cardinal virtue was extolled in the second volume of the cycle, appropriately entitled "Le porche du mystère de la deuxième vertu," cast in the form of a monologue by Madame Gervaise. Hope, she said, was the most difficult of all virtues and therefore most pleasing to God. Faith and charity came spontaneously, but "in order to hope, my child, one must have been happy indeed, one must have obtained, [and] received great blessings." [53] This call on

> Hope, the little child . . .
> who goes to sleep every evening
> in its crib
> after having duly said its prayer,

was continued in the "Mystère des saints innocents," which appeared in March 1912. Hope now shone as the most exalted of virtues, a divine command without which there could be no life, no freedom, no redemption.

> If there be justice, who shall be saved.
> If there be mercy, who shall be lost.[54]

Thus Péguy concluded by achieving faith in divine understanding. A merciful God would not deny him what human associations had failed to provide.

With mankind Péguy continued to fight many wars. His wife would not allow their children to be baptized. The Church refused to recognize his secular marriage and took the view that the convert, as well as his children, continued to live in sin. Péguy would either have to bring his family around or leave

[53] *Cahiers*, XIII, No. 4 (1911), 29–30.
[54] *Cahiers*, XIII, No. 12 (1912), 53.

them. The first was out of the question, the second insupportable. Seeing that the Church would not compromise, he refused to go to Mass or take the sacraments. This alienated his Catholic friends. He became estranged from Maritain, who had never shown much tolerance for Péguy's inability to be master in his own house. Ernest Psichari, the grandson of Ernest Renan who had turned to the faith under Péguy's influence, abandoned him in 1913.

These same friends could not understand why Péguy's association continued to be as eclectic as before his reconversion and why the *Cahiers* continued to be a free, rather than a clerical publication. The difficulties of his socialist years were re-enacted as he found it impossible to submit to the discipline of Catholicism.

Most conspicuous among Péguy's secular associates was the anti-Bergsonian rationalist philosopher Julien Benda. In 1911 and 1912 Péguy published Benda's two-volume novel *L'Ordination*. Its central theme, adultery, was so utterly distasteful to the priggish Maritain, that he asked André Bourgeois not to send him such issues in the future. Péguy, infuriated, canceled Maritain's subscription.

Péguy's friendship with Benda likewise brought to a head his growing differences with Georges Sorel.[55] For many years this bearded sage among the intellectual vagrants of the new century had been the center of Thursday afternoon open houses at the editorial offices of the *Cahiers*. There he would sit and pontificate with fluency and authority on any topic of the hour. Whether "those who listened to him . . . owe it to him that a changing world did not take them by surprise," may be argued.[56] But

[55] Here, as in the case of Péguy's quarrel with Lucien Herr, the investigator is confronted by differing versions of the same event. For Péguy's, see Marcel Péguy, "La rupture de Charles Péguy et de Georges Sorel," *Cahiers*, XIX, No. 12 (1930), 7–61. For Sorel's, see Jean Variot, *Propos de Georges Sorel* (Paris, 1935), 250–68.

[56] Halévy, *Péguy and the Cahiers de la Quinzaine*, 75–78; for an interesting contemporary account of Sorel's sermons at Péguy's establishment, see Henri Massis, "Les idées sociales de M. Georges Sorel," *Mercure de France*, LXXXIII (1910), 610.

many of his monologues were an impressive performance, judging by the transcripts of Jean Variot. Péguy's own meetings with "*notre maître M. Georges Sorel*" were not confined to the Thursdays. On Friday they went together to Bergson's lectures, and during their years of intimacy they would meet as often as two or three times each week. Nevertheless, there was gradually building up in Péguy a resentment against Sorel's eclectic dilettantism. Syndicalism, furthermore, conflicted with his own idealistic concepts of the sacredness of work. Regarding the *syndicat* he once exclaimed: "The poor workers! For a long time they have been harassed by their employers. Now they have to put up with union secretaries as well." [57] After the publication of the "Mystère," it was Sorel's turn to object to the inconsistency of Péguy's religious stance. Unlike Maritain his reservations were tempered by compassion. He offered to discuss Péguy's special difficulties with Comte Albert de Mun, the outstanding exponent of conservative, social Catholicism in the chamber, and plead for understanding on the Catholic side. But Péguy flew into a rage and told Sorel to mind his own business. As Sorel became increasingly interested in the Church as a useful social institution, the convert Péguy drew away from him. The older man's insistence that the former disciple clarify and rationalize his position made the Thursday afternoons increasingly embarrassing for the other participants. The debates lengthened, and the less eloquent Péguy, often at a loss for a quick answer, would stomp out of the room to sulk in his back office. "Notre Jeunesse," published shortly before the *Mystère,* afforded a glimpse at these rhetorical contests when Péguy wrote: "There are many things I should have liked to say at the *Cahiers* on Thursday afternoon, if the talk were less loud, and if I were occasionally permitted to hold the floor." [58]

These smouldering fires were fanned into a bright blaze when Benda's *L'Ordination* was nominated for the Prix Goncourt. Péguy learned that Sorel had undermined his friend's chances, reportedly having told a member of the jury not to consider "the

---

[57] Maurice Reclus, *Le Péguy que j'ai connu* (Paris, 1950), 266–67.
[58] *Cahiers*, XI, No. 12 (1909), 218.

little Jew" for the award. Benda did not get the prize and Péguy at once blamed Sorel. He wrote him a short note to the effect that his visits to the *Cahiers* were no longer welcome.

III

Ironically, the very work that expressed a transformation from which Péguy derived so much private sorrow was the cause of the only major public success he was to enjoy. "Le Mystère de la charité de Jeanne d'Arc" was showered with critical attention, a great deal of which was praise. Early in 1911, Bernard Grasset published an anthology of Péguy's work, which earned the author a nomination for the Grand Prix Littéraire of the Académie Française. The foremost rival of Péguy's *Oeuvres Choisies* was none other than Romain Rolland's *Jean Christophe* which had also first seen the light of day in the *Cahiers de la Quinzaine.* These portents of glory led to naught, however. The judges were unable to decide between the two candidates, and the Académie decided against making the award. The very substantial consolation prize which Péguy received instead was to be the only mark of recognition ever bestowed on him by the "forty immortals."

The reason for the ephemeral nature of Péguy's success obviously resided in his ability to lose friends and acquire enemies. Most of the praise for the "Mystère" came from Clericals, Nationalists, and Conservatives who welcomed his glorification of Joan with exclamations of triumph and rapture. But he confounded his new admirers when, in "Notre Jeunesse," he reaffirmed his solidarity with the Dreyfusard associations of his youth. He described how the cause in whose service he found himself had been degraded by politicians. He went on to accuse the modern world of habitually degrading every ideal. "Everything," he thundered, "begins as an ideal and ends as a plank in a political platform." [59] His newfound friends were dumbfounded, and they dropped him without delay.

In 1911, Péguy for the first time declared war on the Catholic hierarchy. In the pages of the sedately Catholic *Revue Hebdomadaire* the critic François LeGrix had objected to what he

[59] *Cahiers,* XI, No. 12 (1909), 27–28.

considered Péguy's unhistoric approach to the passion of Joan of Arc. He insisted that even a poet or playwright should base his work on the documented episodes of a hero's life, in this case the evidence accumulated in the course of the trial at Rouen. Péguy replied with a polemic of three hundred pages entitled "Un nouveau théologien, M. Fernand Laudet" in which he not only questioned his adversary's thesis, but his honor and the integrity of his Christian faith as well. Not satisfied, he blasted the *Revue Hebdomadaire* and its editor, Fernand Laudet. As a Catholic he went on to argue that miracles needed no documentation. One believed in them, or one did not. Documents were irrelevant to those who were truly full of faith. The public life of a saint or hero consisted of his superhuman accomplishments, not of documents. Taking the life of Christ in support of his case, Péguy pointed out the many sacred days on the Christian calendar, Christmas included, which commemorated events in His life that could certainly not be documented by LeGrix's standards. He believed that the essence of Christianity was contained in its legends. If faith had any meaning, it could be displayed only in connection with those aspects of a set of religious beliefs that transcended reason. A Christian who needed proof for every canon and a legal foundation for every command was no Christian at all.[60] Péguy's appeal to the efficacy of faith found no echo among the hierarchy. He was not destined to lead a new Catholic reformation. The only result of this exchange was that critics henceforth abandoned him to silence, rather than risk incurring his overpowering wrath.

What the Church denied, Péguy, according to his own testimony, ultimately received directly from God. A profound crisis, induced by the many personal and spiritual controversies that converged upon him, was capped in 1912 by the serious, near-fatal illness of his son Pierre. The sickly child was stricken by typhoid fever, and Péguy—in keeping with an earlier vow for just such an eventuality—resolved upon a pilgrimage to Chartres to put his children into the care of the Holy Virgin. Although the boy was out of danger by March 5, his father set out in June to

[60] *Cahiers*, XIII, No. 2 (1911), 16–20.

keep his promise and repeated the pilgrimage in July of the following year.[61] The two journeys on foot across the plains to the gates of the great cathedral were this solitary Christian's answer to a Church that denied him the sacraments and to friends who were disappointed by his inability to submit to regular Catholic discipline. Through a ritual of his own choosing Péguy simply turned to God, convinced that if man was lost it was not because the Creator had not heard him, but because man had not called Him. "Thereafter everything went well. Naturally."[62]

Thus toward the end of a brief existence consumed in a struggle against evil in the state and complacency in the Church, Péguy became a mystic who had spoken to God and a lonely prophet of French virtue. In 1913, his two essays "L'Argent" and "L'Argent (suite)" wistfully recalled the "old France" into which he claimed to have been born. It embodied the undefiled purity of the French revolutionary tradition and a national greatness that found its highest expression in the little man's daily rededication to honest toil.

Péguy found political refuge in conservative anticapitalism. He supported the romantic vogue against mass production, mass distribution, and the anonymous capital power of the corporation. The manager and mediator who produced nothing directly, but appeared to become rich merely by satisfying a desire to "make money," symbolized to him the decline of an ancient civilization whose pride of workmanship was now replaced by pride in one's bank balance. Another manifestation of this retreat into a past of questionable historicity was Péguy's abandonment of modern free verse for the sonnet and the alexandrine. His last three poems, "La tapisserie de Sainte Geneviève et de Jeanne d'Arc" (1912), "La tapisserie de Notre Dame" (1913),

---

[61] Germaine Péguy, "L'Enfance," *Témoignages sur Pierre Péguy* (Paris, 1949), 10–15; Mabille de Poncheville, *Vie de Péguy* (Paris, 1945), 138–39. For the most authoritative review of the pilgrimages, see Auguste Martin, "Péguy, Pélerin de Chartres," *ACPFM*, No. 5 (1949), 4–6.

[62] "Le porche du mystère de la deuxième vertu," *Cahiers*, XIII, No. 4 (1911), 58–62; "La tapisserie de Notre-Dame," *Cahiers*, XIV, No. 10 (1913), 104.

which included the moving account of his pilgrimage to Chartres, and *Ève* (1913), were cast in a rigid mold. But in Péguy's work, tradition and revolt continued to live side by side. In his prose he lauded tradition while railing against the institutions it had established. His poetry revealed him to be restive under the confinement of orthodox verse forms. The eighth sonnet in "La tapisserie de Sainte Geneviève et de Jeanne d'Arc" consisted of 2 quatrains followed by a torrent of 327 tercets, while the process of poetic iconoclasm was reversed on a more modest scale in the last poem which consisted of 29 quatrains and 2 tercets.

In his poetry as in his prose Péguy heaped image upon image, verse upon verse to drive home one thought by dint of many multiformed and multicolored repetitions. Form and medium were only vehicles for the transmission of ideas. If existing forms became too confining, he destroyed them and constructed new ones. In his last great poem "Ève," in which he invoked the mother of men as the ancestral mother of Christ, Péguy presented his readers with a stout volume of four hundred pages of alexandrines. Even his most faithful friends were stunned by this colossal package, whose pages few of them took the trouble to cut.

As the years wore on, Péguy paid an increasingly stiff price for the privilege of being his own master. After a visit to the Rue de la Sorbonne in February, 1913, Romain Rolland wrote in his diary: "His material situation is of the worst. Since October, the *Cahiers* have lost 150 subscribers. His work is nowhere accepted. The *Revue des Deux Mondes* has rejected three sonnets . . . the *Correspondant* . . . has refused to take a longer work. The *Nouvelle Revue Française,* which paid 1,000 frs. to the Tharauds for their *Fête Arabe,* offers him 400 for a far more extensive work." The lack of recognition in his own home weighed upon Péguy even more heavily. Neither his wife, nor his mother in Orléans, attached any value to his writings. "They would prefer it if he received his degree and became a professor." [63]

[63] Romain Rolland, *De Jean Christophe à Colas Breugnon, pages de journal* (Paris, 1946), 93–94.

By 1914 visitors found the office of the *Cahiers de la Quinzaine* quiet and deserted. It seemed to Péguy that he met rejection wherever he turned. The freethinkers stayed away from the religious mystic; the liberals were disconcerted by the militant chauvinist; the nationalists distrusted the unreconstructed Dreyfusard; the Catholics repudiated the nonconformist. Péguy had reached a dead end. Though not friendless by far, he had come to occupy a political and ideological position so uniquely tailored to his own emphatic convictions that no one else seemed ready to follow him. Struggle and frustration had exhausted him. "I have fallen into a pit of fatigue out of which I have not been able to climb these past two months," he wrote André Suarès in the spring of 1914.[64]

Given the opportunity, however, Péguy was still spoiling for a good fight. Early in 1914 the major works of his friend and master, Henri Bergson, were put on the Index. The editor of the *Cahiers* went to his defense at once. On April 26 he published his "Note sur M. Bergson et la philosophie bergsonienne" in which he praised his mentor at the expense of Descartes. This blow is said to have been felt as far away as Rome, and some of Péguy's Catholic friends feared that he would be excommunicated in turn. His only response was to make his case even more explicit. In the "Note conjointe sur M. Descartes et la philosophie cartésienne," he countered with a furious attack on the Index as such. Censorship, he said, was useless in dealing with non-Catholics and an unnecessary restraint on true believers. Catholics needed no signposts, he affirmed; they knew their way. Only the priests, who had lost the habit of walking, required guidance.[65]

Péguy was working on the "Note conjointe" when France mobilized for World War I. He put down his pen in the middle of a sentence when he received his call to the colors on August 1. Although he was forty-one years of age and about to become a father for the fourth time, he volunteered immediately for front-

---

[64] "Correspondance Péguy-Suarès (suite et fin)," *ACPFM*, No. 75 (1960), 21.

[65] Charles Péguy, *Oeuvres complètes* (Paris, 1917–55), IX, 329–31.

line duty. The news of this summons was the exhilarating release from the proliferating sorrows of temporal existence. He closed his shop and put all civilian feuds behind him.[66] He took leave of his family on the same day and spent the next two in the city, seeking reconciliation with the many friends with whom he had quarreled. On August 4, at 1:30 in the afternoon, he left on a troop train, surrounded by his reserve company of two hundred men, shouting, drinking, and singing exuberantly, casting himself daily into the void that was to swallow all but a handful of them.[67]

In the staging area Péguy was assigned to the 19th Company of the 276th Infantry Regiment. He reached the front with his unit on August 18 and was in sporadic contact with the enemy until the beginning of the great retreat on the twenty-third. On the twenty-seventh he learned of the evacuation of Alsace and the defeat at Charleroi. Cruel days ensued. A train took his regiment back into the interior. Bar-le-Duc, Vitry-le-François, Châlons, Reims, and Soissons passed until the men detrained eighty miles from Paris. From here the retreat continued on foot. During the next twenty-four hours Lieutenant Péguy and his men marched some thirty-five miles with the enemy hard on their heels. On September 2, they saw Senlis under German fire. They halted at a road sign which informed them that they were now a mere fifteen miles from the capital which they had left less than a month before.[68]

It was time to stop the invader's advance, and to that end the regiment took up its position in the vicinity of Meaux on the morning of September 5. In their blue uniforms these Frenchmen were perfect targets for the attacking enemy, but the murderous fire which rapidly thinned their ranks did not cause their lines to collapse. Members of the 19th company of the 276th

---

[66] Jacques Rivière, "Notice sur Charles Péguy," *Nouvelle Revue Française*, XIII (1919), 161–62.

[67] Jérôme and Jean Tharaud, *Pour les fidèles de Péguy* (Paris, 1927), 126–31.

[68] Victor Boudon, *Avec Charles Péguy de la Lorraine à la Marne* (Paris, 1916), *passim;* Lucien Christophe, "En Lorraine à la trace de Péguy," *ACPFM,* No. 80 (1960), 17–18.

Regiment, led by Péguy, gave a good account of themselves, fighting and firing as long as they had life. At two o'clock in the afternoon a bullet struck down their commander, and at the end of the day only thirteen members of their group had survived. None of them realized that their sacrifice was part of that First Battle of the Marne whose setback the invader would never be able to overcome.

On September 6, a staff officer visited the battlefield near the village of Villeroy. There he found the body of a lieutenant of infantry, amidst his fallen men. Reading the papers a year later on the anniversary of Péguy's death, he concluded that he had seen none other than the lamented poet.[69] The corner of France which these men had defended with their lives, and in which they were to be buried together a few days later, was quiet now; and for the remainder of the war no sound of battle would disturb their repose.

Péguy, too, was finally at rest. To a man as steadfast and stubborn as he was, life was bound to be without peace and without armistice. His stay on earth had been brief, outwardly undramatic, yet full of struggle and conflict. "Socialist in his aspirations, Christian by nature, a hero by his sacrifice," [70] he early acquired the habit of intellectual independence and never abandoned it.

Péguy's unchanging spirit and the successively changing positions into which it led him can be observed from a systematic examination of his work together with the conflicts and crises that inspired it. His writing years extended from 1895, when he began his first literary labors, until August 1, 1914, when France's mobilization is said to have halted him in the middle of a sentence. His maturity was spent between the Panama scandal which became public when he was eighteen and the First Battle of the Marne which claimed him as the first casualty among the ranks of the Third Republic's intellectual elite. He found his

[69] Henry d'Estrée, "D'Oran à Arras, feuilles détachées d'un carnet de guerre," *Le Correspondant*, CCIX (1915), 1054; Henry d'Estrée, "Comment j'ai recontré le corps de Péguy," *Figaro*, November 8, 1932.

[70] Jacques Copeau, "Charles Péguy," *ACPFM*, No. 44 (1955), 22–24.

mission during the 1890's when France had become uncertain of hers. Amidst charges of public corruption and fears of anarchist revolution; before the specter of treason called forth by the conviction of Dreyfus; confronted by the confession of weakness implied by the alliance with Russia (1893) and confirmed by the retreat at Fashoda (1898), where Britain successfully pressed her claims in the Sudan, France stood trembling for want of competent leaders. Péguy's *Cahiers* were founded on the morn of the great Republican reaffirmation under the leadership of René Waldeck-Rousseau, which coincided with the dawning of new material, social, and intellectual progress usually summarized by the term *la belle époque.* His journal alternately flourished and languished through fourteen years that nevertheless reverberated with the abuse exchanged by clericals and anticlericals, republicans and nationalists, friends of peace and apostles of war, social reformers and economic conservatives. Péguy listened to and participated in the acrimonious debates between the dogmatic acolytes of scientific progress and their pessimistic detractors who insisted on an inevitable decline of morality in a materialistic world. From his dark office in the shadow of the Sorbonne, the editor of the *Cahiers de la Quinzaine* watched the continuous parliamentary game of ministerial chairs which might at one moment elevate to the presidency of the council a nonentity like Jean Sarrien, only to reverse itself with equal caprice a few months later and save France once again through the craggy, sardonic Georges Clemenceau. He observed the Boxer rebellion, watched the progressive Europeanization of the Dark Continent, and pondered the impact of the Russian Revolution of 1905. Throughout, he remained bitterly sensitive to the seesaw battle between national frustration and exaltation in his own country; and he may have died knowing that out of these trials had at last come for France a capacity for sacrifice which halted a superior enemy at the portals of victory and thereby confounded the gloomy predictions of bitter-end conservatives and resurgent monarchists.

Péguy's writing and suffering encompassed almost two decades that were part of the great creative harvest gathered throughout Europe during the late nineteenth and early twentieth centuries and to whose yield France contributed as great a diversity of fruit as any nation. It was a time during which the practitioners of the Fine Arts looked to Paris as they never had before. Impressionism had become mature and respectable. As *cause célèbre* it began to be overshadowed by a host of new iconoclasts: the *Fauves,* among them young Henri Matisse, whose emergence made the autumn *salon* of 1905 unforgettable, and the outrage of cubism visited only three years later upon an indignant world by Pablo Picasso and Georges Bracque.

The same breathtaking and baffling variety characterized the world of music. The charming Camille Saint-Saëns continued to regale the *bien pensants* with such elegant offerings as his Fourth and Fifth Piano Concertoes, and opera buffs welcomed the new century's advent with the premiere of Gustave Charpentier's inoffensive *Louise.* But here revolution was brewing, too. Young Maurice Ravel had just finished his *Pavane for a dead Infanta* which began the most solidly productive period in his life, culminating in the great String Quartet on the eve of the war. In 1902, Claude Debussy's *Péléas et Mélisande* elicited laughter, hoots, and profanity from an unappreciative audience at the Opéra Comique. And yet, what harmless manifestations these were, including the austere productions of the master of the Schola Cantorum, Vincent d'Indy, compared to Igor Stravinsky's *Sacre du Printemps* which shook the rafters of the Opera in 1913 under the vigorous direction of the prodigious Pierre Monteux.

And what a golden age of letters that said farewell to Émile Zola, sat at the feet of the two great irreconcilables—Maurice Barrès and Anatole France—and discovered the divergent talents of André Gide, Paul Claudel, and Gillaume Apollinaire! These were years when style for its own sake was still practiced in the prose of a Charles Maurras and an Émile Faguet. These times were no less hospitable to a bursting romantic energy that flooded all established dams of traditional form, as revealed by Romain Rolland's popular and endless *Jean Christophe,* by Alain-Fournier's murky and mysterious *Grand Meaulnes,* and at last in Péguy's own work. Jules Romains and Roger Martin du

Gard were making their debuts, and Alain (Émile Chartier) was publishing his first *Propos* which eventually identified him as the tragic oracle of the fading Third Republic.

Even at close range many landmarks become indistinguishable from each other, such was the richness of these years. Aging masters, vigorous newcomers, suave practitioners of convention, and reckless destroyers of traditional practice crowded each other on the musical, theatrical, and literary stage of a Paris which could truly lay claim to being the cultural capital of the world. Not only in a climate of political and moral conflict but amidst this surfeit of genius Péguy sought a hearing; as one of this host of rebels and reactionaries he dwelt, often in utter and incomprehensible loneliness. It was as an emigrant to this metropolitan purgatory of the human spirit that he began to think of, plan, and finally complete his first ambitious work: *Jeanne d'Arc*.

II

Écuyer de Jeanne d'Arc

WHEN Péguy began his research on Joan of Arc, twenty-five years had passed since the death of the Second Empire. In 1875, by a numerical majority of one vote, the National Assembly had accepted the Republic. Soon the electorate returned more substantial republican majorities, and Jules Grévy's election to the presidency in 1879 revealed a thoroughgoing transformation of the public outlook.

The 1880's witnessed the emergence of a distinctly new policy line, but this evolution of a *régime* into a *system* bred controversy rather than cohesion. The imposition of secular controls on the schools accentuated the division between clericalist and secularist France. The occupation of Tunis in 1881 substituted a policy of overseas expansion for a diplomacy based on bitter memories, but public reaction was also divided. Not all Frenchmen were prepared to accept indefinitely the amputation of Alsace-Lorraine. As late as 1895, Georges Clemenceau, the Radical, and the Duc de Broglie, the Monarchist, expressed doubts about the wisdom of imperialism in strikingly similar terms.[1]

[1] Duc de Broglie, "Vingt-cinq ans après (1870–1896)," *Revue des deux Mondes,* CXXXV (1896), 5–44. For a confrontation of two similar views, see Jacques Saint-Cère, "Quelques réflexions imposées par M. M. de Broglie et Clemenceau," *Revue Blanche,* VII (1896), 58–60. Note also the spate of articles of detailed historical retrospection, of which Etienne Lamy, "La fin du Second Empire," *Revue des deux Mondes,* CXXVII

The division on issues was soon complicated by the drama of personalities and prejudices. The collapse of the financial empire of the *Union Générale* in 1882, in itself a symptom of spreading depression, gave rise to the charge that this debacle exposed a sinister financial conspiracy between Free Masons and Jews.[2] From 1886 to 1889 General Georges Boulanger became the hero of unregenerate *revanchards* and attracted the discontented of all factions. His charisma was enhanced by the revelations of the scandalous sale of offices and decorations by Daniel Wilson, President Grévy's son-in-law. Amidst the resulting tumult, Edouard Drumont published his corrosive anti-semitic tract *La France Juive,* whose thesis, that "the only one to whom the Revolution [of 1789] was profitable was the Jew,"[3] cast a shadow on the entire republican heritage. In 1891 the circumstances and misdemeanors leading to the collapse of the Panama Canal Company confirmed the suspicions of monarchists, clericals, conservatives, and anti-semites. Drumont the pamphleteer became Drumont the editor whose newspaper *La Libre Parole* editorialized both against the Republic and its presumable corruptors.

Not all attacks on the Third Republic came from the Right. In 1886 the strikes at the mines of Décazeville began a new and dramatic phase in the step-by-step alienation of the industrial worker from a republican order that was agonizingly slow in the espousal of social reform. The rate of protest grew, and in 1893 alone 634 work stoppages were recorded in France. The observance of May 1st as the day of labor, begun in 1890, led to more clashes; and on the first anniversary of this new ritual twelve participants lost their lives in encounters with troops and police. Anarchist activities, often mistakenly identified with parlia-

---

(1895), 70–96, 316–53, 787–822; G. Valbert, "La candidature du Prince Leopold de Hohenzollern," *Revue des deux Mondes,* CXXVIII (1895), 684–95, and Benedetti's "Ma mission à Ems," *Revue de Paris,* II (1895), 225–57, are only a small sample.

[2] Jean Bouvier, *Le Krach de l'Union Générale, 1878–1885* (Paris, 1958), 1–4.

[3] Edward R. Tannenbaum, *The Action Française; Die-hard Reactionaries in the Twentieth Century* (New York, 1962), 16.

mentary socialism and the aspirations of organized labor, took ever more terrifying forms. On December 9, 1893, the anarchist Vaillant threw a homemade bomb into the Chamber of Deputies. At Lyons, six months later, the Italian Caserio sought to avenge Vaillant's execution by plunging a knife into the breast of President François Sadi-Carnot. Far from showing remorse, the assassin, when asked at his trial whether the King of Italy and the Pope had been next on his list of victims, replied nonchalantly, "Not at the same time. The two never go out together."

These manifold threats to the social order began to generate a noticeable panic even on the Paris Stock Exchange which had remained stolidly unaffected amidst the thunder of siege guns during the winter of 1870–71. On the other hand, the various demonstrators, whether strikers in the ranks or assassins in the street, justified their deeds of violence as overdue protests against a government which simply refused to recognize the industrial revolution. Unlike Germany, France had not found a leader who appreciated the need for reform as a barrier against social revolution; and so the Left, no less than the Right—though obviously for different reasons—viewed the Panama scandal as the natural concomitant of a society which was hopelessly held captive in the golden claws of Mammon. The conspiratorial alliance between venal politicians and Jewish bankers was accepted as incontrovertible fact by socialist and conservative alike.

But the regime survived. The elections of 1893 returned only 76 monarchists, as compared with 210 in 1889. A republican center of 278 deputies was joined by 140 Radicals, and for the first time by 50 socialists,[4] who like Adolphe Thiers had discovered that loyalty to the political institutions of the Third Republic divided them least from each other and from the rest of France. The unpredictable succession of cabinets, the untoward revelations of political corruption, and social unrest capped by the murder of a president constituted in no sense crises (at least not yet) but merely transitory flaws in a workable system.

It was in this fluid atmosphere of acceptance and protest,

[4] Ligou, *Histoire du socialisme en France,* 122–24.

under this imperfect but elastic order, that Péguy formulated his life message. He wrapped it in a large and heavy volume, cardboard-bound and printed on paper that had "limited edition" written all over it. On the front "Jeanne d'Arc" is embossed in red letters. The spine is completely blank except for the dates "1412–1431" in black. There is no title page. After several blanks the reader encounters a dedication "to those who shall have lived" and "to those who shall have died to remedy universal ills." At its bottom are the names "Marcel et Pierre Baudouin." Marcel, the brother of Péguy's wife, died before the work was completed. The author eulogized him here with the concession of a co-authorship for which there is otherwise no evidence and by taking the same family name for his own *nom de plume*.

At last one turns the first page of *Jeanne d'Arc* proper, a dramatic trilogy in eight parts, carefully and meticulously printed, with generous intercalations of empty pages whose purpose was to allow the reader to think as he turned them.[5] This is Péguy's "first Jeanne d'Arc, too little known and so revealing of his innermost being."[6]

Péguy's interest in the heroine was, one might almost say, inborn. The sensitive, educated Orléanais grew up with the memory of the city's liberatress, and the annual procession on May 8 was one of the few bright memories in his dour childhood. As she had freed his forbears from the bondage of the invader she freed him, ever so fleetingly, from the day-to-day harassments of poverty and—perhaps—from the stinging memories of 1870–71.

The decision to write about Joan can be traced to 1894. On November 2, Péguy borrowed Henri Wallon's biography of the *pucelle,* together with Jules Quicherat's *Aperçus nouveaux sur l'histoire de Jeanne d'Arc* (1850). From March to June of the

---

[5] Johannet, *Vie et mort de Péguy,* 69; Halévy, *Péguy et les Cahiers de la Quinzaine,* 41–43; Tharaud, *Notre cher Péguy,* I, 142.

[6] Romain Rolland to Frantisek Leichter, April 14, 1925, in F. Leichter, "Péguy avec des lettres inédites de Romain Rolland," *ACPFM,* No. 58 (1957), 8.

following year he pored over Quicherat's edition of the trial.[7] At this point the form his work was to take still remained uncertain. Letters to friends, written in 1895 and 1896, tell of copious taking and sorting of notes, a laborious *"travail d'historien"* which was to result, according to one communication, in a history of the "inner life" of the maiden.[8] During his year of leave from the École Normale (1895–96), he visited Domrémy and the Meuse country.

Over a period of three years Péguy consulted every printed authority within reach,[9] but among all the chroniclers and artificers to whom he turned in search of insight, Jules Michelet undoubtedly stood out.[10] It has been noted that this great nineteenth-century precursor of Charles Péguy and Anatole France once himself toyed with the thought of writing a play on Joan of Arc, and that his outline [— the first act at Domrémy, the next three reconstructing her campaigns and her capture, and the last describing trial and execution—] foreshadowed Péguy's triptych: *Domrémy—Les Batailles—Rouen.*[11] But Michelet's impact goes deeper than that. Joan's voices, her battles, and her trial constitute three obvious climaxes in a short and miraculous life, around which any reconstruction, whether historic, dramatic, or poetic, would have to revolve. What is important is that Michelet imparted to them a meaning which Péguy, in turn, accepted after him. His relatively few pages on the Maid of Orléans are the most important single source of *Jeanne d'Arc.*

The great romantic historian saw 1429 and 1789 on the same

[7] "Les sources de la 'Jean d'Arc' de Péguy," *ACPFM,* No. 32 (1953), 31.

[8] Béguin, "De la Jeanne d'Arc de 1897 au Mystère de 1909," 12; Auguste Martin, "Charles Péguy, Lettres à Léon Deshairs," *ACPFM,* No. 38 (1954), 19–20; Auguste Martin, "Lettres de Péguy et Albert Lévy à Théo Woehrel," *ACPFM,* No. 56 (1957), 20.

[9] Marcel Tricaud, "Les sources de la 'Jeanne d'Arc' de Péguy," *ACPFM,* No. 37 (1954), 3–9.

[10] For a review of the interpretations of Jeanne d'Arc by those authors on whom Péguy chiefly relied, see Egidé Jeanné, *L'Image de la Pucelle d'Orléans dans la littérature historique française depuis Voltaire* (Liege, 1935), 62–166.

[11] Tricaud, "Les sources de la 'Jeanne d'Arc' de Péguy," 6.

plane, as two moments in which the French nation discovered itself. As a result, he endowed the shepherd girl from Domrémy with a special kind of sainthood, which began to have a renewed and ambiguous significance for the generation born in the shadow of the defeat of 1871 and facing the end of France's isolation in international affairs. For two years before Péguy began his work, the year 1892 had added a new and as yet incalculable dimension to the dialogue between the die-hard advocates of the recovery of Alsace-Lorraine and the new empire builders. A secret military pact had been concluded with Russia. The next year, units of the czar's fleet were accorded a frenetic welcome in Toulon; and on October 5, 1896, Nicolas II became the first Christian monarch to visit the capital of the Third Republic.[12] Step by step these successive visits revealed the closeness of an agreement whose range was the subject of extensive speculations. The full meaning of the *entente* became apparent only when President Faure returned the Russian autocrat's call in April of 1897 and toasted him as "friend and ally." The popularity of this alliance between incompatibles indicated that France had, if nothing else, adjusted to her inability to stand alone either as neighbor or as enemy of Imperial Germany. The age of Boulanger was past and with it the time when the *royaume de France* could be freed by any liberator risen from the ranks of the people.

What could Michelet's Joan therefore mean in the 1890's? As he presented her, she was holy in the eyes of the nation rather than the Church. The kingdom of France which she had saved was not a dynastic creation like the other great states of Europe; it was born of the strength and the will of the people. Thus the *pucelle* was identified with a community, democratic in the purest sense of the word, and this identification compelled her to choose compassion over aggression. To Michelet, the romantic revolutionary, this was an inescapable conclusion. The people were not grasping like a dynastic ruler. Their morality eschewed conquest, he believed, and preferred to build bridges between

---

[12] For a sample of this reaction, see Anatole Leroy-Beaulieu, "Le voyage du Tsar," *Revue des deux Mondes,* CXXXVII (1896), 549–69.

nations. While Joan of Arc, a true daughter of the people, had taken up the sword in defense of her country, she could still weep at the sight of the dead, forbear to attack a retreating enemy, and be more concerned with the welfare of the souls of the departed than with avenging the depredation of the living. But in the 1890's when Péguy discovered her, albeit largely through Michelet, the democratic nation had decided to lean not on the sword of popular enthusiasm, but on the cannons of an absolute ruler from abroad. What would Péguy make of the contradiction between the ways of her heroine and the ways of Republican diplomacy?

This gap between Péguy's historical ideal and the realities of his day was equally relevant to Michelet's portrayal of Joan as a good anticlerical Christian. Her call had come from the King of Heaven. She could serve no earthly institution, the Church included, except in accordance with the commands she had received from Him directly. It will surprise no one that God would make a pure and simple daughter of the people the vessel of His will, rather than the pharisaic *docteurs* of the theological faculties. When taunted by them: "Do your voices forbid you to submit to the militant Church?" she faced them squarely and replied: "They do not forbid it at all, provided our Lord be served first." God's service, as she saw it, demanded the liberation of France. This was the great cause which the Church had refused to recognize during the Hundred Years' War, just as it had fought on the side of the enemy during the campaigns of the great revolution.[13]

In this respect the Third Republic of the middle 1890's also provided an atmosphere in which the positions of Michelet were no longer wholly relevant. Anticlericalism was losing its momentum as Pope Leo XIII urged French Catholics to abandon their nostalgic monarchism.[14] Although the immediate political repercussions of this appeal apeared negligible—a major party

[13] Jules Michelet, *Histoire de France* (Paris, n.d.), VI, 165–258.

[14] For the most recent treatment of the events leading to this important departure, see James E. Ward, "The French Cardinals and Leo XIII's 'Ralliement' Policy," *Church History,* XXXIII (1964), 60–73.

representing republican clericalism did not materialize until 1945—the gulf between clericals and skeptics seemed to be narrowing. In an address before the chamber on March 3, 1894, the minister of public worship, Eugène Spuller, recognized the new spirit emanating from Rome and promised that it would meet an equally tolerant accommodation in Paris.

In the intellectual realm, the almost simultaneous passing of Hyppolite Taine and Ernest Renan in 1893 had removed the two men who had guided a generation allegedly beholden to a staunch faith in science. Their immediate successors, the intellectual innovators of the next decade, attempted to reverse the spiritual course of France almost at once. They rejected "the whole tendency to discuss human behavior in terms of analogies drawn from natural science." [15] "The soul is about to rediscover its antecedents," wrote the critic René Doumic in 1895.[16] "The supernatural is recovering its rightful place, and the appreciation of the mysterious has been given back to us," to which the philosopher Alfred Fouillée added: "After passing through a period during which . . . the intellect rebelled against the heart, we are entering another where the heart rises against the intellect." [17]

The most influential and in his day also one of the most polished spokesmen of this intellectual reaction became Ferdinand Brunetière, member of the Academie Française and editor of *La Revue des Deux Mondes*. In a notable essay on the relation between science and religion he substituted for the current variations on the Darwinist theme the hypothesis that the two constituted two distinct and unrelated spheres. "It no more behooves science to deny or affirm the 'proofs of religion,' " he declared, "than it is the task of religion to reject or debate the

[15] H. Stuart Hughes, *Consciousness and Society, 1890–1930* (New York, 1961), 35–36.

[16] In a review of J. K. Huysman's new novel *En route, Revue des deux Mondes,* CXXXIII (1895), 467. On the same subject, see also René Dumesnil, *La publication d' 'En route'* (Paris, 1931), chaps. VII and VIII.

[17] Alfred Fouillée, "Le mouvement idéaliste en France," *Revue des deux Mondes,* CXXXIV (1896), 276.

. . . findings of Egyptology." [18] This new option of coexistence appeared to captivate the young academic generation in particular whose members, as one observer saw it, were "beginning once more to extoll morality and religion with the same enthusiasm which the young people of 1848 had accorded science and free thought." [19]

And yet, the Joan of Arc of Michelet—democratic, pacific, anticlerical, and devout—was obviously a kindred spirit to the generation of 1870. She reflected Michelet's modified Jacobinism, which embraced a mystic faith in popular virtue; she illustrated that his view of war was conceived in terms of the traditions of 1793—defense of the soil and dissemination of the gospel of liberty; and she emphasized his skeptical contempt of the hierarchy coupled with an abiding devotion to a God who would never forsake France. To Péguy's generation these beliefs continued to be part of French civism and religion, even though the nature of their practice might have changed. The Third Republic was democratic, although democracy had descended from the barricades and put on a top hat and a frock coat. The Third Republic was peace-loving; but the defense of its soil depended, in addition to the strength of an incompatible ally, on a professional army, even though the gospel of liberty was being preached at home and abroad by a strange succession of missionaries from Marshal Bugeaud, the conqueror of Algeria, to Marshal Lyautey, the "pacifier" of the rest of North Africa. The Third Republic was secular; but in the 1890's the clerics who were ejected during the preceding decade of educational secularization were returning, and the faith they represented was more deeply rooted among the established elite of the Academy and the major editorial offices than it had been a century earlier.

Raised in a national environment that rested on these attitudes, Péguy could admire Michelet's Joan because she em-

[18] Ferdinand Brunetière, "Après une visite au Vatican," *Revue des deux Mondes,* CXXVII (1895), 111. See also by the same author, "La moralité de la doctrine évolutive," *Revue des deux Mondes,* CXXIX (1895), 136–62, and a good secondary treatment in J. Van der Lugt, *L'Action réligieuse de Ferdinand Brunetière, 1895–1906* (Paris, 1936), 55–70.

[19] Edouard Rod, *Les Idées morales du temps* (Paris, 1897), 308.

bodied ideals that were recognizable to his time—ideals which he apparently shared: love and respect for the people, love of peace coupled with national strength, approval of the civilizing mission overseas, and a religious tradition that embraced both Robespierre and Christ, in which his own specific position remained at this point admittedly obscure. They provided the air that breathed life into his own *Jeanne d'Arc.*

A complementary vision of tolerance spoke to Péguy from the pages of Alfred de Vigny's *Eloa.* Here he encountered the fallen angel who rebelled against the irreversible sentence of eternal damnation and who offered herself as a substitute sacrifice which would redeem the lost. As Eloa descends to Satan's level, an angelic chorus sings the glory of those who die for the salvation of others.[20] Like Joan of Arc, De Vigny's heroine was moved by an abiding love for the stricken:

> Et toujours dans la nuit un rêve lui montrait
> Un ange malheureux qui de loin l'implorait.[21]

The knowledge of Satan's suffering in hell, like the knowledge of France ground under the heel of the English, would not let either heroine rest until she had fearlessly sacrificed herself.

Péguy derived an even more powerful and persistent inspiration from the martyrdom of Antigone as portrayed by Sophocles. Polynices has invaded the *polis* and has been killed in the ensuing battle. In retribution the law denies him the honor of a ceremonial burial. Dog and carrion will devour his remains, wind and sun will bleach his bones. To save his soul from the horror that follows such desecration of the flesh, Antigone elects to brave the wrath of man and the gods and bury the outlaw brother. The penalties do not deter her. To leave her duty undone and die a peaceful and hence ignoble death is infinitely worse than the most cruel punishment.

Michelet, De Vigny, and Sophocles: three diverse and powerful impulses guided the young *normalien* absorbed in the mystery

---

[20] Alfred de Vigny, *Oeuvres complètes: Poèmes,* with notes by Fernand Baldensperger (Paris, 1914), 38.
[21] Quoted in Maurice Paléologue, *Alfred de Vigny* (Paris, 1894), 23.

of Joan of Arc and caught in the realities of a period of transition. He read them before he wrote; Sophocles certainly was a discovery of the early nineties. He read them to prepare; that is without doubt true of Michelet. And he read De Vigny as he wrote.

In March of 1897, two months before *Jeanne d'Arc* was completed, Péguy finished a "sketch of a study of Alfred de Vigny" [22] which, insignificant as it is—a mere college composition—nevertheless contained in embryonic form the views that provided direction for his entire adult life. That they first emerge here does not make the sketch a document of De Vigny's "influence." Rather, for the first time Péguy found himself by reacting to someone he despised. He rejected De Vigny's scale of human values which were rigged so that the poet was bound to emerge supreme. De Vigny loved all "virtues beyond the call of duty," thus avoiding, in Péguy's opinion, the performance of those which society imposes on all. He embraced the unattainable out of sheer moral laziness. He fled reality, finding refuge in a nihilistic pessimism. To De Vigny the world was bad, and everything ended in nothingness. Péguy scorned this self-indulgent world-weariness. He granted that the world was redolent with evil, but his immediate response to its imperfections was the desire to improve it.

In *Jeanne d'Arc* Péguy affirmed this concern in human terms: "Men are what they are, but we must consider what they should be." [23] "We *must* consider" was the crucial phrase, for *Jeanne d'Arc* was above all a gospel of duty.

In the first part of the play—*Domrémy*—Joan and her friend Hauviette symbolize the opposing forces of devotion to duty and egoistic timidity, much like Antigone and Ismene in the opening scene of the Sophoclean tragedy. Hauviette hopes that the city of Orléans may soon surrender to the English so that peace can

[22] Chares Péguy, "Ébauche d'une étude sur Alfred de Vigny," *Cahiers,* XX, No. 7 (1931), 11–35.

[23] Charles Péguy, *Oeuvres Poétiques Complètes* (Paris, 1951), 1152–53, hereinafter cited as Péguy, *OPC.* Since the original, privately printed edition of *Jeanne d'Arc* lacks pagination, all references to the play are documented from this recent version.

return to France. Joan protests. There can be no peace until a wrong has been righted, until the strangers have left the country. The homeland must be saved. Frenchmen cannot serve foreign masters, nor can they depend on alien allies to do their work for them. Freedom must be earned, it cannot be enjoyed as a gift. The victim's own strength alone must justly punish the aggressor.[24]

Part two—*Les Batailles*—shows these principles in action. Called by God, the girl's confidence knows no bounds. When asked whether she wishes to participate in a council of war, she cannot see in this query a gracious concession to an unskilled novice by experienced warriors. Instead of shyly accepting, she answers coolly: "I will gladly come and tell you what must be done." [25] That the king's lieutenants may not take kindly to being told how to fight battles gives her little pause. God has instructed her, this makes any council superfluous: one argues with neither the wisdom nor the authority of the Lord.[26]

Victorious, the maiden has her way; but before the battle of Paris, where her fortunes turn, the theologians—by all odds the villains of the piece—begin to whisper of witchcraft and heresy. In the field, discipline begins to deteriorate. The soldiers resume the habit of looting as the novelty of her inspiration wears off. Gilles de Rais scoffs at her love of peace; booty is what the soldier seeks, not pacification. To these counsels of moral defeat, Joan replies as readily as to Hauviette's posture of appeasement: France cannot be saved through wrongdoing. If her freedom could be restored only through an appeal to human baseness, it were better that she remain in bondage.[27]

At Rouen, finally, the *pucelle* has ceased to be an active protagonist. The saintly shepherd girl, Péguy's symbol of human perfectability and perfection, is now the object of a battle between the forces of good and evil among her judges. Frère Mathieu Bourat suspects that her trial, ostensibly for heresy, has

[24] Péguy, *OPC*, 978–80.
[25] *Ibid.*, 1037.
[26] *Ibid.*, 1073.
[27] *Ibid.*, 1073.

a predominantly political purpose. If Joan is to be tried by the Church, why is she kept in a prison of the temporal power? Maître Nicolas L'Oiseleur, the exponent of evil expediency, explains the uses of a divided jurisdiction. Joan is the prisoner of an alliance in which everyone's sensitivities must be duly considered. Bourat does not follow that argument. "The Church, maître, need not consider temporal hierarchies, the subordination of man to man. She is . . . the only sovereign and every man is her vassal." [28] As the *pucelle* languishes in her cell, he seems to represent temporarily her spirit on the stage, echoing even her iron concept of duty. "Men are what they are, and they do what they do," he concludes the argument with his adversary in canon law; "that does not concern us. What does concern us is what *we* must do." Like Joan, he proceeds immediately from principle to action. Why this deviousness against the heretic unless there is doubt about her guilt? If she has sinned against God she must be punished by the Church, and the Church must insist on it. If she has merely run afoul of secular forces or, worse, if she is guiltless, the Church must break with her persecutors. As matters stand, Bourat will not be judge in a trial whose nature is equivocal. But he, after all, is not Joan; he does not fight; like Pilate he merely washes his hands.

After Bourat's departure Joan returns to the stage. Her judges charge her with transgressions against the laws of the Church. She replies that she does not know what they mean by "the Church." She has obeyed God. After it has been patiently explained to her that the Church has no other purpose but to do likewise, that obedience to it is the mark of a good Christian, she agrees: "I, too, am of the Church, as you say, because I am a good Christian. . . ." [29] Delighted, the inquisitors seek to extract from her a declaration of complete submission. Péguy's Joan replies in the words of Michelet's heroine: "I do want to serve the Church . . . provided, be it understood, that our Lord God be served first." [30] Discouraged and annoyed, her

[28] *Ibid.*, 1123.
[29] *Ibid.*, 1159.
[30] *Ibid.*, 1161.

questioners wish to know whether she considers herself saved. Again, the words of the learned are meaningless to the pure, humble servant of God. Only He counts. If she is in a state of grace, may He preserve her in it; if she is not, may He, in His infinite mercy, grant it to her.[31] In the final analysis, "Church" is to her an empty word. Joan, who has been called by God to perform a duty, can only serve Him who is infinitely above her judges. Like Antigone, she cannot act otherwise. She cannot sin in order to save herself. She cannot submit to men, only commit herself to her maker. As she goes to her death, she is sustained by her righteousness; and the curtain falls as she calls on Him to "save us all." [32]

From beginning to end *Jeanne d'Arc* is a call to duty without compromise. Saddened unto death by the sufferings of war, by the depredations visited upon her country, by the engulfing specter of damnation incarnate in many physical and spiritual shapes, Joan first contemplates her own "potential" as savior: "Who must be saved? How must we save?" she asks.[33] Do we save by giving food to the hungry, or by taking up the sword for France? She finds both efforts futile. Charity will not last, and hunger will soon overtake the destitute once more.[34] Fighting for France arouses nothing more lofty than greed and lust for blood. During the lifting of the siege of Orléans, Joan is horrified by the killing of a captured enemy before he has had the opportunity to make his peace with God. Later at Rouen the memory of this crime haunts her and with it the fear that she may have incurred damnation without saving others in the process.[35] But neither deeds of charity nor of bravery can save anyone. Man's only hope is to bring himself closer to salvation by his integrity. On the battlefield, Joan clasps the royal standard. "I loved that standard forty times more than my sword." [36] Three

---

[31] *Ibid.*, 1163.
[32] *Ibid.*, 1204–1205.
[33] *Ibid.*, 1024–25.
[34] *Ibid.*, 960.
[35] *Ibid.*, 1192.
[36] *Ibid.*, 1150.

times she rejects the temptation of compromise. She is willing to risk all in order to save France, while Hauviette prefers comfort with dishonor. At war she faces and overcomes the condescension of the regular army man who challenges divine strategy and the counsel of the cynical freebooter to let the soldiers loot. "Avoid trouble. Let men do what they have always done," she is advised. But Joan refuses a tarnished victory. Nor will she abandon her goal in adversity. After her failure to enter Paris, Father Claudet urges her to take the reverse as a sign that her mission is completed. She has crowned the king. Perhaps this was all she was meant to accomplish. Again she is unyielding. Her voices have told her to drive the English from France. They did not promise that she would succeed.[37] She must obey at any risk and at any cost. Abandoned at last by an indolent king and tried by clerical collaborators, Joan faces the supreme temptation: to save her life by telling the court what it wishes to extract from her. But she cannot commit blasphemy by admitting a guilt which consisted of serving God.

There is an answer to the question, "Who must be saved?" The last two lines of the play appeal to God and His son "to save us all for eternal life." There is no answer to the question, "How must we save?" We cannot save; and nothing on this earth, no power and no act, can save us. Our only hope is divine mercy. In all we undertake, victory belongs to Him alone.[38] This is what Péguy tells us in *Jeanne d'Arc*. De Vigny was wrong. Life is not nothingness. There is duty for man. There is mercy from God.

Nevertheless, Albert Béguin, the editor of the Catholic monthly *Esprit,* wrote in 1956 that the Christian *motif* in *Jeanne d'Arc* was injected more for the sake of historical accuracy than from the compulsion of deep feeling.[39] It is difficult to accept such reasoning. Péguy chose a mystic heroine whom God had called. If her inspiration and her destiny had not been meaningful, would he not have chosen a different subject? The annual procession in the maiden's honor had been a part of his child-

---

[37] *Ibid.,* 1097.

[38] *Ibid.*

[39] Béguin, "De la Jeanne d'Arc de 1897 au Mystère de 1909," 17–18.

hood. The ritual that impressed him was religious. The subject was religious. Had Péguy wished to deny that ingredient in his own heritage, had he wished to extoll some social utopia on the stage, Robespierre or Babeuf would have served him much better. Yet he re-created a heroine who was sensitive to physical suffering, who loved her country and her king, and who placed herself and all that was dear to her in the care of God. Social, patriotic, and Christian, that was Péguy's Joan. To eliminate any one of these attributes would have meant changing a subject which Péguy after all—and not Béguin—had chosen.[40]

Béguin was repelled by Christian anticlericalism. To a committed Catholic, it must be both paradox and heresy; and if he at the same time admires Péguy, as Béguin did, a dilemma results from which he has every reason to desire an escape. But the difficulties of Péguy's position were inescapable in his own life, and they remain inescapable to his biographers.

Joan of Arc was revealed to Péguy through the eyes of a Michelet who had passed through the purgatory of the Revolution of 1830 and—a decade later—through the hellfire of deep personal tragedy, the death of his wife. When he was completing the volume which included the glorious portrait of the Maid of Orléans, he had, in fact, nothing left but his work—history—, his faith—revolution—, and his suspicion of the clergy.[41] Michelet claimed to be sustained by his confidence in the civilizing mission of his country and yet displayed an insatiable spiritual hunger which the past glories of France could not satisfy. The rigor of his anticlericalism, at the same time, was sharpened by his belief that religion permeated history, that it oozed into every corner of every life. Civilized man, i.e. Michelet himself, constantly strove to clarify his relation to religion as an institution, and to religion as the summation of his understanding of the origin and nature of creation. Religion to him meant asking

[40] But note Jean Onimus, "Le patriotisme de Péguy," *ACPFM*. No. 57 (1957), 3. ". . . the heroine of the drama which Péguy composes in 1896 never utters the word 'fatherland' and hardly ever the word 'France.' "

[41] Oscar H. Haac, *Les principes inspirateurs de Michelet* (New Haven, Paris, 1951), 10.

the same questions again and again without hope of an answer.

This vitality of doubt was matched by Michelet's appreciation of the vitality of Christianity. Still, he could not accept what he considered to be its central postulates. The belief in original sin repelled him; and the assertion that "weakness keeps us in humility, in consciousness of the necessity of grace, in the spirit of prayer" [42] would not have prompted him to be weak. He took pride in man's freedom to be and to do good.

The certitude of death was another Christian *kismet* which Michelet denounced. Eternal life was physical as well as spiritual. Rebirth and continuity were the abiding truths of universal history. Finally, since life was eternal and the quest for immortality a metaphysical redundancy, every conflict ended in resolution. All things could eventually be reconciled: church and state, faith and reason, religion and morality, all races and all cults.[43] Perhaps he scored Christianity most for its failure to accept this design, for, as he once complained, "Christianity is not Christian enough."

At this juncture the anticlerical in Michelet was joined by the anti-intellectual. Christianity had become untrue to itself because a desiccating scholasticism had overcome the spirit of love and devotion. The Church had forsaken the noblest ranks of mankind, the people. It had become a coterie of theologians whose intellectual convolutions alienated the people's good sense. Personal nearness to God, expressed in the heroic folly of Joan, roused an abandoned nation,[44] as it inspired Michelet, as it gave voice to young Charles Péguy.

If the republican Michelet was the man whose vision of the Maid of Orléans became the major model for Péguy's *Jeanne d'Arc,* then one need hardly speculate about the religious essence of the trilogy. Both mentor and disciple were rooted in the same national tradition which reconciled patriotism and Christianity.

[42] Francois Petit, O.P. *The Problem of Evil* (Twentieth-Century Encyclopedia of Catholicism, v. 20) (New York, 1959), 92.

[43] Mary-Elizabeth Johnson, *Michelet et le Christianisme* (Paris, 1951), 238–39.

[44] Jeanlouis Cornuz, *Jules Michelet: Un aspect de la pensée réligieuse au XIXe siècle* (Geneva, 1955), 168.

Both revered a revolutionary past, as a result of which spiritual and temporal salvation became curiously intertwined. By coincidence Péguy wrote *Jeanne d'Arc* at a time when the same accommodation between spiritual and social justice was beginning to be propagated by the Church itself. In 1892, Leo XIII's great encyclical *Rerum novarum* had proclaimed that "evangelical morality had a social dimension which none of the faithful had a right to overlook." [45] A Joan of Arc weeping for the hungry was not at odds with a Joan of Arc praying for the salvation of all.

But the case propounding the religious essence of the trilogy is immeasurably strengthened if one proceeds from the source and from the arguments of historical coincidence to the work itself. What specific internal evidence is there of the devotional nature of *Jeanne d'Arc,* other than the historical subject itself? Most obviously, the shift from prose to verse whenever the heroine prays. These prayers are not formally liturgical. They are spontaneous and evangelistic, sudden verbal outbursts addressed to God. They are the poetic buds that will later bloom into the epic mysteries of Péguy's mature years. The shepherd girl pleads with the Creator to vouchsafe France a great captain. She asks forgiveness for leaving home without her father's permission. Reminiscing soliloquies on the beauties of the Meuse valley constitute the first lyric attempts of the young Péguy. Every utterance points toward an epic culmination, the heartrending last plea to "save us all." To stress the loftiness of the virgin's meditations, Péguy derogates ritual prayer. When Monsignor Pierre Cauchon opens the session of the tribunal with the Lord's Prayer and the Ave Maria, both are printed as prose. The impropriety is deliberate and demonstrates the very opposite of Béguin's contention. Joan's search for religious verity is not introduced to complete a historical tableau; Cauchon's ritual is. To have him mumble prescribed formulae before the trial constitutes the touch of historical realism. Joan's appeals to God, on the other hand, are the contributions of the poet who relives

[45] A. Latreille, et al., *Histoire du Catholicisme en France* (Paris, 1962), III, 479.

history through his imagination and whose vision makes of *Jeanne d'Arc* more than an unusual condensation of Quicherat's trial record.

The aforementioned blank pages, the unusual pauses in a closet play, point in the same direction. Obviously they are interjected at the end of each act, when the reader naturally halts to consider what he has just read. But there are other blanks, even in the very middle of a scene. Is it unreasonable to suggest that they occur after Péguy has put into the mouth of his protagonist words of unusual importance? If so, what utterances precede, or follow, such untoward pauses?

There is that moving passage expressing Joan's love for mankind, which concludes:

Et j'aime le regard humain quand il s'envole
Ainsi qu'un trait vivant droit au ciel désirable,
Encore plus douloureux et doux que la parole,
Vaillant, vite et fidèle, et beau, prèsque admirable. (p. 969)

Péguy forces one to pause in mid-action again after Joan has bid Hauviette farewell with the first intimation of her calling: "There is news [not only from the battlefield] but also from beyond" (p. 982). And again a moment later in the midst of a soliloquy after the portentous passage,

mais puisque les Anglais
Ont décidé d'aller à l'assaut d'Orléans
Je sens qu'il est grand temps que je décide aussi.

Here Péguy takes infinite pains to make us perceive the juncture at which Joan's despair over her country's suffering becomes more than the simple hurt of the frustrated patriot and grows into the terror man inevitably feels as God's will is about to be revealed to him. The first outcry following this silence reveals the overwhelming magnitude of what has happened meanwhile when the girl intones,

Moi, Jeanne, je décide que je vous obéirai.

Later the *pucelle* persuades her uncle to aid in her departure under the pretense of an innocuous visit to his home. Once plans are made, they separate, each to make his preparation for the journey. As he leaves her, he exclaims, *"À tout à l'heure et que Dieu nous pardonne,"* and Joan cries out *"Hélas!"* as she sinks to her knees. Again Péguy commands silence, to resume with the famous soliloquy so reminiscent of Schiller's *Jungfrau von Orleans:*

> Adieu, Meuse endormeuse et douce à mon enfance. . . .

Here Joan's anguish at deserting her family to follow His call, the barest hint of an underlying wish to be spared a mission which begins with a lie, lends poignancy to the characteristic dramatic device. She is not yet possessed by her later certitude that the service of God places her beyond the reach of human judgment. All she can feel is an overwhelming despair at being forced to commit a wrong before she can do right.

The same agonizing paradox which forces Péguy's heroine to transgress in order to assure the victory of virtue leads him to inject a long silence into the first act of the second part of *Les Batailles*. Jeanne has impressed upon Raoul de Gaucourt and Gilles de Rais the fact that Paris must be taken by storm. At the same time discipline is breaking down, and the good cause is being defiled by murder and rapine. Her voices tell her to press on. The maiden is caught between two kinds of death-dealing— banditry and war. Left alone by the two disgruntled warriors, she meditates in anguish before raising her voice to God:

> O mon Dieu, je savais la douleur des batailles. . . . (p. 1062)

Les Batailles, of course, moves rapidly, although much of the action occurs offstage. There are fewer soliloquies; Joan is rarely alone with her God. In the fourth act, after the failure of the assault on Paris, she attempts several times to pour out her heart in prayer:

> Il ne peut savoir ce que mon âme est lasse,
> Lasse de la bataille et lasse du conseil. (p. 1093)

and again:

> Mon Dieu pardonnez-moi si j'ai l'âme si lasse, (p. 1099)

and finally:

> O mon Dieu faudra-t-il que je sois toute seule? (p. 1101)

Each time, however, she is interrupted by one of her lieutenants, two of whom are leaving the encampment rather than obey the King's armistice with the Burgundians.

The central part of the trilogy ends as the heroine goes forth on the raid that will result in her capture. With God? Without Him? Against Him? Who is to say?

Rouen is the sequel to Joan's defeat. The trial and her fate are one kind of balance sheet drawn from the good and the evil she has wrought. What is the heart of the matter here, as far as Péguy is concerned? Where will he now require us to stop and reflect? Certainly none of the words spoken by her enemies can give us pause. None of her testimony before the human judges is edged by silence. But in the second act, when the shepherdess' unwillingness to submit elicits from her tormentors dire threats of damnation, Guillaume Evrard delivers the only verse not assigned to the heroine as he describes the torments of hell in strident tones (pp. 1181–82). This intimation of the terrible fate of man leaves the accused and the court dumb. After a brief silence Joan is led wordlessly from the chamber, the curtain falls, and the stage directions call for an intermission of forty seconds in the middle of the act.

Returned to her cell, Joan is left alone; and after another short pause in which the reader is not so much called upon to reflect on what has passed as to prepare for what is to come, the *pucelle* sobs out her despair:

> Oh, j'irais dans l'enfer avec les morts damnés,
> Avec les condamnés et les abandonnés. (p. 1187)

The last years pass in review, the battles, the dead, and finally the betrayal of her king, against whose express command she has led the second unsuccessful attack on Paris. When constrained to ask herself whether she is not lower than Judas the arch-traitor, her flow of words stops abruptly. As if to change a subject that has become intolerable, she returns to memories of childhood and of home. But the shadow of betrayal darkens her mind even here:

> O comme il me souvient de l'enfance passée (p. 1188)

that childhood which also ended with a lie, stealing from home without parental blessing.

The device of the dramatic pause is brought into play during the crisis in each part of the trilogy. In *Domrémy* as Joan hears and follows God. In *Les Batailles* during those junctures in which she obeys her voices even after they have led her into defeat. In *Rouen* when she confronts in succession the human and the divine judge, as she wrestles with the fear of death and the torments of her conscience. These fragments of a dialogue with God constitute the moments when Péguy insists that the reader think as he turns the page.

Thus *Jeanne d'Arc* reveals Péguy's theocentricity at the very outset of his creative, adult life. All roads lead to God, all questions and answers emanate from Him and lead to Him; only He can judge, only He can save. Pursuing this path of analysis, one comes upon the other constants of Péguy's world view.

The revelation of God to Joan occurs without intercession. One major villainy of the clergy in *Jeanne d'Arc*, therefore, consists of its meddling in a sacred relationship between the creator and a chosen human being. Thus, it is more than officiousness, it is blasphemy to insist upon interpreting the will of God after it has been addressed to His pure and innocent handmaiden at Domrémy.

At one point in this running attack on the clergy, which is mainly concentrated in the last part of the play, Péguy echoes briefly, but poignantly, Michelet's charge of treason. In the first act of *Rouen,* as the tribunal files in, one protagonist discovers among the judges an English theologian, William Haiton. He voices surprise. But Maître Nicholas L'Oiseleur reassures him that one of the glories of the universal Church consists of disregarding the human distinction between French and English.[46] Since the young socialist Péguy professed to believe in the brotherhood of man, it is strange to see him attack the Church as an international body. One glimpses here another facet of Péguy's universe. Even in this essentially religious drama, the young poet reveals his hatred of strangers who have designs on

[46] Péguy, *OPC,* 1135.

the inviolability of his country and his nation and of priests who, under the guise of Christian solidarity, promote the interests of France's enemies.

Still, there are occasions when Péguy treats the enemies of his heroine with a certain disdainful, condescending charity. He grants that it is possible for them to mean well, but shows, too, their limited understanding. Why should it be surprising that they doubt her voices? No God has ever spoken to them. There is one limitation which these theological inquisitors will never be able to overcome: the narrow mind of the reasoning intellectual. Under the impress of Michelet's romantic imagination, Péguy fortifies his distrust of the clergy with a stout dose of anti-intellectualism. The fact that the hierarchy leads the doubters of Joan's source of inspiration is merely incidental. But in diverse dramatic and oratorical embellishments Péguy accumulates the hard evidence which convicts the intellectual and the *clerc* in priest's clothing in particular.

Péguy's youthful anti-intellectualism reflected more than a reading of Michelet and the superficial crosscurrents of republican harmony. Behind the measures of French rejuvenation in international affairs and reconciliation at home, he, in harmony with many of his contemporaries, responded to the major intellectual innovators of the 1890's who "were profoundly interested in the problem of irrational motivation in human conduct."[47] This aspect of the movement to free the soul from the prison of reason derived much of its strength from foreign cultures.[48] The tremors that followed the explosive discovery of Russian literature through Melchior de Vogüé's *Le Roman russe* (1886) had not abated after two such disparate heroes as Feodor Dostoevski and Leo Tolstoi unleashed a host of new and strange emotions in this searching generation.[49] The intermittent intellectual love

[47] Hughes, *Consciousness and Society*, 35.

[48] For a contemporary assessment of literary influence from abroad, see André Hallays, "De l'influence des littératures étrangères," *Revue de Paris*, II (1895), 874–94.

[49] On the prolonged after-effects of De Vogüé's book, see Joseph Paul-Boncour, *Entre deux guerres; souvenirs sur la Troisième République* (3 vols.; New York, 1946–47), I, 63–64.

affair between France and Germany gained new intensity as Nietzsche took France by storm, and pilgrimages to Richard Wagner's musical temple in Bayreuth became the rage even among such nationalists as Maurice Barrès. It was of course comforting and respectable to discover the Russian ally to be civilized, but Nietzsche and Wagner had to be justified as representatives of a more universal culture than that of the country of their origin. Accordingly, the French crusaders at Wahnfried were not Germanophiles but rebels against naturalism in search of a new idealistic mystique.[50] As a result they were able to convince themselves that their seasonal treks across the Rhine were undertaken for the sake of strengthening and purifying France. The spark of Wagner's genius did indeed generate both imitation and opposition. His work had long been accepted in Paris, but now it gave rise to a school of consciously nationalist composers including Saint-Saëns, Vincent d'Indy, and Gabriel Faure.[51]

The pleasures derived from the reading of Nietzsche were likewise elaborately justified. He was said to sustain a "generation disgusted with democracy."[52] In this instance this would include the revolted aristocrat á la Gobineau as well as the bearded anarchist intellectual of the *Revue Blanche*. A growing flight from the "disarray of modern life" by "the social and intellectual anarchy of the present" was proffered as another justification by the same disciples, who claimed that Nietzsche provided answers which made such escapism unnecessary.[53] But most important was the contention that in welcoming Nietzsche, France was offering asylum to the work of a man who preferred her civilization to his own and who lived in a state of rebellion

---

[50] J. M. Carré, *Les écrivains français devant le mirage allemand* (Paris, 1947), 116–17.

[51] Claude Digeon, *La crise allemande de la pensée française (1870–1914)* (Paris, 1959), 454–58.

[52] Halleys, "De l'influence des littératures étrangères," 883; also the testimony of Jacques Bainville in Jacques Morland "Enquête sur l'influence allemande en France," *Mercure de France*, XLIV (1902), 299–300.

[53] Guy Batault, "Nietzsche prophète," *Mercure de France*, LXXX (1909), 411.

against the empire which had been built on France's surrender in 1871.[54]

Less influential, but in step with this Teutonic invasion, was the arrival of Henrik Ibsen, the translation and performance of whose plays likewise left a clear mark on the 1890's, both as theater and as the recognized exhortation toward an individualism both chaste and dynamic.[55]

Liberators from corruption, liberators from vice, liberators from lassitude, these foreign prophets were also acclaimed as liberators from academic tyranny.[56] Again it was Nietzsche in particular who was credited with leading the young above and beyond the stultifying atmosphere of dark classrooms and the dreary pursuit of degrees. Even though his alternative to these intellectual conventions never emerged clearly, his appeal was irresistible,[57] for after all, as Barrès confessed, it was not a new doctrine which this generation sought—the Republic had provided an abundant supply of those—but an activating enthusiasm simply to keep on living.[58]

To Péguy such an enthusiasm flowed from the example of Joan of Arc. She provided the escape from the academic prison of the École Normale whose stifling rigors he sought to escape almost as soon as he had won the prize of admission. And so, while it can no longer be determined which aspect of the anti-intellectual fashion compelled him to pen his first assaults on the academic bastion—for Péguy even in the 1890's wrote few letters—*Jeanne d'Arc* also served as the cover from behind which he was able to direct a barrage against his academic wardens.

[54] Digeon, *La crise allemande de la pensée française*, 457; Carré, *Le mirage allemand*, 123.

[55] Jules Lemaître, "De l'influence récente des littératures du Nord," *Revue des deux Mondes*, CXXVI (1894), 853–54; Halvdan Koht, *The Life of Ibsen* (2 vols.; New York, 1931), II, 270–73.

[56] Rémy de Gourmont in Morland, "Enquête sur l'influence allemande," 336–37.

[57] Cf. *The Journals of André Gide*, trans. Justin O'Brien (3 vols.; New York, 1948), I, 301.

[58] Paraphrased in Henri Drain, *Frédéric Nietzsche et André Gide* (Paris, 1932), 24.

In the most striking expression of this hostility, two learned members of the tribunal discuss the forthcoming trial of Joan. In pompous detail L'Oiseleur impresses upon an older colleague the academic eminence of some of the younger judges. They count among themselves twelve doctors of theology, at least five doctors of civil and canon law, six or seven bachelors of divinity, and a corresponding baccalaureate array versed in the statutes of Church and State.[59] It is a design of grim comedy: a formidable artillery park of learning amassed at Rouen to reduce to subjection an illiterate shepherd girl from Lorraine. How feeble must book learning be that it requires such superiority in numbers, and in diplomas! What a scathing vote of contempt on Péguy's part against the pretensions and insufficiencies of conventional education.

Such sentiments, expressed at this particular point in the poet's life, reveal also that his later feud with the Sorbonne was born of more than the resentment over his own academic failures. Written during his leave from the École Normale and completed after his return, this passage suggests that his commitment to an academic career was even then considerably less than complete. Not only did he treat university honors with contempt, his heroine also preferred action to deliberation. There is no room for councils of war in her conduct of operations. This sentiment is echoed by Jean, Duke of Alençon, who contemptuously calls Charles VII "a wise King, who often sits in council, especially on days of battle." He, together with the *condottiere* La Hire, is one of the lesser heroes of the play who rejects the armistice with Burgundy, characteristically announced at the very moment when substantial forces in Paris were willing to surrender the city. Péguy always takes the side of the activist, and puts the mediator, the negotiator, and the compromiser in an unfavorable light. The men who weigh the issues and the effects appear tarred with the brush of cowardice.

Lastly, Péguy's Joan, once again returning to the model of Michelet, mirrors the socialism he was about to embrace. What position he took within that divided movement will be considered

[59] Péguy, *OPC*, 1080.

in the next chapter. For the moment one may merely suggest that *Jeanne d'Arc* offers no clue to an answer. Nothing in its pages would allow one to label Péguy either as a Marxist, a Possibilist —that peculiar French form of revisionism—as an Allemanist or Syndicalist. All one can hope to accomplish at this point is to relate Michelet's social gospel to Péguy's first literary effort. The two men shared humble origins and they both had ambitious parents. Michelet's artisan father helped his son become a bourgeois professor, Péguy's widowed mother, mending her chairs and saving her sous until she became a *propriétaire* of substance in her section of Orléans, helped her son attain the company and comradeship of the sons of the *grande bourgeoisie*. Both men could safely discourse on the virtues of a humble station and on the merits of earning one's livelihood by manual labor. In so doing they both assumed the position of the *rentier* who opposes the reduction of the working day, lest idleness result in the corruption of the morals of others.

Still, Michelet's and Péguy's respective poses rested on sincere convictions. The former's romantic populism of 1848 was reborn in the latter's heroic shepherdess whose pure instincts remained undefiled by rationalist corruption, who recoiled at the sight of bloody ruin wrought by war before and after her voices had called on her to don armor. Joan was sensible, clean, good, and compassionate. In the very first scene of *Jeanne d'Arc* she suffers for the children whom the war has disinherited:

". . . I saw two children pass, quite alone, descending the path below, the older of the two pulling the other along. They were sobbing: 'I am hungry, I am hungry, I am hungry. . . .' I could hear them from up here. I gave them to eat. They fell over the food like animals and *their eagerness was agony that made me think of all the hungry who are not eating.*" [60] As she goes on to bemoan how little one piece of bread contributes to the stilling of their hunger, Péguy pleads through her not only for man's recognition of his eternal dependence on God, he likewise speaks for the indigent whom no single act of charity can redeem.

[60] *Ibid.,* 952. Italics mine.

The shepherd girl's incorruptible, kind heart is not calloused by the sights of battle. To her the duty to drive out the English is no license to kill. Before she launches the first attack she pleads with the enemy to relinquish peacefully what is not his. Nor does she forget her place and her allegiance after passing her days in the company of princes and nobles. She refuses to join these great men at their council of war, but she has time to reminisce with a humble cannonsmith like her from Lorraine.[61] Theirs becomes a relationship of loyalty, unknown to the powerful makers of history. Maître Jean, her countryman, does not desert her, but joins the last sortie during which she is captured.

The *Jeanne d'Arc* of Péguy is a strange and arresting document. Form and content, structure and message mirror the spiritual ferment, the reconciling harmonies and the disconcerting confusion of the times during which it was written. The observant reader senses that the mixture of humanitarianism and chauvinistic militancy, of conservatism and rebellion, faith and reason, the seemingly contradictory emphases on both spiritual and material salvation stamps it as a major historical monument. This historical significance exceeds its literary virtues. It has the Wagnerian proportions of a first work whose proliferations were not pruned by a cold-blooded editor. One feels neither surprise nor indignation upon learning that its publication went all but unnoticed. Only the *Revue Socialiste* reviewed the volume, doing so at considerable length but without revealing the identity of "Marcel et Pierre Baudouin." [62] Five years later, Péguy was offering the innumerable unsold copies as a bonus to attract new subscribers to the fledgling *Cahiers de la Quinzaine.* Even then the high cost of mailing this heavy, luxury-papered tome made the gift prohibitively expensive for the giver. This trivial fact, on which Péguy commented with a rare sally of wry humor, completes the story of a well-rounded failure. What a contrast between Péguy's first drama and its exact contemporary Edmond Rostand's *Cyrano de Bergerac* which "exploded like a clap of

[61] *Ibid.,* 1034.
[62] *Revue Socialiste,* XXVII (1897), 246–48.

thunder" [63] on the Paris stage on December 28, 1897! What a difference between one play whose printed version was only with difficulty given away and another that sold 220,000 copies in two years while making its author at thirty-three the youngest member of the French Academy! But the essential distinction between these two contemporaries lay in Péguy's anguished attempt on the one hand to ask and answer the questions that agonized an age, while Rostand's success, in the words of one admirer, rested on "the courage to be intelligible and clean." [64] Rostand was an entertainer; Péguy sought to be a prophet. Therefore neither neglect of his monumental, even monstrous work nor its doubtful quality as a play constitutes any real measure of its significance. It represents Péguy's first program. In it we encounter the mystic who is closer to God than ordinary men. It proclaims the refusal to accept damnation of either soul or body. Péguy confesses his "faith in devotion, in sacrifice, in the great community where all sacrifice for all," namely *la patrie,* [65] and at the same time affirms his disdain for the doctors and clerks who cannot see the truth for learning. Ultimately he emphasizes that to the elect, whom divine guidance has shown the way, compromise and deviation are the worst of crimes. Once the voices have spoken, there remains nothing to do but their bidding.

Jeanne d'Arc foreshadowed a determined and solitary Péguy, a passionate and inflexible man who gave early warning of all the conflicts and inconsistencies of his nature. It bore the marks of a far closer kinship with yet another literary fruit of the year 1897, *Les Déracinés* of Maurice Barrès. This aggressively chauvinistic novel by the up and coming young drum major from Lorraine completes in a real sense the spiritual portrait of the mid-nineties in France. In this account of the moral misfortunes of seven young men from his own province who live in the Parisian cesspool of iniquity, Barrès like Péguy extolled the memory of

[63] J. W. Grieve, *L'Oeuvre dramatique d'Edmond Rostand* (Paris, 1931), 49.
[64] Oskar Langer, *Edmond Rostand* (Linz, 1901), 56.
[65] Jules Michelet, *Le peuple* (Paris, 1846), 360.

Lorraine as the birthland of France's savior and the overpowering virtue of men and women close to the soil of every province. Like the heroine of the witch-hunt at Rouen, he inveighed against the "false teachings" of a treacherous expediency.[66] Like Péguy's *Jeanne d'Arc, Les Déracinés* sought to indict the corruption of French youth by the academicians.

Thus one is left with a suggestive triangle, Michelet-Péguy-Barrès. The values and principles of these three men were superficially identical, but the nuances were shifting until one day the heirs of 1848 would emerge all but unrecognizably as the heralds of 1914.

Jeanne d'Arc was the work of a child of the times: its author was the citizen of a republic seemingly secure because of the Russian alliance abroad and the political prowess of her supporters at home, but he was also the member of a society under whose thin façade of political stability spiritual revolt was brewing. The political leaders of France might be cast in the mold of the Jacobins and Girondins, but the intellectual was rapidly drifting away from this ideology; and under the influences of new demigods both foreign and domestic, a new irrational and activist *Weltanschauung* was challenging the traditional assumptions of 1793.

As 1897 was drawing to a close the cracks in the edifice of the Third Republic were once more beginning to show through the whitewash of electoral compromise, thanks to the eruption of the Dreyfus scandal; and Péguy, who shared in this crisis, faced the opportunity of taking his program and testing it on the streets and in the meeting halls. To the vassal of Joan of Arc would soon be added the character of Jaurès' lieutenant, attempting to translate his literary visions into political reality.

[66] Pierre Boisdeffre, *Maurice Barrès* (Paris, 1962), 72–75.

III

Citizen of Utopia

TO say that *Jeanne d'Arc* was written by a socialist is patently meaningless. The dramatic trilogy was not political. It was a personal confession, written after Péguy had opted for socialism. However, since the poet was unable to synchronize his religious and political beliefs, the biographer must eschew any attempt to do it for him, lest he reconstruct the model of an order which never existed. One has no choice but to contemplate a thinking and suffering man and describe him as he appears in a variety of successive postures and attitudes.[1]

Young Charles Péguy is said to have broken with the Catholic faith of his fathers in 1891 while under the influence of the blacksmith Boitier, who taught him the verses of Victor Hugo and the ballads of Béranger. To this down-to-earth *petit patron,* the deterministic cerebrations of Marx were so much irrelevant balderdash. Boitier's influence made of socialism a liberating experience. He freed Péguy from the authority of his ambitious mother and from the social limitations within which the orphaned son of the *douanier* Désiré Péguy would be expected to spend the rest of his life. Socialism meant not a commitment to a set of social and political goals but the freedom to step outside the conventions of the petty bourgeois existence for which young Charles seemed destined.[2]

[1] Cf. Basil Guy, "Notes on Péguy the Socialist," *French Studies,* XV (1961), 28.

[2] Alain Archidec, "Péguy et les socialistes du groupe Jules Guesde," *ACPFM,* No. 69 (1959), 16; No. 70 (1959), 7.

The exploitation of this freedom became easier with each ascent on the scholastic ladder. The possibilities became seemingly unlimited once the young prodigy from Orléans reached the École Normale. But now he met a different kind of socialist, men who were national leaders rather than cracker-barrel sages. The spectrum of socialist leadership was rendered all the more brilliant by the well-known multiplicity of divergencies. It began with Jules Guesde, the Moses of the French movement who had received the commandments from Marx himself. French revisionism was founded by the printer Jean Allemane, a veteran of the labor movement under Napoleon III and of the Commune. In 1890, however, Allemane seceded from that nucleus of peaceful socialism, leaving it under the leadership of the "possibilist" Paul Brousse. Closest to Péguy's own inclination came a brilliant group of unaffiliated or "independent" socialists who constituted the largest component of the socialist group of forty deputies elected to parliament in 1893. Most conspicuous among them was Jean Jaurès, like Péguy a *normalien,* a member of Parliament since 1885 when he had become the youngest member of the chamber. Most influential may have been Lucien Herr, a strange shadowy personage, librarian of the École Normale, never emerging from the dimness of his stacks, never fated to hold positions of eminence either in the party or the republic, always a critic, never an author, but nevertheless credited with effecting a vast number of conversions. Among these converts none proved more spectacular than Jaurès, who led the party from 1905 until his assassination in 1914, and Péguy, who was attracted by the integrity which he presumed to be the reason for their professed independence. "Socialism," he wrote in 1892, "is a new life, not merely a political program. . . . My friends and I will act without compromise." [3] But did his "friends" see socialism in this light? Was there ever a real meeting of the minds between Péguy on the one hand, and Herr and Jaurès on the other; or did the former merely see in them and in the party what

[3] Charles Péguy to Camille Bidault, February 27, 1892, in Auguste Martin, "Exposition du Centre Charles Péguy: Les premières années de Péguy à Paris," *Courrier d'Orléans,* No. 12 (1963), 18.

he wanted to see? Had Péguy really penetrated and absorbed the ideas of socialism before he committed himself to the movement?

These questions are hard to answer because it is difficult at any point in his early life to identify Péguy's political position in terms of surrounding influences. The year he had fallen under the spell of Boitier, Benoit Malon, the editor of the *Revue Socialiste*, summarized his vision of "integral socialism" in a staggering two-volume tract whose form and weight gave it every appearance of a French answer to *Das Kapital*.[4] There is no evidence that Péguy ever read it. There is no way of confirming that he had ever perused a page of Marx.

The Tharaud brothers, on the other hand, whom Péguy met at the Lycée Ste. Barbe, recall in their memoirs of him that their generation read the revolutionary classics of Mikhail Bakunin and Alexander Herzen as well as current anarchist works such as Prince Peter Kropotkin's *Les paroles d'un révolté* (1885) and Jean Grave's *La société mourante et l'anarchie*, whose publication had earned its author a two-year sentence in prison plus a 1000-franc fine.[5] These recollections constitute a worrisome paradox: the future teachers and leaders of France, holders of state scholarships were immersed in the work and thought of men who were associated in the popular mind with a succession of ruthless deeds of violence. Were Péguy and his friends really interested in the works of proscribed advocates of assassination? Were they deliberately exposing themselves to a revolutionary message which even the Socialists had rejected at the Zürich Congress in 1893?[6] One must recall that historical reality was less dramatic. Certainly the assassination of President Sadi-Carnot in 1894 had led to the confiscation of all known anarchist publications and the arrest and trial of thirty of the most prominent members of the movement, including Sébastian Faure and Jean Grave. Yet, the year 1894 was a turning point in the history of French

[4] Benoît Malon, *Le socialisme intégral* (2 vols.; Paris, 1891).

[5] Jean Maitron, *Histoire du mouvement anarchiste en France (1880–1914)* (Paris, 1951), 232 n.

[6] Patricia van der Esch, *La deuxième Internationale (1889–1923)* (Paris, 1957), 29–30.

anarchism. "The era of individual assassination attempts ended." [7] A fair trial exonerated the thirty defendants from complicity with Vaillant or Caserio and they were released, though kept under continuous police surveillance. In 1895 the appearance of *Les Temps Nouveaux* gave back to anarchism a vigorous if not always effective voice.

One may therefore accept as plausible the testimony of the Tharauds. Some *normaliens* preferred anarchist authors as the spokesmen of a libertarian rather than terrorist ideology. The replacement of the state "by an entirely free and spontaneous cooperation among individuals, groups, regions, and nations," [8] signified to them a paradise of freedom whose attractions were apparent even to those down-to-earth minds who had long despaired of its attainment. Here was the antithesis to the ruthless world of Darwin and Spencer, compellingly synthesized by the motto of "mutual aid" in Peter Kropotkin's vision which insisted that all creatures were cooperative rather than competitive[9] by nature. The notion of a society in which individuals should provide for each other protection and justice "based on mutual respect of [universal] moral obligations," [10] came to be understood as the basis of anarchism and constituted the essence of its attraction to those young men in particular who were preparing for a career in teaching and letters.

Is there, on the other hand, any evidence that Péguy participated in this reading of Kropotkin and Grave and that it affected his views? The attempt to answer this question should begin with a consideration of another letter, written to a friend in the provinces in May, 1895, in which he labeled socialism as spiritual liberation. In a socialist society, according to Péguy, every individual would be free to contribute his tithe to "mankind's loftiest labors: Philosophy, Art, and Science." Such an order wasted no effort and no talent because it distributed equally

---

[7] Maitron, *Histoire du mouvement anarchiste,* 241.

[8] Oscar Jaszi, "Anarchism," *Encyclopedia of the Social Sciences,* II, 46–53.

[9] Cf. G. D. H. Cole, *A History of Socialist Thought* (London, 1953–61), II, 339.

[10] Van der Esch, *La deuxième Internationale,* 24.

work, leisure, and the blessing of self-realization. "To accomplish this, I am joining the socialists," he concluded. Félicien Challaye, a classmate at the École Normale, later cited this letter as evidence of the "anarchist hue" of "Péguy's youthful ideal." [11] Péguy may have been echoing Grave who likewise insisted that true revolution must not be the work of hungry men, but of citizens both sensitive to and jealous of individual rights. [12]

At the same time it is possible to read a call to violence into this letter. Péguy listed the enemies of his dynamic, utopian socialism: the churches, the banks, big industry, high finance, and the army, all allies of a *bourgeoisie gouvernementale* which, he believed, would stop at nothing to preserve its preëminence. At the outset of revolution, these powers would resist with arms, and mutiny alone would overcome them. There is other evidence that he did not expect the birth of the universal socialist republic to be accompanied without bloodshed. Two months after his marriage in October, 1897, he hinted to a friend that his apartment contained a secret hiding place and concealed exits for use in the event of a revolution. [13] Another witness recalls that Péguy chose his dwelling place on the Place de l'Estrapade because "on the day of revolution the working masses descending from Montrouge and the student bands ascending from the Latin Quarter might clash" on that very street. [14]

Nevertheless all evidence points to the conclusion that Péguy counted on moral and spiritual rather than violent persuasion. His views paralleled those of Jean Jaurès, who "did not entirely rule out the possibility of a future social revolution" but "believed that the existence of political democracy in France made possible the realization of a socialist order without recourse to [violent] revolutionary action." [15] Péguy's letter to his provin-

[11] Charles Péguy, "Un premier état de la 'Cité Socialiste,' Lettre à Collier," *ACPFM*, No. 10 (1950), 1–3; Challaye, *Péguy socialiste*, 38.

[12] Jean Grave, *La société mourante et l'anarchie*, preface par Octave Mirbeau (Paris, 1893), 25.

[13] Jean Maxence and Nadeshda Gorodetzkaya, *Charles Péguy* (Paris, 1931), 104.

[14] Challaye, *Péguy socialiste*, 84–85.

[15] Noland, *The Founding of the French Socialist Party*, 38.

cial correspondent Collier resumed in a different tone when he concluded: "Meanwhile, since it is only sensible to attain Utopia without talking unduly of the pains one may suffer along the way, I follow *for now and no doubt for some time to come,* the footsteps of the French socialists." [16] One must remember that Péguy was a *normalien* when he addressed himself to this friend. Having pursued academic honors with conspicuous success so far, he was now writing to a former companion who had apparently been less successful. His attitude was a trifle pompous and schoolmasterly. He appeared to be showing off as he expatiated on the risks he was willing to countenance in order to assure the coming of the millennium. This may account for a letter which was in part entirely out of character with Péguy's outspokenly pacific tendencies in the years before and after it was written.

By autumn of 1895 Péguy seemed to have become more sure of his commitment to socialism. In August he wrote to another acquaintance that he was a socialist and expected to remain one for the rest of his life. "To me, this conversion will perhaps be the greatest event of my entire moral existence." [17] His participation in party activities, furthermore, engendered in him an evident sense of belonging, which constituted a new and exhilarating experience in the lonely boy who had heretofore known only the uncomprehending company of an illiterate grandmother and an unschooled mother whose own life had been bleak and cheerless. No wonder that Péguy saw himself as living in an "epoch of renovation. Everything is changing around us and begins to develop for the best." [18]

As Péguy became immersed in *Jeanne d'Arc,* however, and contemplated the triumph of evil in the tragic history of his heroine, lights and shadows mixed. To his later lifelong associate, André Bourgeois, he wrote in March of 1897 that France was sick and dying of her "bourgeois customs and her bourgeois laws." [19] One wonders whether this could mean that he sud-

[16] Italics supplied.
[17] Péguy to Woehrel, August 7, 1895 in "Lettres de Péguy et Albert Lévy à Théo Woehrel," *ACPFM,* No. 56 (1957), 8.
[18] *Ibid.,* 17.
[19] Péguy, "Lettres à André Bourgeois," 5.

denly lost faith in the miraculous powers of socialist salvation, and if so, why?

Péguy's divided feelings in 1897 mirrored a divided existence. *Jeanne d'Arc* on the one hand revealed him as the artist completely lost in the ecstatic process of creation. At the same time he began to contribute reviews and articles to the *Revue Socialiste*, since 1885 the major revisionist organ of the movement. He emerged both as a poet and, on a modest scale, as a political journalist. The socialist party had also just completed a two-year span of equivocal evolution. That same autumn of 1895, during which Péguy had become certain of his socialist convictions, confronted his comrades in parliament with the question of whether they should support Léon Bourgeois, who had just formed the first Radical government in twenty years. An overwhelming majority decided to support this departure from tradition, and the coalition policy was expanded and applied with conspicuous success in the municipal elections of 1896. Socialist mayors were elected in major cities like Marseille and Lille, while the total socialist vote of 1,400,000 was more than twice that polled in the parliamentary contest of 1893. In the wake of this triumph of compromise was born the Saint-Mandé Program, proclaimed by Alexandre Millerand at a victory banquet in Paris on May 30, 1896. It held unalterably to the progressive socialization of the means of production, exchange, and distribution; proposed the attainment of these socialist goals by a legally constituted majority; and reaffirmed that socialists believed in national solidarity as well as the brotherhood of man. In a different context Jaurès restated the case with characteristic eloquence a year and a half later: "The working class not only has for its mission the assumption of power and the creation of a more equitable social order, but it also should have, while awaiting the inevitable hour of social revolution, the mission of safeguarding all that is good and noble in the human heritage." [20]

A socialist movement retreating into moderation provided the atmosphere in which Péguy decided that he was a socialist and furnished the opportunity for him to make his journalistic debut

[20] Quoted in Noland, *The Founding of the French Socialist Party*, 65.

in the *Revue Socialiste.* His first article was a review of Léon Walras' *Étude d'économie sociale,* a pioneering work in mathematical economics. The young reviewer appeared alternately attracted and repelled without quite understanding his divided heart. Walras also sought "the ideal society and the means of achieving it," and Péguy approved. But the young idealist who responded to Jaurès' faith in "the inevitable hour of social revolution" and who joyfully prepared to add his strength to the defense of "all that was good and noble in the human heritage" could neither understand nor sanction a utopia expressed in mathematical formulae. Péguy's exposition of Walras' method was uneasy and confused. Almost irrelevantly, he concluded that Walras' entire *Weltanschauung* could be summarized by the maxim: "Keep your faith and add science to it." [21] The review revealed more about Péguy than about his subject. His own confidence in socialism was too new to be critical. It was too early for him to admit that he could not accept everything propounded by every articulate comrade. Walras' *Étude d'économie sociale,* on the other hand, was to him both alien and disconcerting. As a way out of the confusion propagated by this strange encounter, Péguy constructed an *ad hoc* compromise of his own: faith in the inevitability of a just society which rested on a mixture of science and morality whose exact proportions he was unwilling to measure or describe.

If faith and science constituted a strange socialist recipe, it was no more extraordinary at the time than Millerand's call for social revolution without violence or his assertion that French patriotism and socialist internationalism could harmoniously live as two souls in one breast. Saint-Mandé made Millerand no less of a socialist than before. Péguy's indecision upon confronting Walras did not becloud his basic conviction that he was and remained a member in good standing of the working class movement.

The content of Péguy's next essay, on the affairs of the Near East, only confirmed the earnestness of his partisanship. This

[21] C[harles] P[éguy], "Un économiste socialiste, M. Léon Walras," 174–86.

article was primarily a commentary on the Armenian massacres and their implications for the Franco-Russian alliance. From the very outset France's socialists had stood almost alone in their opposition to this pact. They flayed the secrecy that shrouded its negotiations. They considered the alliance with the czar revolting and humiliating. Once more it was the vocal Millerand who added the patriotic consideration when he prophesied inevitable doom if France should "on any pretext" become "the mere tool of the policy of a foreign power." [22] The soundness of his objections was confirmed in socialist eyes when France failed in the autumn of 1894 to support English pleas for intervention in Armenia, where Turkey was wreaking bloody havoc while suppressing a local rebellion. The reason for French reserve was regard for Russia's interest, which demanded the disciplining of Turkish Armenians in order to discourage the Armenian subjects of the czar from following their example.

Péguy's essay gave new voice to these criticisms. By 1897 France's passivity had been compounded by a deliberate effort to hide these bloody memories behind a cloud of silence. France, Péguy claimed, had stifled her traditional humanitarian impulses in order to protect czarist policy. The author of *Jeanne d'Arc,* then approaching the completion of his work, echoed Millerand by attacking this subservience to a foreign power, not merely because he belonged to a party to whom Nicholas II represented evil incarnate, but because the Armenian tragedy illustrated to him how the alliance of incompatibles obstructed France's civilizing mission. If France, building on her revolutionary tradition, could not look forward within twenty years to becoming a nation of 50 million socialist missionaries, then, Péguy insisted, any and every alliance would have been concluded in vain. Yet, how could his country even dream of accomplishing this high purpose if it accepted the official thesis that its existence hinged on the consortium with a semi-barbaric power? For the sake of her Jacobin past, for the sake of her socialist future, France must

[22] Georges Michon, *The Franco-Russian Alliance, 1891–1917,* trans. Norman Thomas (London, 1929), 76 n., 81–84.

depend on her own strength alone, or perish.[23] Joan's counsel to Hauviette was repeated for the benefit of the government of Jules Méline, which also chose to disregard it.

In November, 1897, the *Revue Socialiste* asked Péguy to review Emile Durkheim's *Le suicide*. Again, as in the case of Walras, he faced a work whose spirit and method were totally alien to his own. Durkheim had attracted considerable attention in 1893 with his thesis *De la division du travail social* in which he analyzed the changing nature of social conformity in an industrial world. Assuming that the social mind was "exterior, superior, and independent of the individual mind," he postulated that the pressure to conform to its dictates was no longer exercised by the entire cultural unit as in primitive society, but by the occupational group, which Durkheim saw as the agent of social order in the urbanized and industrialized universe. Thus he came very near to providing an exclusively "mechanist interpretation in which the element of conscious direction [was] eliminated." [24] Two years later, as professor at the University of Bordeaux, Durkheim delivered a series of lectures on the problems of socialism in which he concluded condescendingly if not unkindly that "socialism is not a science . . . it is a cry of pain." As such it appealed to those who suffered, but neither explained nor cured their agony. A social scientist, therefore, must view it with "reserve and circumspection." [25]

To this record and to this position was now added Durkheim's study of suicide as a social phenomenon curable by social agencies. Just as he saw conformity as a reflection of social integration so he viewed suicide as a reflection of the opposite,[26] as a collective phenomenon brought about by a society's proclivity toward disintegration. Tendencies of such decline, according to

[23] "Pierre Deloire," "A propos des affaires d'Orient," *Revue Socialiste*, XXV (1897), 258–61.
[24] Harry Elmer Barnes, "Durkheim's Contribution to the Reconstruction of Political Theory," *Political Science Quarterly*, XXXV (1920), 239–44; Georges Davy, "Emile Durkheim," *Revue française de Sociologie* I (1960), 21.
[25] Quoted in Hughes, *Consciousness and Society*, 79–80.
[26] Davy, "Emile Durkheim," 16.

Durkheim, might be the result of economic disaster, which accelerates the rate of self-destruction among both rich and poor, or of more specific causes, such as the permissiveness of certain religious groups which provided little shelter against ultimate despair.[27]

Such notions appalled Péguy. In his review of *Le suicide* he objected vigorously to such a collectivist and statistical study of social developments. Durkheim, he charged, was a mere cataloger of external phenomena who could never hope to penetrate to the heart-causes of human despair. Péguy's own faith as a socialist and as a humanist was of necessity anthropocentric. He wanted to lay bare the roots of human misery, from individual to individual, and tear out the entire malignant growth. Durkheim, in his view, lacked the compassion without which sociology could be no more than a biological analysis of the human condition. Durkheim's scientism furthermore implied an attitude in which the author presumed himself to be on a level well above those whose conduct he was explaining. Thus Péguy added the charge of arrogance to that of superficiality. In his concluding opinion he granted the book not the merit of explaining the social causes of suicide but of exposing the moral shortcomings of the author.[28]

As a socialist Péguy cringed under the coldly statistical blasts of social science. He decided to do his part in improving the atmosphere. Shortly after the completion of *Jeanne d'Arc* in 1897, he began his search for a cure against social injustice and the distempers that had given rise to the kind of investigations pioneered by Durkheim. The first result of this anabasis was a sketch entitled "De la cité socialiste" which appeared in the August, 1897, issue of the *Revue Socialiste*. Péguy's utopia would have been a state where everyone worked for the common good under a minimum of pressure, where everyone was educated and as a result accepted the postulate of human solidarity.

[27] Emile Durkheim, *Le suicide* (Paris, 1897), 271–272; Barnes, "Durkheim's contribution," 237 n.; M. A. Elliot and Frances E. Merrill, *Social Disorganization* (New York, 1934), 386–87.

[28] "Pierre Deloire," "Durkheim *Le suicide, étude de sociologie*," *Revue Socialiste*, XXV (1897), 635–36.

On that basis the ideal society could succeed in banishing the twin demons of competition and misery from its territory. Competition had no place in Péguy's socialist commonwealth because it was incompatible with order. Competition divided men; it made them work against each other; it was the first cause of all violence. Misery would disappear only if the noncompetitive *cité* granted everyone the opportunity to develop his gifts.[29]

In conjunction with Péguy's critiques of Walras and Durkheim, "De la cité socialiste" read like a refutation of mathematical economics and the statistical investigation of social problems. In point of time it preceded by three months the appearance of his essay on Durkheim, and it is unknown whether he fashioned the first design of his socialist state before or after the reading of *Le suicide*. In any case "De la cité socialiste" portrayed social harmony as resting on the twin assumptions of voluntary individual subservience to a common pursuit of perfection and of the entire cultural unit of the *cité* superseding both the individual and the occupational group as the fulcrum and end product of flawless social organization.

Even if "De la cité socialiste" antedated both the reading of and the attack on Durkheim, one may well wonder whether *Le suicide* did not contribute to Péguy's resolve to expand this short essay. It may have prompted him to hasten the completion of the far more ambitious *Marcel. Premier dialogue de la cité harmonieuse* in which the original sketch grew into a full portrait. If so, the handful of Péguy's contributions to the *Revue Socialiste* in 1897, though very modest in size, forms an interesting bridge between *Jeanne d'Arc* and the years of combat that followed. *Jeanne d'Arc*, if viewed as an essentially religious profession, pointed to a dead end in Péguy's work. It had no immediate sequel. At the same time, the thoughts occasionally and haphazardly woven into the pages of the *Revue Socialiste* revealed Péguy's sensitivity to the dangers threatening man's temporal salvation. A shabby foreign policy threatened France's civilizing mission. False economics and a heartless sociology were inter-

---

[29] "Pierre Deloire," "De la Cité Socialiste," *Revue Socialiste*, XXV (1897), 186–90.

posed between man and his physical welfare. Leaving Joan on the threshold of heaven, beyond which he could neither carry nor pursue her, Péguy rushed to defend the human prospect of material happiness.

In June, 1898, Péguy presented to an indifferent world his first (and last) "dialogue of the harmonious commonwealth," a universal utopia from which no man was to be excluded.[30] By the time the manuscript was completed, the apprehensions generated in his mind during the reading of Walras and Durkheim had been intensified into a *cause célèbre* by the revival of the Dreyfus case. The doubts of Mathieu Dreyfus concerning his brother's guilt had been substantiated by Colonel Georges Picquart, whose attorney in turn had gained the ear of a number of influential members of parliament. Major Charles Walsin-Esterházy had been openly accused as the author of the document which Alfred Dreyfus had been convicted of writing; and although a military court exonerated Esterházy in a secret proceeding on January 11, 1898, the doubters were not appeased.

Most leading socialists, even the Independents, maintained a cautious indifference toward this *querelle de bourgeois;* but when Émile Zola's famous open letter to the president of the republic appeared on the streets three days after Esterházy's acquittal, Péguy was prompted to give vent to his own revisionist convictions. An accolade which he addressed to Zola on January 21 voiced his first doubts about the integrity of socialist leadership. Their duty was not to stand aside, but to lead the socialist "march for every just cause which has not yet triumphed" and to assume command of the future citizens of the socialist commonwealth, which included "all artisans, manual workers and intellectuals, . . . who have left their daily pursuits to fight for the

---

[30] The following exposition is based on the original edition of "Pierre Baudouin," *Marcel. Premier dialogue de la cité harmonieuse,* which was printed in the same elaborate and painstaking fashion as *Jeanne d'Arc,* likewise without pagination. Another edition was published by Marcel Péguy (Paris: Desclée de Brouwer, 1933). He discussed the surprising reasons for this revival in "Les prophéties de Charles Péguy; essais sur la valeur prophétique du premier dialogue de la Cité Harmonieuse," *Le Journal Vrai, Organ des Amis de Charles Péguy,* I, no. 1 (1929), 1–32.

complete recovery of justice."[31] To Millerand he added with blunt hostility: "We demand that socialist principles be preserved in their entirety, not merely the poses [customarily] classified as socialist on election day." His angriest expressions of doubt and discouragement remained hidden from his contemporaries. Some time in February, 1898, he dashed off an essay "L'Épreuve," not published until 1930,[32] which was probably his immediate reaction to the news that Zola had been convicted on February 7 of having libeled both government and army. Péguy had expected no more from the courts, but widespread public support of the verdict shocked him. The crowds in the streets, a majority in both houses of parliament, and the civilian and military leaders of the executive appeared to him caught up in a bloodthirsty rage. Everyone seemed to applaud the violation of justice, and no effective voice was raised in the defense of the just.[33] Thus for months before the publication of *Marcel*, Péguy revealed a growing fear that his conception of the millennium had few supporters and could expect to make few converts among the corrupted multitude. The fact that he persisted in completing its writing and printing merely revealed that he was not a man to surrender after the loss of one battle.

Marcel describes a city where tasks are performed by all able-bodied men. The labor of women is outlawed because it destroys the family; the work of adolescents and children is rejected because it unravels the entire social fabric. Work in the commonwealth, furthermore, is performed to satisfy needs rather than to obtain riches. Péguy condemns the pursuit of luxury which deprives man of the leisure without which his spirit, the most precious property of the *cité*, cannot flourish. The end of work is survival on a high level, not competition for distinctions. The *cité harmonieuse* knows no rivalry. Accordingly, the community charges no price and pays no salaries. Men labor; they do

[31] In October, 1898, Péguy expressed the same view in a letter to an Orléans paper. See Jules Riby, "Une polémique de Péguy avec le 'Journal du Loiret.' Octobre, 1898," *ACPFM*, No. 22 (1951), 1–13.

[32] "L'Épreuve," *Cahiers* XX (1930), 48–59.

[33] Not even that of the Jews, according to Léon Blum's *Souvenirs sur l'Affaire* (Paris, 1936), 25.

not sell themselves. Since all perform to satisfy the needs of survival, their contributions are of equal value; they are all equally indispensable. Management, for instance, is considered a distinctive but not a higher function. The *cité* recognizes inevitable differences of occupation; it approves no variety of status. All products are grown or manufactured for the commonwealth and distributed among the members in accordance with their needs. No one may make any additional claims. "The workers donate their labor to the community; the community donates its products to its citizens." There is no property and no inheritance, only the storage of surplus by workers assigned to this task. The *cité* neither buys nor sells; it merely distributes.

Up to this point *Marcel* constituted a materialistic utopia, of which modern French political thought since St. Simon and Fourier provided Péguy with an ample supply of models. Bakunin's *Future Society,* with its contention that a truly free society knew no conflict of interest, might equally well have been a forerunner of the *cité harmonieuse*.[34] Pierre Joseph Proudhon's uncompromising dedication to inviolate freedom and to the proposition that the perfect society grows only from voluntary commitments, easily stamps him as another precursor of Péguy.[35] Finally, the first part of *Marcel* might have been an amplification of the last pages of *La Société mourante et l'anarchie,* in which Jean Grave proclaimed: "Since authority and property have been abolished, and society has ceased to be . . . based on conflicting interests, but contrariwise on the closest solidarity of men whose morrow is secure, who no longer hoard to provide for the future, men will now cease to regard each other as enemies ready to devour one another in pursuit of a mouthful of bread or a job with an exploiter. Since the causes of struggle and hostility have been destroyed, social harmony will be established." [36]

[34] Maitron, *Histoire du mouvement anarchiste,* 474–80.
[35] Cf. Jacques Bougeat, *Proudhon, père du socialisme français* (Paris, 1943), 220–21; Henri de Lubac, *The Un-Marxian Socialist: A Study of Proudhon* (New York, 1948), 34, 131.
[36] Grave, *La société mourante,* 270.

Even now, however, Péguy can see neither paradise nor hell in exclusively material terms. His egalitarian commonwealth has not only a spiritual substance with curiously hierarchical distinctions, it has in fact an exclusively spiritual purpose. At the very outset, one discovers in this city without alienation, where status is unknown, an acceptance of spiritual evolution. There are two orders among souls: mature and adolescent. The mature souls belong to humans, the adolescent souls to animals. With strikingly stubborn logic the commonwealth, which rules out labor by human adolescent bodies, also rules out the exploitation of animal labor, that is, the exploitation of adolescent souls. In the realm of the mature soul Péguy distinguishes between the soul of the individual, the soul of the family, and the soul of the city. Every social organism, in other words, has a nonmaterial essence.

This puzzling metaphysic which cannot be conveniently labeled, nor readily tied to any movement at large or any preceding or subsequent terrain feature in Péguy's spiritual universe is part of a general discussion of the intellectual's role in the commonwealth. This is the most original and elaborate part of *Marcel*. In it Péguy again reveals and betrays himself. The moment he abandons himself to the voices and visions of his genius, he drops the socialist pose, at least in the conventional and political sense. His *cité* is the guardian of the entire human heritage. The founders of all faiths, the saints of all religions, and the heroes of all civilizations may claim its citizenship. It will close its gates to no man, it will not deny entry to any idea. All it seeks to exclude is the unwholesome.

The intellectual himself is completely free to pursue his work. Since he can do this in an atmosphere that is free of rivalry, jealousy, or hate, he entertains no unwholesome thoughts himself and is manifestly incapable of creating any work that could harm the city. Unwholesome ideas, tending to generate rivalry, jealousy, or hate and introduced from without, will die from lack of nourishment once they have crossed the threshold of utopia.

Péguy's realm of harmony, furthermore, thrives in a climate of cool, objective detachment. There are no hard codes of justice since injustice is unknown. The impulse of charity does not exist because no citizen of the commonwealth is needy. The *cité* is without pity because no one in it is pitiful.

The work of the creative artist, finally, is the ultimate manifestation of the model universe. His work is totally unmotivated, performed to safeguard the existence of neither the city—which is assured by the labor of its citizens—nor the artist himself who is safeguarded by the city in turn. Like all his fellow citizens, the artist strives to accomplish as effectively as possible that which nature endowed him to accomplish. He seeks not to excel, he does not pursue fame. "The work of the artists comes to them from within, their within," and the same is true of the scientist and, last and loftiest of all, of the philosopher whose "philosophy is the art of science." When a work has burgeoned toward perfection in the creative soul, it is brought forth, a product not of the will but of innate necessity.

Péguy's *Marcel,* his first and last dialogue of the perfect society, gained its author no particular renown but, in the light of the poet's subsequent thoughts and actions, it has at least attained the stature of a major document. In the context of socialism the *cité harmonieuse* is a collective which manages the resources of its territory and distributes them according to individual need, thus creating an atmosphere of harmony whose proudest result is complete spiritual freedom.[37] To the ideas and ideals furnished by the preceding socialist and anarchist utopias of the nineteenth century, it contributed an attempt to define and describe an ethos which Péguy considered to be the inevitable result of the unconditional application of his particular socialist vision.

Marcel, like *Jeanne d'Arc,* portrayed an ideal presented and defended without hint of compromise; but unlike the drama its reality was not limited by history nor was its content devoid of the interplay between the sun of success and the shadows of failure. Péguy said nothing about the process by which his collectivist paradise might come into existence or about the conditions that would precede its creation. Unlike Bakunin's future society, it followed no period of collapse or insurrec-

[37] Guy, "Notes on Péguy the Socialist," 18.

tion.[38] It bore all the earmarks and imperfections of a day-dream, an escape from the knowledge that in the fifteenth as well as in the nineteenth century the utterly pure became the victims of injustice. Perfection in *Marcel* simply appeared as the inevitable result of human virtue. Péguy had built himself a refuge from the doubts expressed in *Jeanne d'Arc,* doubts which socialist equivocation during the Dreyfus Affair and the Zola trial had accentuated. In conjunction with the shock of seeing the people cheer injustice, volubly expressed in the pages of "L'Épreuve," these crises challenged his humanist optimism. Henceforth, he had to wrestle not only with an increasingly hostile reality, but with more persistent harbingers of gnawing doubt. As one turns next to the slighter literary harvest of 1899 and views it against the background of the affairs of the Librairie Georges Bellais,[39] of the new Dreyfus trial, and of the new verdict at Rennes, one learns to expect a serious moral and emotional crisis. Obviously, the time is approaching when Péguy must either give in to reality, or go forth alone into the wilderness of human hate and corruption.

Péguy's connection with the *Revue Socialiste* ended in February, 1898, shortly before he began work on *Marcel.* It was not until the beginning of 1899 that he resumed his career as a journalist, this time at the *Revue Blanche.* This substantial publication, nominally anarchist, became during its short life of twelve years a focus of intellectual discontent and, as such, a significant precursor of André Gide's *Nouvelle Revue Française* and Jacques Bainville's *Revue Universelle.* "Among those whom fame overtook during the years before the first world war, there are few who did not publish a text, an article or a poem in the *Revue Blanche.* From Marcel Proust to Pierre Louÿs, from Alfred Jarry to Guillaume Apollinaire, and including André Gide, Paul Claudel, Léon Blum, Julien Benda [and] Charles Péguy, the list is indeed long." [40]

---

[38] Cf. Maitron, *Histoire du mouvement anarchiste,* 475.

[39] See above, pp. 11–13.

[40] A. B. Jackson, *La Revue Blanche, 1899–1903* (Paris, 1960), 148; see also Evelyn Nattier-Nathanson, *Les amitiés de la "Revue Blanche"* (Vincennes, 1959), *passim.*

Péguy's contributions, printed under the rubric "Social and Political Notes," expanded from relatively brief observations into eloquent and elaborate commentaries on the political crisis of 1899. A recent, long overdue appreciation of these notes views them primarily as the work of a young visionary, still under the illusion that a "revolution of sincerity" would soon bring men to the threshold of the socialist commonwealth.[41] This judgment, like Béguin's narrow assessment of *Jeanne d'Arc,* falls short of encompassing the range and meaning of Péguy's efforts. In his contributions to the *Revue Blanche,* Péguy wrote as the engaged observer, the thrust of whose ideal clashed in mortal combat with the forces of evil. What were the events, what the issues that kindled this succession of increasingly acid commentaries?

The year 1899 provided the backdrop of multiple crisis. The short period of Péguy's association with the *Revue Blanche* from February 1 to November 15, 1899, began with the bitterness of retreat at Fashoda. Tensions grew when President Félix Faure, sometimes called *le président-soleil* because of his love of pomp and pleasure, collapsed and died after enjoying the company of one of the demi-mondaines he so assiduously pursued. A Moderate known to favor the revision of Dreyfus' sentence, Emile Loubet, was chosen as his successor. His politics were closer to the Left, his morals more conventional. Faure's funeral generated a convulsive nationalist campaign against the new chief executive whom the anti-Dreyfusard press dubbed without palpable reason "Panama I." Paul Déroulède, the leader of the recently revised League of Patriots, prepared an uprising for the day of the funeral. Once more the Republic appeared to be in danger. But when the great day came, the projected coup turned out to be the work of one fevered brain rather than of a well-disciplined revolutionary élite. The troops returning from the interment heeded their general's call rather than Déroulède's hysterical exhortations and returned to their barracks. Arrested and tried, the would-be *putschist* was even denied the satisfaction of martyrdom. A court ingloriously acquitted him of all charges. Ludicrous as this episode has appeared to subsequent chron-

[41] Boisserie, "Les Notes Politiques et Sociales de Péguy dans la 'Revue Blanche,'" 21.

iclers,[42] it served to perpetuate an explosive atmosphere, additionally charged by the news, announced four days after Déroulède's trial, that the Court of Appeals had ordered a new trial for Dreyfus.

The next day at the Longchamps race track, a well-known dandy of monarchist persuasion, Baron Christiani, smashed President Loubet's top hat with his cane, another incident which accurately reflected the feelings and the level of political intelligence of the malefactor as well as the quality and quantity of weapons stored in the antirepublican arsenal. And once more the republican reaction, a march of tens of thousands of good citizens to the scene of the assault, seems disproportionate in retrospect.

The chain of reactions would not break. Angry interpellations ensued in the chamber and nine days after the ordering of a new trial for Dreyfus, the Dupuy cabinet tumbled. It took fourteen days to replace it. Finally, on June 26 after numerous abortive attempts, the Moderate Senator René Waldeck-Rousseau emerged with a coalition of "Republican Defense," embracing the socialist Alexandre Millerand as minister of commerce and industry and General Marquis Gallifet, the grim executioner of the Communards later converted by Gambetta into a good republican, as minister of war. It was almost too much for a smooth take-off, and the vote of confidence (263 to 237) presaged another cabinet crisis around the corner. Some credited Waldeck-Rousseau's minimal margin to the 25 socialist votes cast in support of the controversial Millerand; others ascribed the decisive role to a splinter of the Progressives, a group of economic conservatives who were soon to rechristen themselves the *Alliance Républicaine Démocratique*. Combining incompatible forces, the new premier survived, thanks to the support of incompatible factions. The backbone of his alliance, however, was clearly provided by what came to be known as the Left bloc: Republicans, Radicals, and Radical-Socialists, who were to govern France for the next forty years.[43]

---

[42] Most recently to Siegfried Thalheimer, *Macht und Gerechtigkeit, ein Beitrag zur Geschichte des Falles Dreyfus* (Munich, 1958), 522–25.

[43] This is the very plausible interpretation of Waldeck-Rousseau's in-

No sooner had the government cleared port when the time came for Dreyfus' retrial before a military court at Rennes. From August 7 onward, as witness succeeded witness at the bar, the hopes of the revisionists gradually turned into certainty of defeat. The defendant's glacial aloofness jarred the romantic expectations of many who had come to weep for and rejoice with him. The military witnesses doggedly reiterated their conviction of his guilt. Most of the judges in uniform agreed, and on September 9 a vote of five to two convicted Dreyfus a second time, though with extenuating circumstances. To a revisionist government the verdict was rendered all the more offensive by its patent absurdity. What "extenuating circumstances" could be admitted when considering a charge of treason?

But now the Dreyfusard high command was divided. Should the fight for acquittal continue, or should the president's power of pardon terminate this prolonged abuse of justice? Mathieu Dreyfus pleaded with his brother's friends that Alfred could not endure further imprisonment. Clemenceau remained obdurate, but Jaurès and Joseph Reinach agreed. The appeal to Loubet went out, and a pardon ended six years of incarceration for an innocent man. "The incident is closed," General Gallifet sternly told his army. But it was not. Dreyfus had regained his freedom; another seven years would pass before he would regain his commission and his good name.[44]

A deceptive calm settled over France, unruffled by the renewed arrest and imprisonment of Déroulède in November. The country was ready to sweep the debris of multiple unpleasantness under the rug and put up a festive front for the impending World's Fair of 1900. But the battles for Dreyfus and for republican defense had rekindled the fires of socialist division, and on a smaller stage an equally furious encounter pitted faction against faction even after the specter of civil war had been exorcised. Millerand had joined the cabinet on his own

vestment in Jacques Chastenet, *La république triomphante, 1893–1906* (Paris, 1958), 168.

[44] On the pardoning of Dreyfus and Jaurès' part in it, see Harvey Goldberg, *The Life of Jean Jaurès* (Madison, Wis., 1962), 524.

responsibility. Jaurès and Lucien Herr, though aware of the dangers of ministerialism, agreed that the defense of a democratic republic exacted this sacrifice.[45] When the showdown came in the chamber, only twenty-five socialists supported Millerand, but the rest abstained. In one way or another Herr's argument had convinced everyone that the Republic must be defended by giving it at least a government.

Uneasily the socialists lived between peace and undeclared internecine war. Those who subscribed to the Possibilist slogan, "The safety of the country is the supreme law," [46] were too conscious of having sacrificed principle to be at ease. The supporters of Jules Guesde, meeting in August at Épernay on the other hand, were unable to agree on a condemnation of Millerand. The only decision to which all socialists finally agreed was to meet in December to arbitrate the divisions over the ministerial issue and to discuss once more the formation of a single socialist party. When the congress met, on December 3, Péguy was no longer writing for the *Revue Blanche;* and by the time he set down his impressions of the unity conclave, he had ceased to play an active part in the socialist movement.

Thus Péguy's articles in the *Revue Blanche* encompass the period from the death of President Faure to the second trial and imprisonment of Paul Déroulède. How did his conceptions of utopia and his uncertainties concerning human virtue develop amidst this recurrent tumult? Despite the doubts expressed in "L'Épreuve" his faith in the people apparently had suffered no lasting diminution. In his account of President Faure's funeral he ascribed the failure of Déroulède's coup to the patriotic good sense of Frenchmen of all ranks. The general did not hesitate to lead his men back to their *caserne.* The men did not hesitate to follow his command of loyalty and moderation. Through Péguy's eyes the reader next saw the inauguration of President Loubet as a merry *fête populaire* in which honest, stalwart citizens enjoyed the sunny weather, the parades, and the display of power and fashion with pure-hearted insouciance.[47] Their gaiety and their

[45] *Ibid.,* 254–55.
[46] Noland, *The Founding of the French Socialist Party,* 93.
[47] "Quelques égarés," *Revue Blanche,* XVIII (1899), 384–86.

easy good conscience was justified, for they were in fact celebrating the beginning of the saving of Dreyfus.

Péguy likewise saw the trial at Rennes and the subsequent pardoning of the degraded captain in this optimistic light. This succession of events provided release for the prisoner. It signified a triumph of justice and a victory for the people. "What saved us from confusion, catastrophe, and perhaps defeat as well," he wrote in September, "was the wisdom, stoutness, health, the common sense, frankness, and uprightness of the French workers and peasants. The soldiers of the socialist army, like the soldiers of most armies, were worth more than their leaders." [48]

By "their leaders" Péguy meant, above all, the intellectual luminaries of socialism, whom he rated no more highly than the doctors and magistrates who had presumed to judge Joan of Arc at Rouen and of whose indecision he spoke in the harshest terms. While the people had flocked into the streets to save the Republic, Péguy maintained, socialist scholastics and scholars had argued fruitlessly over whether or not supporting Dreyfus was compatible with their particular brand of political sectarianism. Instead of joining the people's fight for freedom, they had attacked Millerand for joining Waldeck-Rousseau's coalition in defense of the Republic. These remarks revealed that Péguy had forgiven the new minister of commerce for his earlier procrastination. The second Dreyfus trial seemed to have brought about a complete realignment of Péguy's world. There were Dreyfusards and anti-Dreyfusards. It was that simple. Like the Possibilists, he believed dogma to be unimportant when the country was in danger. To Péguy the summer of 1899 was a time when every man worthy of his mettle belonged on the firing line. At this point Péguy went so far as to decide that it was better to die for the Republic without knowing exactly what it represented than to write learnedly and rationally why others should lay down their lives for the cause. Sincerity alone counted in a crisis, and some leaders of the party had been found wanting that virtue. The sincere alone were just, Péguy pontificated, because they accepted without reflection the mandate of their convictions. They

[48] "L'Affaire Dreyfus et la crise du parti socialiste," *Revue Blanche,* XX (1899), 133.

alone could be considered intelligent because they alone knew what had to be done.[49]

Without sincerity, furthermore, there could be no justice. Without justice no cause had integrity. Péguy believed that the Dreyfus Affair had divided Frenchmen into three parties. There were, first, the enemies of Dreyfus who made a religion of inequity. Every action of theirs was camouflaged in ritual. The charges in court had been mysterious and obscure. The sentence had been equally mysterious and as merciless as an edict of God. It inflicted eternal hopelessness on the defendant and limitless agony on the deity forced to condemn those he had created. The punishment was infernal, coming as close to reproducing hell as any human judgment could. The justification that all was done to protect the honor of the army was repeated again and again until it became a sacred litany, a ritualistic defense of the judicial crime.[50] Again the reader is transported into the chamber at Rouen, whose proceedings Péguy castigated in the same spirit: a judicial crime concealed behind prayer, service, and plain chant. The conclusion is still the same. Péguy rejects the collective and formalized approach to the seat of God, and he refuses to take damnation for an answer. In this light he views the enemies of Dreyfus not merely as enemies of the Republic and of justice but—like the judges of *Jeanne d'Arc*—as men whose false beliefs have alienated them from the company of good men and the intentions of God.

Péguy's second party was composed of those socialists who had violated the precepts of his humanism. They would not defend the accused—the human cause—because Dreyfus and many of his defenders were members of the propertied classes. To avoid an alliance with the just, they became the passive allies of the unjust. Their neutrality was a crime, like any neutrality in the struggle between good and evil.

Finally, there were the Dreyfusards. The manner in which Péguy identified them confirms once more the breadth and vagueness of his humanitarian socialism. In "La crise et le parti

[49] "La crise et le parti socialiste," *Revue Blanche*, XIX (1899), 463–65.
[50] "L'Affaire Dreyfus et la crise du parti socialiste," 128–29.

socialiste," he used Dreyfusard and Socialist interchangeably. The Dreyfusard-Socialist took his stand without thought of material interests. His only certainty was that he risked his and his children's bread. He was not motivated by class-consciousness; "he did not even ask whether the Dreyfus Affair would aid socialism." [51] Thus, the Dreyfusard-Socialist established solidarity of all good causes. Good men fighting for justice constituted the vanguard of the socialist city. They bore witness to human progress by engaging themselves wherever evil and oppression struck. They recognized a "staggering extension of responsibilities." [52] The Dreyfusard-Socialist, in other words, was a latter-day apostle of the morality embodied by Joan of Arc.

The morals of the Dreyfusard-Socialist appeared to Péguy to be molded in the patriotic image of Joan of Arc. In addition to exacting a clear-cut commitment to the postulates of justice, the Dreyfus Affair, as Péguy saw it, raised this question: "Will France remain faithful to her revolutionary past or will she go the way of Spain?" [53] The answer was of the highest significance, for it would affect the reaction of the world to this *cause célèbre*. Were it not for France's position as a cradle of civilization, the fate of the Jewish captain would certainly not have attracted much notice abroad. But under the circumstances, everything happening in France was of universal importance. A Nationalist victory, therefore, would doom Dreyfus and destroy France as a power in civilization.[54] During the first week of the Rennes trial Péguy warned that condemning the prisoner a second time was in fact tantamount to betraying the fatherland.

It did not take the Rennes verdict to persuade Péguy that the army and its supporters were traitors to France's cultural mis-

[51] "La crise du parti socialiste," 466.
[52] "La crise du parti socialiste et l'Affaire Dreyfus," *Revue Blanche*, XIX (1899), 631. Cf. this contemporary comment: "The progress of Socialism, despite its materialistic aspects, is an idealistic flight towards superior justice and morality," in Alfred Fouillée, *Morale des Idées—Forces* (2nd ed.; Paris, 1908), 376. "Enseignements," *Revue Blanche*, XIX (1899), 211–12.
[53] "L'Affaire Dreyfus et la crise du parti socialiste," 128.
[54] "La crise du parti socialiste et l'Affaire Dreyfus," 631–32.

sion. As early as March, 1899, he had written, "At present the wayward are those who seek to undermine the country's confidence in its institutions." [55] This was aimed directly at the opponents of revision, military and civilian, whom he suspected of being basically intent upon destroying the Third Republic. On the other hand he was equally outspoken in extolling socialist patriotism. It was true that socialism opposed any instrument of offensive warfare, particularly the kind of collective violence which France's army had been guilty of in Algeria, Tunisia, and Tonkin. "But" he added, "it is because we are good Frenchmen, that the colonial massacres perpetrated by bad Frenchmen fill us with remorse. Because we are *French* internationalists, the crimes of General Gallieni pain us more than English, German, or American crimes." The ideal instrument of patriotism, as Péguy saw it, was the nation-in-arms called by a national convention to defend national liberty. This militia, he asserted, was in effect a counter-army, a people rising to punish aggression and prepared to smother tyranny. [56]

To a significant degree the Péguy one encounters in the *Revue Blanche* is still the defender of Joan of Arc, wrestling now with France's contemporary problems but as ardent, uncompromising, outspoken, and patriotic as before. The issues of socialist unity do not appear to have concerned him. The details of coalition politics, absorbing so many energies around him, are never specifically discussed. Péguy's eyes are riveted on Dreyfus, who emerges in his prose as an ideal rather than as an existence. The young polemicist does not go to Rennes. He does not report the trial; he fails to report the arguments of either side. The captain on the stand is a symbol of virtue whose downfall shall exalt evil and thrust the French nation into an abyss of degradation. Categorically and abstractly, Péguy discusses the events and

[55] Quelques égarés," 386. Compare this charge with a similar attack in Urbain Gohier's *L'Armée contre la nation* (Paris, 1898), quoted by Pierre Dominique (pseud. Pierre Lucchini), *Les polémistes français depuis 1789* (Paris, 1962), 340–43.

[56] "Service militaire," *Revue Blanche*, XIX (1899), 217–19. For a general comment on the Affair and military policy, see R. D. Challener, *The French Theory of the Nation in Arms* (New York, 1955), 61–63.

imposes his conclusions. As he does so, the historian discovers another facet of his complex character. In *Jeanne d'Arc* he recreates history, in this instance the deeds of the dead. *Marcel* is a figment of the imagination. The articles in the *Revue Blanche* treat current issues and describe living men, and for all of Péguy's moral posturing they reveal him for the first time as a man attacking for the sheer joy of the attack. In them he becomes aggressive, acid, even defamatory.

This side of Péguy's nature appeared in September after Dreyfus' second conviction. Shamed and shocked he turned with icy fury on the socialist leader who had remained indifferent to the "bourgeois quarrel" and who had condemned both Millerand's and Jaurès' support of the Republic in distress. Péguy turned his fire on Jules Guesde whom he pictured as an aging prima donna and a collaborator of "forgers, traitors, assassins and hangmen." [57] He accused France's foremost Marxist of feigning illness when the battle for Dreyfus was first joined. Not indifference but cowardice had imposed silence on him. "I feared that he might suffer a relapse at the very moment when the struggle for justice would erupt once more. Events have justified that fear." Guesde's followers, Péguy went on, were no better. They had been preparing a social revolution when this captain, this bourgeois, had had the temerity to intervene with his trifling misfortunes, unforeseen by and disconcerting to the pompous high priests of socialism. Well might these proud determinists curse him. Nothing like the Affair had been prophesied in their sacred scriptures; nothing like it had ever happened before.[58]

Péguy's were strong and ill-timed words to be uttered while the party was attempting to close ranks. His most important biographers—Halévy, Johannet, Sécretain, and Guyon—have understandably surmised that they nettled a leadership intent on minimizing internecine differences. Yet, the available evidence only allows the conclusion that Péguy's words were taken more seriously by the author than by the audience. When the December Congress of Socialist Unity imposed limitations on freedom

[57] "L'Affaire Dreyfus et la crise du parti socialiste," 133–34.
[58] *Ibid.*, 134–35.

of expression in order to reduce the risks to unity, Péguy moved out of the socialist mansion into his own annex, the *Cahiers de la Quinzaine*. No one told him to leave.[59] No one ever suggested his expulsion. The explanation for this can best be gleaned from another series of standard sources: the histories of French socialism by Alexandre Zévaès, Aaron Noland, and Daniel Ligou, and the biographies of Jaurès by Marcel Auclair and Harvey Goldberg. The most they reveal is that Péguy was a nuisance, but a relatively unimportant one. The party could have lived with this burr under its saddle, and it managed to survive his defection with ease.

To Péguy, on the other hand, the crisis of 1899 was an event only matched by that of 1908, the year of his presumable religious conversion. One's reading of his last two articles for the *Revue Blanche* confirms it. Their tone provided the orchestration of the change that he was preparing and whose momentum pulled him along uncontrollably at the same time. The attack on Guesde revealed to what extent he was acquiring the habit of merciless judgment and of passing sentence in a manner that men found unforgivable. What he was indicating in his scathing denunciation of the grand old man of French Marxism was that henceforth *his* conception of justice took precedence over every other consideration. He warned an indifferent party that he would not follow it into any pact with imperfection and compromise. Since he had no power to threaten, this was a first long step into solitude.

Two months elapsed between the assault on Guesde and Péguy's last and longest article in the *Revue Blanche*. During the interim he had concluded that he could not continue to work for the Société Nouvelle de Librairie et d'Édition. On the public front the Dreyfus Affair had been temporarily shelved with the presidential pardon. Nationally and individually Frenchmen were living through the morning after. Péguy's commentary on this *tableau* was appropriately titled "Le ravage et la réparation." The battle had subsided, and, overwhelmed by sudden revulsion, Péguy turned from all the combatants. Whereas he had earlier

[59] See above, p. 14.

in the year praised the ranks at the expense of the generals, he now considered everyone contemptible. In humble pursuits the people were admirable, but in the hour of decision they "lie like generals, betray like cabinet ministers, and forge like a general staff." The people, Péguy realized with a sudden shock, were insensitive to moral decay. As a result they lusted after the power of the privileged and were perfectly ready to imitate the immorality of the elite. An aristocratic general lied, but a citizen-general felt honored when democracy presented him with an opportunity to sink to the same depths. Men became ministers after a succession of betrayals, Péguy explained. Nevertheless the petty bourgeois rejoiced when he had reached the same eminence where he, too, could play the role of Peter. This stolid callousness of the people had come to be reflected in their children: "I shall remember all my life those grade-school children, unleashed in the streets at four o'clock, walking home in small groups and cheeping, 'Death to the Jews.' "[60] The people whom Péguy had heretofore praised as Dreyfus' only reliable defenders were now made to share the collective guilt for an unspeakable crime.

To Péguy, much of this moral deterioration stemmed from the people's misunderstanding of democracy. They equated popular government with the opportunity for social and economic advancement. If a man of humble origin rose to become a colonel, an eminence once reserved for aristocrats, all the lower classes derived a vicarious pleasure from his success. Once the foes of privilege, they had become satisfied with imitating the corruption of the Old Régime.[61] No wonder democracy had lost its luster. No wonder it had failed, for failed it had. Dreyfus was not saved by democratic institutions, but by a pardon from the president, "that monarchic residual."

Péguy hints that man's purity only extends as far as his first temptation. The people are clean until they have the opportunity of defiling themselves. Historians are incorruptible until they deal with revelation. Critics are rigorous in their standards until confronted by a sacred text. Yet life is made of one piece, and

---

[60] "Le ravage et la réparation," *Revue Blanche*, XX (1899), 418.
[61] *Ibid.*, 422–23.

integrity is unqualified and unlimited, or else it is an illusion. Toward the end, like a despairing swimmer struggling in waters that threaten to carry him beyond reach of the comforting shore, Péguy tries to recapture his lost innocence by invoking one of his house gods: "Michelet alone, son of poor people, having experienced misery, thought as one should. Let us again read Michelet." [62] But the creeping malaise of disillusionment could not be cured by re-reading the *Histoire de France*. Péguy would never again be the same; and a short, turbulent, and heady era of his life was coming to an end. He cut the last ties himself. As early as November 21, 1899, he had resigned from the Société Nouvelle, but retracted after Lucien Herr pressed him to stay. His second withdrawal, on December 26, was final. [63]

Significant moment though this was in retrospect, none of the protagonists then quite realized it, least of all Péguy. On that last Christmas of the nineteenth century, the gloom of November had lifted. The world might no longer be as full of hope as he had once believed, but neither was it as ravaged as he had described it in his last assessment of the Dreyfus Affair. "I am leaving for a while," Péguy wrote Herr. "I leave like a faithful colony of the motherland. I have always considered my plans as a reinforcement of socialism, and of the Société Nouvelle in particular." He expected to visit, to call, and to write his old friend and teacher; and he did throughout much of 1900. [64] The personal ties with Herr, and the emotional ties with socialism could not be cut by one controversy. Péguy likewise did not take leave of utopia when he moved from the Rue Cujas to new quarters and to a new enterprise. He was unaware that he would never write a sequel to the first dialogue of the harmonious city.

The two years that followed the completion of *Jeanne d'Arc* confirmed the assumption that Péguy belonged to no man and to no group and could not subject his convictions to the discipline of any movement. The paternity of his political philosophy

[62] *Ibid.,* 429.

[63] Isaac, *Expériences de ma vie,* I, 197–98, 215.

[64] Cf. Auguste Martin, "Lettres de Péguy à Lucien Herr," *ACPFM,* No. 11 (1950), 1–11.

remained a riddle. His socialism of spiritual liberation was no more and no less than a synonym for his ardent humanism. The intensity of his commitment to the party was always doubtful.

The years of the Dreyfusard action left in Péguy's political writings evidences of a recurring vacillation between exaltation and despair. In 1895, he calmly predicted the foreseeable coming of the millennium; yet a letter to André Bourgeois, written in 1897, expressed fear for the future of a moribund, bourgeois France. *Marcel* re-affirmed his faith in human perfectability; "L'Épreuve" mirrored a far more discouraging reality. The failure of Déroulède's coup in 1899 confirmed his faith in the people; the actions of the Socialist Congress of 1899 threatened to destroy it. Péguy's view of the world changed from mood to mood, but it always came out either white or black. Light and shadow never met on the same canvas of opinion.

What remained constant was Péguy's abiding concern for the salvation of all men. Even when he felt tempted to abandon all hope, his love of country and his undiminished belief in spiritual and intellectual freedom persisted. In this respect the great sermon in *Marcel* on the freedom of the human mind pointed to the work that was to fill the remainder of his life: the *Cahiers de la Quinzaine.* On November 19, he submitted a sequel to "Le ravage et la réparation." It was rejected by the *Revue Blanche* for being too long. "It is long because it tells a long story," Péguy replied stubbornly. Seven weeks later he published it in the first issue of his *Cahiers.* Henceforth, he would decide when and how his views were to be presented to the public.[65]

---

[65] Challaye, *Péguy socialiste,* 106.

IV

The Cahiers de la Quinzaine:
The Bitter, Lonely Road,
1900–1908

THE new century was born amidst fanfares, many of whose echoes have since faded. The souvenirs of 1900 in Paris are a curious mixture of pomp, bad taste, shrill innovation, and continuous tension. For the first time since the year 1000, when apocalyptic prophecies unleashed the panic of an impending *fin-du-monde,* a chronological barrier was crossed in full consciousness that a *fin-de-siècle* must be duly observed as the overture to a new era.

Thousands of visitors flocked to the Paris World's Fair and gaped at the architectural atrocities of whose number the Pont Alexandre III is the best known and possibly the least offensive survivor. Electric trains and rolling sidewalks facilitated the progress from one hideous edifice to another. The opening of the subterranean *Chemin de Fer Métropolitain* on July 16, 1900, quickened the pulse of movement in and out of the metropolis and its monster exposition.

Falling in with the spirit of technical progress, the Academie Française, after due deliberation, agreed to accept the word "automobile" as part of the French language. (Perpetuating a record that revealed an almost unfailing preference for mediocrity, the same select gathering received into its ranks not a great or even popular man of letters, but the urbane president of the senate, Paul Deschanel, the best-dressed parliamentarian of his day.) After closing hours a never-ending procession of fans sat at the feet of the great Sarah Bernhardt whose presence made of Edmond Rostand's *L'Aiglon* the first great theatrical event of the new century.

In 1900 France took stock of her position as a power. By chamber of commerce standards the World's Fair, bringing visitors from afar and from the provinces by the tens of thousands, confirmed Paris as the capital of the world. But the discerning observer of the multifarious exhibits was forced to conclude that the host country, while still a leader in wealth, was being overtaken in achievement by her ambitious neighbor to the east. The anticipated congregation of foreign heads of state, furthermore, failed to materialize. Emperor William II of Germany would gladly have come—his love for grandiose occasions was notorious—[1] but the French government refused to take the risk of entertaining so unpopular a guest. Nicholas II, on the other hand, was unwilling to jeopardize his safety among the unruly Parisians whom he distrusted even more than his own subjects. As on past occasions, the public had to be satisfied with the Shah of Persia and a monster banquet attended by over 20,000 mayors from the provinces.

France wanted to shine, but without taking chances and without giving up her cherished prejudices. Her investors continued to prefer government bonds to more hazardous industrial issues, and most of her politicians luxuriated in their dislike of the Germans and their inveterate Anglophobia. The people booed the Prince of Wales, while they cheered the president of the Boer Republic. The shallowness of these attitudes is ironically underscored when one remembers that the most celebrated literary import of 1900, Henryk Sinkiewicz' *Quo Vadis?*, a camouflaged Polish *J'accuse* of Russian oppression, was welcomed as a "work of absolute art." [2]

On the domestic scene, cheers and whistles likewise became

---

[1] Cf. the successful effort to keep him from visiting the Columbian Exhibition in Chicago, Adolf Wermuth, *Ein Beamtenleben, Erinnerungen* (Berlin, 1922), 160–70.

[2] Paul Morand, *1900* (Paris, 1931), 168.

louder. Many a contemporary expressed the concern that France's political life was becoming increasingly radicalized and that the "best orators belonged to the extreme parties." [3] In the salons the Dreyfus Affair, though ostensibly liquidated by presidential fiat, provided a continuing subject for controversy. The habitués of the most brilliant drawing rooms would press around the literary critic Jules Lemaitre, president of the rightist League of the French Fatherland, if they wished to continue the fight against the Republic and its supposed Jewish masters. The friends of the tragic captain, on the other hand, frequented a different address to rejoice with Anatole France in the hard-won victory of justice. At the book stalls the disgruntled Nationalists found solace in Maurice Barrès' *L'Appel au soldat,* reveling with its author in the recollection of those distant days when General Boulanger had hypnotized the nation with the prospect of an early *revanche.* The republicans fortified their resolve with a reading of France's *M. Bergeret à Paris,* which presumed to expose the monstrous plots from which the Republic had only been saved recently.

New prophets emerged from this ferment. Charles Maurras' *Enquête sur la monarchie,* its title notwithstanding, sought solace not in the past but in a future revitalized by the return to kingship. In a real sense it was anti-Boulangist as well as anti-Dreyfusard because it demanded a head of state who would defy money and the mob. [4] A different pied piper, whose appeal likewise cut across the divides separating the "two Frances" of the Dreyfus Affair, suffered both death and resurrection. Friedrich Nietzsche's passing unleashed a bitter struggle between reactionaries, socialists, and anarchists over his equivocal legacy. At the Collège de France, finally, there appeared Henri Bergson, recently promoted from his professorship at the École Normale Supérieure. To the *eris* between tradition and revolt, between church and state, Bergson gave rational and comprehensive answers by introducing new concepts into the philosophers' search for truth. To the artificiality of time he opposed the reality

[3] *Ibid.,* 49.
[4] Tannenbaum, *The Action Française,* 74–76.

of duration, infinite and immeasurable and therefore only comprehended intuitively. In *Matière et Mémoire* (1896) he next distinguished between the brain as the mechanism through which we measure time and the spirit as the creative force through which we understand the limitless *durée*. Amidst the quarrels of literary coteries, parliamentary factions, and political parties, Bergson's steady, calm voice called men to the pursuit of ultimate and irrefutable truth.

Péguy had not yet discovered Bergson in 1900, but it would almost appear as if this son of Polish expatriates was the only voice that reached meaningfully into the solitude with which the fellow-townsman of Joan of Arc was about to surround himself. During the next half decade Bergson became the spiritual mentor whom he accorded respect and admiration. During these years which saw Péguy abandon old positions and attitudes and adopt new stances with the vigor and intolerance of the convert, Bergson alone remained the fixed star in his ideological firmament.

Péguy was now "an alumnus of the École Normale without degree, a professor without a chair, a master without disciples, a leader without followers, a poet without readers, a publisher without clients, a socialist without a party, an orator without an audience, [and] a mystic without a religion."[5] Only the lack of an audience was temporary. Though he never had an opportunity to preach to the masses, Péguy was never without readers for long. Many of his former schoolmates became charter subscribers of the *Cahiers*. Joseph Lotte sent copies to his brother-in-law who perused them while sailing on a French merchantman.[6] Daniel Halévy proselytized Marcel Proust, who subscribed although he considered Péguy devoid of talent.[7] Romain Rolland persuaded his old friend Malwida von Meysenbug to become a regular reader of Péguy's "audacious truths."[8] Louis Gillet

[5] Robert Avice, *Péguy, pèlerin d'espérance* (Bruges, 1947), 53.

[6] *Pour les fidèles de Péguy,* 183.

[7] Robert Proust and Paul Brach, *Correspondance générale de Marcel Proust* (Paris, 1932), IV, 738.

[8] Romain Rolland, *Choix de lettres à Malwida von Meysenbug* (Paris, 1948), 281.

joined him in repeated attempts to persuade socialists of all ranks to support the maverick *Cahiers*.[9] Georges Sorel, by 1900 convinced of the bankruptcy of the socialist movement, was an early sympathizer of Péguy's new enterprise, though hardly the first to recognize his talents, as one of his biographers has claimed.[10] In the summer of 1901, Péguy met Jacques and Jeanne Maritain whose mother, Geneviève Favre-Maritain, became in time one of his most faithful partisans.[11]

Otherwise, Péguy's situation conformed to the description of failure, which was, however, not an impasse created by a merciless fate but a path deliberately chosen. He pledged the *Cahiers* to tell the truth, no matter how much pain or discomfort it might cause.[12] This course was physically and economically risky; it could make many enemies. It was morally hazardous; not every statement painful to others was for that reason necessarily accurate. In any event, what truth or whose truth was Péguy about to proclaim? He made it clear that he would assume full responsibility for everything printed in the pages of his review: "I speak for no minority, no majority, no unanimity, no group, no society, [and] no party," he affirmed.[13] To André Bourgeois he put it less rhythmically, and more brutally: "The *Cahiers* oppose all liars and skunks (*salauds*), that is to say the overwhelming majority of all parties." [14] Yet this was hardly a sufficient answer. Cut adrift from all visible political moorings, whither had he set sail?

"The city whose birth we are preparing," was a city of all men.[15] Socialization of goods and production would encompass

[9] Mme. Louis Gillet and Mme. Romain Rolland (eds.), *Correspondance entre Louis Gillet et Romain Rolland* (Paris, 1949), 109–13, 118.

[10] Michael Freund, *Georges Sorel; der revolutionaere Konservatismus* (Frankfurt-am-Main, 1932), 113.

[11] Favre, "Souvenirs sur Péguy," 146–48; R. Maritain, *Les grandes amitiés,* 96; Henriette Psichari, *Ernest Psichari, mon frère* (Paris, 1933), 78.

[12] "Lettre du Provincial," *Cahiers,* I, No. 1 (1900), 9.

[13] "Réponse provisoire," *Cahiers,* I, No. 2 (1900), 6.

[14] "Lettres à André Bourgeois," 8.

[15] "Réponse brève à Jaurès," 17.

everything and benefit everyone.[16] "We [socialists] do not admit that men may be treated without humanity. . . . We shall not grant that there may be men turned back on the threshold. . . ."[17] Conflict and competition continued to be anathema to Péguy. War and the pursuit of fame were the essence of the bourgeois ethic. Acceptance of the inevitability of class struggle, therefore, was a socialist concession to the bourgeoisie, "just as arming a peaceful people is, in a sense, a concession to its belligerent neighbors." Then Péguy described the worker's state which was evolving from the destruction of the middle-class as bourgeois socialism in much the same way as disillusioned later generations unmasked the Soviet Union as being founded on state capitalism. The social revolution must be brought about through "the universalization of socialist civilization; that is to say, harmoniously [and] humanely."[18] Péguy was convinced that the adherents of the inevitable class struggle, Guesde above all, were not leading France to social revolution. They were fighting a rear-guard action for the bourgeois revolution of the eighteenth and nineteenth centuries.[19]

These commentaries left no doubt that a deep chasm had opened between Péguy's socialist ideology and the politics of the momentarily united socialist movement. At the Congress of Socialist Unity (December 3–8, 1899) and the succeeding international congress which convened in 1900, ministerialism was condemned even though the sentence was hedged with qualifications and even though Millerand left neither the party nor the government. But there is no evidence that either this issue or its treatment concerned Péguy. What caused his secession and perpetuated his alienation were the concomitant results. He abhorred the powerful central committee, dominated by the followers of Guesde, with its authority to supervise the action of socialist deputies and the content of the socialist press and with its power to suppress recalcitrant journals that challenged party

[16] "Préparation du congrès," *Cahiers,* I, No. 3 (1900), 71–72.
[17] "Encore de la grippe," *Cahiers,* I, No. 7 (1900), 31.
[18] "Préparation du congrès," 34–35; "Réponse brève à Jaurès," 31–34.
[19] "Réponse provisoire," 9.

decisions. The unanimity with which the national congress adopted such stringent measures after a brief and desultory debate undoubtedly deepened Péguy's disappointment and confirmed his conviction that this was no longer his party.[20]

For Péguy socialist civilization continued to find its supreme expression in the freedom of the mind. His projected revolution "will not give us socialist art, it will give us art that is free." [21] On the road to utopia truth must prevail, and the habits of liberty must be cultivated. This duty was first of all incumbent upon the socialists who were the most conspicuous apostles of social change. Péguy repeatedly expressed stupefaction at the attempts of the congress of 1899 to tamper with the freedom of written discourse among the socialist factions. "The perfect equanimity with which this congress suppressed the freedom of the press, merely to serve the internal needs of the Socialist Party, left me speechless. . . . No sovereign . . . has the right to pronounce against truth." By closing the mouths of its journalists, moreover, the party was condemning them to unemployment or dishonor. It was slamming the doors of the *cité* in their faces.[22] Worse, it seemed to surrender altogether the quest for perfection. "It is not enough to preach socialism. One must first know what socialism is, and this we shall never learn without free discussion." [23]

What contributions did the *Cahiers* propose to make to the progress of socialism? Péguy repeated publicly what he had written to Lucien Herr: "I have never intended to institute an economic or intellectual competition between the *Mouvement [Socialiste]* and the *Cahiers*. I ask that people subscribe to the *Mouvement* and then to the *Cahiers*. If they cannot subscribe to both, I ask that they first subscribe to the *Mouvement*, and I shall send them the *Cahiers* regardless." [24] His publication constituted a part of a collective effort; nothing unique or competitive.

[20] Noland, *The Founding of the French Socialist Party*, 102–14; Alexandre Zevaès, *Histoire du socialisme et du communisme en France de 1871 à 1947* (Paris, 1947), 291–93.

[21] "Réponse brève à Jaurès," 10.

[22] "Lettre du Provincial," 12–13.

[23] "Réponse provisoire," 10.

[24] *Ibid.,* 4–5.

During the first year, free subscriptions outnumbered all other categories of readership, and announcements in the first and eighth issues assured Péguy's clientele that paying for the *Cahiers* would confer no additional rights or privileges.

The Péguy of *Marcel* and the *Notes politiques et sociales* did not change during the first year of the *Cahiers de la Quinzaine* except that he found a freedom of action and expression which the board of the Société Nouvelle had never accorded him and which he could not have enjoyed as contributor or editor at the *Mouvement Socialiste* or the *Revue Socialiste*. By publishing his own review, Péguy likewise had the opportunity to continue his restless dialogue with God. During the winter and spring of 1900, the religious projection of the *cité harmonieuse* continued apace in a series of dialogues of which "De la grippe" has become the most famous. To his sources and scriptures Péguy now added the writings of Pascal, to whom he accorded a new and unprecedented prominence. The seventeenth-century philosopher, to whom "suffering humbly accepted" was "the sign of spiritual regeneration," [25] had first come within Péguy's ken in 1897 at the Sorbonne during the masterful lectures of Émile Boutroux. Pascal was anything but fashionable then, and Jansenism, as such, exercised no compelling influence on Péguy in 1900 or later. Yet, reading the *Pensées* was a source of great comfort to his divided heart. In these pages he found the same belief in human greatness, tempered by an awareness of man's frailty and misery, which had permeated the hopes and doubts of his own articles in the *Revue Blanche*.

Clearly, Péguy was still trying to decide on a definition of man's true nature. His first fruitful years had produced cyclical vacillations between faith and doubt. This conflict continued to shake his innermost being. When an attack of influenza brought him, as he thought, face to face with death, he read Pascal again, and he grew afraid, not only for himself but for mankind. "I came to look at the universe *sub specie mortalitatis*." [26] Fear of death, as such, was not the essential concern. To die before

[25] Émile Boutroux, *Pascal* (3rd ed.; Paris, 1903), 189.
[26] "De la grippe," *Cahiers*, I, No. 4 (1900), 3–5.

receiving certitude about the hereafter, that was the terrifying prospect. Péguy rejected the idea of the immortality of the soul. Yet, the dogmatic assertion of its mortality, he admitted, rested on no surer ground.[27] In either case he was ignorant of eternity; in either case his life remained without final purpose. Leading an aimless existence rendered him incapable of leading others. Not knowing where he was going, he could not expect others to follow him.

Why was this impasse so distressing? Because Péguy was a collectivist. Both in socialism and in Christianity, all men must be saved in society. If there was salvation after death, all men must partake of it. The certainty he sought was not primarily for himself, but for the *cité harmonieuse.* He must know whether utopia was mortal or immortal.[28]

Concern alone, moreover, furnished no answer. "How can we examine . . . the immortality of the soul, if we have not begun by studying the question of salvation?" Péguy had resumed the posture of Joan of Arc, beseeching the Almighty and All-merciful to "save us all." Yet, speaking for himself, the *licencié en philosophie,* he could not grasp the problem with the peasant girl's innocent simplicity. Salvation involved grace and predestination. The subject was complex and dark. "He who has begun by studying the question of grace and predestination knows quite well at the beginning that he does not know when or where it will all end." [29]

Péguy, in other words, began his stewardship of the *Cahiers de la Quinzaine* by attempting to mold his temporal and spiritual humanism into one comprehensive platform that would guide the destinies of his review. Throughout 1898 and 1899 it had appeared as if he had become wholly absorbed by the desire to attain social justice. Now he recognized that he had merely sketched a schedule that would fill the gap between birth and death. The question of man's purpose on earth had been answered by *Marcel* and the *Notes politiques et sociales.* It dawned

[27] "Encore de la grippe," 6–7.
[28] *Ibid.,* 31.
[29] "Entre deux trains," 24–25.

on him now that every member of the harmonious commonwealth remained mortal. Even after he had resolved the problems of society he must face eternity.

Turning from the contemplation of mortal utopia, Péguy saw
its citizenry individually and collectively entering the unknown
while accustomed to viewing equality and nonexclusiveness as
categorical imperatives. If these principles had been made to
prevail in human society then it was inconceivable to Péguy that
a lesser order should prevail in the presence of God, "whose
hospitality is infinite."[30] Nothing was, therefore, more amazing
and frightening to him than the Christian vision of hell.[31] If the
earthly *cité* admitted all men, heaven could do no less. If there
were limits to divine mercy, on the other hand, the *cité* would
remain a dream forever.

Thus there emerged a desperate article of Péguy's faith that
total collective justice must be followed by total collective salvation. Since man could not make demands on God, it was only
reasonable to accept the vision of the *cité harmonieuse* as di-
vinely inspired. This must mean that the socialist commonwealth
was not merely a hypothesis of perfection—heaven on earth—
but the only possible prelude to man's eventual salvation by an
all-merciful God. This was the conclusion toward which Péguy
seemed to be moving as he meditated on his sickbed.

II

Like *Jeanne d'Arc,* these moving outcries have never elicited
the response their substance would appear to deserve. Their
form, a dialogue of imaginary persons constantly deviating from
and detouring around the subject, may have made them as forbidding as the great trilogy of 1897. The absence of a clear,
simple, black and white partisanship, which excites the reader of
Péguy's later prose, may further have served to put them in the
shadow.

The anticlimactic nature of the next few series of the *Cahiers*
may finally have fortified the impression that Péguy's work

---

[30] "Toujours de la grippe," *Cahiers,* I, No. 7 (1900), 12.
[31] "Encore de la grippe," 38.

during these years deserved the neglect which has been its chief reward. The second year of the *Cahiers,* the next nine series, in fact, contained no sequel to "La grippe." The public dialogue with God was suspended. Instead, it appeared as if the major purpose of the *Cahiers de la Quinzaine* was now to keep readers abreast of the latest development in the editor's own bailiwick. There were regular bulletins announcing the number of subscribers.[32] The seventh issue of the second year declared, categorically, that the editor would "sooner exhaust his finances than give up the service of free subscriptions,"[33] but three months later "the *Cahiers* being very poor," this charity was abandoned.[34] In 1902 readers learned of an elaborate and partially successful attempt to raise a large endowment in order to provide a certain measure of long-range security.[35] Early, Péguy began to cast himself in the role of the virtuous, hard-working editor, of whom it was not clear, however, whether he worked primarily for the salvation of man or the uplift of printers and proofreaders. At any rate he did not spare his readers the fact that he "made packages, glued on stamps, made lists [of subscribers], drew up memorandum slips, arranged orders, and stacked volumes."[36] While he added that he was satisfied to perform such humble work, he nevertheless seemed to expect sympathy.[37] This behavior stood in curious contrast to his insistence that the *Cahiers* claimed, above all, the right to displease. "In order to solicit subscriptions to the *Cahiers* one must never say: Subscribe . . . you will see how you enjoy them. One should rather say: Subscribe . . . because they are serious, sincere, unassuming, and they have a hard time."[38] As was habitual with the head of an endeavor to whom success came slowly, there were the usual attacks on the public—"a new public is yet to be

[32] E.g. I, No. 12 (1900), 5–6.
[33] "Librairie des Cahiers," *Cahiers,* II, No. 7 (1901), 51–56.
[34] "Librairie des Cahiers," *Cahiers,* II, No. 13 (1901), 1–2.
[35] "Emprunt des Cahiers," *Cahiers,* III, No. 16 (1902), 61–69.
[36] "Compte rendu du mandat," *Cahiers,* II, No. 11 (1901), 14.
[37] "Personnalités," *Cahiers,* III, No. 12 (1902), 44–45.
[38] "Bilan," *Cahiers,* III, No. 1 (1901), 36; see also "Personnalités," 36.

created"[39]—and on enemies who alienated support already won.[40]

In the second year of publication, Péguy began to air his recent political quarrels in exhaustive detail. The best part of two entire issues dealt with nothing else.[41] His inability to abandon a subject, even after it had been exposed from every angle, became apparent for the first time. Lesser details, omitted from the great chronicle of the vicissitudes of the Librairie Georges Bellais— *Pour ma maison* and *Pour moi*—were inserted on all conceivable occasions.[42] Not even the news of two subscriptions cancelled by readers of the *Mouvement Socialiste* was too trivial to be mentioned. Péguy magnified the importance of such petty defections by importuning his friends not to do likewise.[43] He made much of turning the other cheek.[44] But if he sought no revenge, why did he spend so much time exposing the wickedness of his enemies? Why did he fail to give credit to their occasional generosity? Was it that he saw in his quarrel with Lucien Herr, for instance, a deeper significance, and in his own resistance the manifestation of a higher cause? It would certainly seem so as one reads his proclamation in the first issue of the third series of the *Cahiers:* "If the custom of true intellectual liberty is to be introduced, maintained, and expanded among us, [then] I declare again that we have begun a revolution far more important than all parliamentarisms with whom we have been blessed in the past."[45]

How did Péguy's increasing egocentricity affect his devotion to the cause of revolution, whose standard he had first grasped at the École Normale? How was it progressing amidst the polemics

---

[39] "Vraiment vrai," *Cahiers,* III, No. 2 (1901), 9–10.

[40] "Pour moi," 50–51.

[41] "Pour ma maison," *Cahiers,* II, No. 3 (1900), 1–27; "Pour moi," 4–51.

[42] "Pages libres," *Cahiers,* II, No. 3 (1900), 50; "Procès-verbaux," *Cahiers,* II, No. 9 (1901), 1–2; "Compte rendu du mandat," 14.

[43] "Note," *Cahiers,* III, No. 16 (1902), 59.

[44] See also the advertisement for the publications of the Société Nouvelle with Péguy's own comment in II, No. 10 (1901), 67–69.

[45] "Bilan," 42.

of 1901–1902? The Socialist party had again split into Marxist and Reformist factions: The Parti Socialiste de France continued to consider itself the party of revolution and rejected "participation in the central power, . . . voting for the budget or . . . alliances with bourgeois parties." The Parti Socialiste Français, on the other hand, warned against neglect of "the great potentialities of legal power." [46] Péguy while continuing to identify himself with revolution unspecified and socialism unqualified, took up an individualistic and solitary position which revealed no commitment to either faction. It could not be otherwise, for when he had joined the party, "it was understood that we would never found a school, but would remain a company of freemen." Socialism had been a promise to do well what one was doing. This implied that "philosophy was philosophical and not socialist, that science was scientific . . . and that art was artistic." Socialism, in other words, meant complete freedom of access to knowledge. It did not mean a new set of doctrines, a new system, or a new religion. "We have given up a religion that forces us to eat fish on Friday. Let us not found one that forces us to eat meat on that day." [47] The convert must give himself unreservedly to the task of self-perfection before he could begin to work as a missionary among the heathen bourgeois and the bourgeoisified.[48] The exigencies of life provided no excuse for deviating from these principles or that plan. True, socialists sought to be effective, and they needed an army of professional politicians. But "revolutionary socialism must not be contaminated by its political army, as the French nation was contaminated by its military army." [49]

Still, one must be prepared at this point in Péguy's life to encounter more than the repetition of views formulated during the previous five years. From the moment Bergson became professor of modern philosophy at the Collège de France, Péguy

[46] Cole, *A History of Socialist Thought*, III, 350–51.
[47] "Note," *Cahiers*, II, No. 1 (1900), 2; "De la raison," *Cahiers*, III, No. 4 (1901), xvi, xxiii.
[48] "Pour ma maison," 20.
[49] "Pour moi," 39–40.

was among the faithful in the crowded lecture hall that was invariably filled before the scheduled hour. Next to him invariably sat Georges Sorel, his elder by more than twenty-five years. In the engineer turned philosopher, whose "ruddy cheeks, white beard [and] flashing blue eyes . . . underscored the brio of his conversation to make an indelible personal impression,"[50] the earnest young maverick from Orléans encountered an unexpectedly kindred spirit. Of humble petty-bourgeois origins, both men had had uncertain and traumatic collisions with socialism and been attracted by its French rather than its German prophets. Both were weighted down by an oppressive certainty that French society was decadent and corrupt. Both advocated moral revolution.[51] Time tightened the bonds of common aversions. They discovered wide areas of specific agreement, "the disintegration of parliamentarism, the demands of virtue [strained] by the decay of bourgeois conventions, the bankruptcy of political socialism." Jean Onimus, in an uncommonly perceptive study of their relationship, has exposed the mercilessly Robespierrist austerity which Péguy and Sorel admired. Their love of antiquity rested on shared ideals of purity and self-abnegation. Péguy's own *cité socialiste* was a city of virtue, not of the good life. The vision was complemented by the two men's contempt for hypocrisy, materialism, and intellectualism, all three of which both identified with the accursed "bourgeois spirit."[52]

"Father" Sorel's attitudes did not represent new revelations to the young editor of the *Cahiers*. Péguy discovered in the older sage an ally who confirmed those doubts and misgivings which he had hitherto entertained and expressed only intermittently. His populism and his distrust of the intellectual continued to exist side by side, but the ascendancy of the latter grew.

Péguy's proud references to his grandmother's illiteracy and to

---

[50] Hughes, *Consciousness and Society,* 180.

[51] Cf. Jack J. Roth, "Revolution and Morale in Modern French Thought: Sorel and the Sorelians," *French Historical Studies,* III (1963), 205–206.

[52] Jean Onimus, "Péguy et Sorel," *ACPFM,* No. 77 (1960), 5–13.

her untutored capabilities as a historian[53] appeared for the first time in the second and third series of the *Cahiers,* and with them the famous affirmation: "I am absolutely not the intellectual who descends and condescends to the people. I am of the people. I chat with the man on the street, man to man, without after-thought. He is not my pupil. I am not his teacher. . . . We communicate. We work together." In the third-class railway carriage to and from Orléans, Péguy listened to the passengers' conversation and heard all that was worth hearing.[54] Was this true? If Péguy was "peuple," was there any need to proclaim it? An old syndicalist, Pierre Monatte, has recently insisted that Péguy, in fact, deserted the people for "the handsome gentlemen of the *Académie*" because he was a professorial autocrat and an egocentric intellectual, completely devoid of any feeling for the man in the street.[55] However that may be, there is enough evidence from Péguy's own hand to make one question the motives behind these frequent professions of love for the people. His praise of the humble invariably became a slashing attack on the university community for having denied him the support and recognition which he felt to be his due. The people were honest, but the academician was phony.[56] The people worked, but the academician was a careerist.[57] Failure to admire Péguy was a serious blemish on the intellectuals' character. Ever since he had struck out on his own, Péguy claimed, the professors had let him down: "When in an outburst of indignation, I began the *Cahiers,* I naïvely expected that my friends from the École Normale and the University would constitute and remain the core of sub-scribers. . . . I had reckoned without the power of envy. I had reckoned without the conformism of the intellectual." While the learned gentlemen deserted him, *"nos abonné peuple"*—never identified—remained true. He viewed this as a demonstration

[53] "Pour moi," 2; "Compte rendu du congrès," *Cahiers,* III, No. 1 (1901), 19–20.

[54] "Pour moi," 31–32.

[55] From a letter to Auguste Martin in "Albert Thierry, Pierre Monatte et la 'Vie Ouvrière,'" *ACPFM,* No. 75 (1960), 26–27, 30–31.

[56] "Personnalités," 29–30.

[57] *Ibid.,* 27.

not so much of spiritual as of economic affinities. The professors with their fine positions and secure incomes knew no loyalty; the people "whose bread, whose family, whose health, whose life, whose liberty, like mine, is threatened every day" were less easily frightened by controversy and remained faithful to the *Cahiers*.[58] Péguy's populism became an arbitrary division of mankind into two categories: those who supported him, the people, and those who did not, the intellectuals. Egocentricity led not to pessimism, as Onimus concludes, but to the misanthropy of failure. Sorel might doubt man's virtue; Péguy merely accused men of not subscribing to the *Cahiers de la Quinzaine*. The poison of selfishness, rather than of doubt, began to be the real corrosive substance that ate away at his former idealism.

In this angry monologue every word must be taken with the proverbial grain of salt. Superlatives of love and hate became the order of the day. At one moment the chatter of the third-class railway carriage became the residue of all wisdom. In another issue of the *Cahiers,* Bergson's lecture at the Collège de France "on Friday at two-forty-five" ushered in the most rewarding hour of the week.[59] Did Bergson ride in third-class railway carriages? Did "the people" attend his lectures? Neither, of course. When Péguy sat in the auditorium he was in the company of Georges Sorel, of Jacques Maritain, of the young physician Robert Debré. He was an intellectual among intellectuals; a frustrated, embittered man, not a man of the people. To that extent, Pierre Monatte's recollections were more precise.

III

This is not the end of the story. Just as the late 1890's witnessed a continuous struggle between Péguy's idealistic drive and his pessimistic querulousness, the years after 1900 produced a kaleidoscopic array of massive essays diluted by petty asides. Great passages of eloquent insight impose upon the reader the obligation of forgiving, if not overlooking, the numerous lapses into strident self-pity. Now the recuperative force of genius

[58] *Ibid.,* 28–29.
[59] "Compte rendu du congrès," 7.

overcame the weaknesses and vanities of the man; then, again, the thrust of genius was throttled by the earth-bound egoist. But Péguy at his best remains so dazzling that one never abandons the hope that one day he might emancipate himself sufficiently from this yearning for recognition to take flight into the realm of pure creation.

Péguy's valedictory to his idealistic past was "De Jean Coste," a seventy-page preface which he wrote to Antonin Lavergne's *Jean Coste, ou l'instituteur de village*. The novel sketched in tones of unrelieved grey the life of a village schoolmaster and dwelt at depressing length on the economic difficulties to which the hero eventually succumbed. Jean Coste's suicide, preceded by the murder of his wife and children, presented to Péguy the extreme of misery. "His last day was a terrifying day. *Dies irae*, day of wrath," he wrote.[60] One can see why Péguy chose this interpretation. Jean Coste was destroyed by a society which had tolerated extremes of inequality. Whereas the experience of temporal equality filled the citizen of the *cité harmonieuse* with confidence that eternity would be no less blissful, Coste's life had merely announced the certainty of hell. Since he had been damned to endure misery on earth, the escape through suicide was an act of unconditional surrender. Hell on earth might be a trial of purification; it might equally be the prelude to eternal damnation.

To Péguy, the socialist, Jean Coste represented misery, "the universal penetration of life by death, the fore-taste of death in all of life."[61] Like hell, misery was without end. The miserable could never be anything else. They were evil, ugly, and feeble. The poor got by, the miserable did not.[62] Even after a *misérable* became poor, petty-bourgeois, or bourgeois, he continued to climb frantically up and up, driven by the memory of his past destitution. In his senseless ambition he revealed how misery had marked him forever.[63]

Once more Péguy was aroused by compassion. Again he

[60] "De Jean Coste," 24.
[61] *Ibid.*
[62] *Ibid.*, 10–16.
[63] *Ibid.*, 35–37.

preached social justice. Preoccupation with the abolition of misery was like the Catholic urge to save. "Damnation has supreme significance for the Catholic, social misery is of supreme importance to us." [64] At the same time he complained that *"ce monde prétendu socialiste"* had become more imbued with the pursuit of pleasure and luxury than the bourgeois world. Everybody spent huge sums on feasts and banquets, meetings, and elections; but when help was asked for a truly socialist project like the *Cahiers de la Quinzaine,* the number of socialists turned out to be microscopic. [65] "Us," therefore, encompassed merely the *Cahiers de la Quinzaine,* presumably representing a socialist elite which was far more sensitive to suffering than the rank and file of the swelling mass movement. Thus, "De Jean Coste" was both a bridge to the past and an expression of Péguy's increasing political isolation, of his separation from the socialist movement which was not accompanied by a corresponding approach to any other organized faction.

One salient theme in this process of political alienation was Péguy's constant reference to the Dreyfus experience. On June 16, 1903, he reminded his subscribers that the "universal, total, perpetual, continuous, continual, constant [and] exact" Dreyfusard, like Péguy, had never accepted the amnesty which had brought the captain back from Devil's Island. [66] This was not quite accurate. In "Le ravage et la réparation" he had described a Dreyfus "saved" by presidential pardon. And while he had even then held that the innocent did not need forgiveness, he had also understood that the weary victim of injustice was entitled to an armistice. What aroused him three years later to the point of denying the past was the revival of the issue and its use as a weapon against the Church during the struggle for separation.

[64] *Ibid.,* 17.

[65] *Ibid.,* 4.

[66] "Réponse politique parlementaire," *Cahiers,* IV, No. 20 (1903), 4. Actually the first hint of dissatisfaction with the pardon can be found in "Les élections," *Cahiers,* III, No. 16 (1902), 35–36, in the wake of the elections of 1902. A month later Péguy wrote to Bernard Lazare expressing his disappointment with the role played by the "Dreyfusard general staff" in the campaign. See Charles Péguy, "Lettres à Edouard Berth, Bernard Lazare, Louis Bompard et autres," *ACPFM,* No. 24 (1951), 4.

In 1898 the Méline government had lost its footing in the hurricane of the Dreyfus Affair and its passing had ended an era of religious harmony. The bloc of the Left which emerged victorious from the elections, and which constituted the sinews of the Waldeck-Rousseau combination, was held together by anti-clericalism. The Moderate prime minister himself became the spokesman of a new secular push when he complained that there were too many intriguers and businessmen among the regular clergy.[67] The wealth enjoyed and the separate school system created and maintained by the Church became the target of a new wave of laic legislation. This change in governmental posture was greeted with thunder from the pulpits and by the same venomous outcries in the clerical press which had characterized official Catholic response to revision of the Dreyfus case. The battle lines of 1898 were not disintegrating; indeed the anti-clericals were so decidedly in the ascendancy that they were determined to proceed from defense to attack.

From 1900 to 1905 the parliamentary majority completed the secularization of the schools and separated church from state. The Association Law, enacted on January 15, 1901, decreed that no religious congregation could function without a bill of authorization passed by both houses of parliament. New congregational schools required a permit from the Council of State.[68] Unauthorized congregations were given three months in which to gain legal recognition. Failing this they had to disband. More than 140 chose the latter course rather than accept the law; members of many others preferred exile to compliance. As it worked out, the *Conseil d'État* kept one eye on the government while dealing with petitions and rejected most of these. The Association Law in effect spelled the end of congregational schools. More than 12,000 had been closed by the summer of 1903.

Meantime the elections of 1902 provided an even more explicit mandate for the government's policy. Amidst unusually

[67] Chastenet, *La république triomphante,* 210.
[68] Charles E. Freedeman, *The Conseil d'État in Modern France* (New York, 1961), 95, 102–103.

heavy electoral participation, the anticlerical bloc (Alliance Démocratique Republicaine, Radicals, Radical-Socialists, and forty-five pro-government socialists) obtained 350 of the 588 seats in the Chamber of Deputies. While the cabinet of Émile Combes, who succeeded the ailing Waldeck-Rousseau on July 15, 1902, no longer included Millerand, its solid majoritary position rested in part on the constant and vocal support of the bulk of socialist deputies, led by Jaurès.

The anticlerical advance continued. A bill enacted in 1904 forbade all teaching by the congregations and provided a ten-year period of grace during which all church schools had to be closed. The last phase of the campaign was introduced in a speech by Jean Jaurès at Rouen in May of the same year: "After secularizing marriage, the family, and the school," the southern deputy promised, "we will finally secularize the state by the great reform we call separation." [69] It is doubtful that Combes wanted to go that far. Like Waldeck-Rousseau, he feared that separation would "render the church free and the state powerless in its regard." [70] But after Jaurès had published the private papal protest against President Loubet's state visit to the King of Italy in *Humanité* and France had broken diplomatic relations with the Vatican, the current toward separation became irresistible. The Act passed the Senate in December, 1905, terminating the Napoleonic Concordat of 1801 and ending state subsidies to the church and clergy.[71]

Péguy watched these proceedings with growing horror. Accustomed to a battle in which clericalism was the enemy, he saw the combat renewed, Dreyfusism corrupted, and the clergy victimized. "You Catholics rejoice," he wrote his friend the Benedictine monk Louis Baillet in 1902. "The persecutions of the Radicals prepare without doubt a rebirth of Catholic faith in France." [72] He realized only too well that the actions of the

[69] Quoted in Goldberg, *Jean Jaurès*, p. 321.

[70] François Goguel, *La politique des partis sous la IIIe république* (Paris, n.d.), 524.

[71] Cf. Louis Méjan, *La séparation des églises et de l'état*, ed. L. V. Méjan (Paris, 1959), 157–207.

[72] *Lettres et entretiens*, 43.

government would, in the long run, benefit those whom they were designed to harm. Anticlericalism was, therefore, a twofold stupidity. It was unjust and unwise.

To find Jaurès among the exploiters of the once hallowed cause, and to see him support acts of increasingly brutal persecution, ranked among the greatest disappointments of Péguy's life. It appeared as if his former hero had become the high priest of a new and vicious political sectarianism.[73] "The great philosopher, the fine artist, the man of wisdom no longer reigns; a minor orator has taken over."[74]

Péguy not only refused to join in the desecration of the *Affaire,* he denounced it. Anticlericalism was even more than unjust and unwise; it was conservative and therefore not worthy of socialist support. Like Catholicism, it was a part of French tradition. The clericals honestly admitted their conservatism; their persecutors were ashamed of theirs. Péguy did not propose to defend the Church. Its discipline and its dogma were as repugnant to him as always. He merely refused to recognize Émile Combes as the champion of that freedom which the Church had sought to subvert when it declared war on the Third Republic. Anticlericalism, in other words, was no weapon against Catholicism. It substituted one regime of oppression for another. Religions could only be mastered by reason; "no command authority, no government authority in particular, is worth anything in a debate of conscience."[75] A *cité socialiste* alone, fashioned to save man, could replace the Church. "A *politique* is no substitute for a religion."[76]

The key in this polemic was the word "oppress." Oppression of justice on the Right had given way to oppression of justice on the Left. The danger lay not in the preponderance of a given party, but in the growth of governmental power as such. As Péguy put it at this point, with his gift for coining striking inaccuracies: "I have regretted for my country the establishment

[73] "Débats parlementaires," *Cahiers,* IV, No. 18 (1903), 4, 34, 43.
[74] Quoted in Goldberg, *Jean Jaurès,* 299.
[75] "Avertissement," *Cahiers,* V, No. 10 (1904), xxxv–xxxvi, xi–xii.
[76] *Ibid.,* xiv.

of an absolute democratic government, just as I should have deplored the establishment of any absolute government." [77]

Here again Péguy rose above himself to see the larger issue. Dreyfusards had been transformed into professional anticlericals; socialists had become statists.[78] Past ideals had been abandoned; principle was about to be sacrificed to the moloch state. The dangers threatening freedom were greater than ever before. The forces of religious bigotry had at least been divided, between themselves and among themselves. The clericals and the nationalists had not seen eye-to-eye on every question. But the state was a monolith. It made war, it concluded peace, it policed the streets, and it collected taxes. Now, through its intrusion into the realm of religion, it had assumed a far more ominous aspect than ever before. It sought to regulate thought. It had grown from a political and social into a "metaphysical" institution.[79] Repeatedly during the next several years, Péguy castigated "the new ideology" as an intellectual monopoly of the most brutal pervasiveness.[80]

In the face of this total threat, Péguy quietly abandoned the *cité harmonieuse* and undertook to defend, by implication at least, the status quo of 1880, the "good old days" before the laic laws. The utopian became a reactionary.[81]

Péguy abandoned the search for the millennium because even the ground on which he stood seemed to be shifting under his feet. Until it had been stabilized, everything else would have to wait. The ultimate goal and the general humanitarian motivation of the search had presumably not changed. But a review of the ambitious polemics against the laic, monolithic, and metaphysical state revealed that Péguy had withdrawn deeper and deeper into impenetrable egocentric solitude. The battery of attacks on the Third Republic revealed that the eloquence of the bard of

[77] "Cahiers de la Quinzaine," *Cahiers,* IV, No. 12 (1903), 199.
[78] *Ibid.,* 202–203.
[79] "Un essai de monopole," *Cahiers,* VI, No. 4 (1904), xi.
[80] "Cahiers de la Quinzaine," *Cahiers,* VIII, No. 11 (1907), 34–62.
[81] This term is here not used pejoratively, but merely to describe a person who wishes to restore conditions which, in his opinion, no longer exist.

Jeanne d'Arc and the visionary of *Marcel* had been pressed into the service of an entirely different crusade.

The reactionary Péguy made his debut in a critical preface to Israel Zangwill's *Chad Gadya,* the French version of that author's *Dreamers of the Ghetto* (1898). Péguy's essay was so massive that it appeared as a separate *Cahier.* Apart from a similarity of attitudes—Zangwill's *Dreamers* were primarily symbols of faith and tradition, not images of historic verity—it was bound only by the most fragile strands to the work it professed to be introducing. Its significance lies therefore in the context of Péguy's own work, for its chief concerns are a rejection of the fashionable assumptions of inevitable progress through science and the revelation of the author's considerable acumen as a literary critic.[82]

Péguy's hostilities coincided with the prejudices of many Parisian literati of his day. The master critics of his time, Jules Lemaitre, Émile Faguet, Ferdinand Brunetière, and the young school of the *Action Française* denied in unison the most widely accepted traditions of French civilization: the Enlightenment, the Revolution, and the positivism and naturalism of the nineteenth century. The more placid and conformist *critique universitaire* offered no sheltering alternative for a man like Péguy who had declared war on academe for the relatively trivial reason that it had refused to support the *Cahiers de la Quinzaine.* Yet he did not adhere to a conservative coterie. He preserved his isolation. Péguy never asked any critic of the Right for a sign of recognition or of community, and he repeatedly snubbed overtures of cordiality from the *Action Française.* Only his critical works henceforth provided any arrows for their eager bows, and his own reckless charges against the emplacements of the "modern world" aided many of their campaigns.

Notably the fathers of scientist scholarship, Taine and Renan, in whose shadow Péguy himself had grown up and who in his view deified man in history, roused him to perpetual indigna-

---

[82] Péguy's eminence in this field was first recognized by Henry Brémond, "Joseph Lotte et les Entretiens de Péguy," *Le Correspondant,* CCLXIII (1916), 470–71.

tion.[83] He accused them of having formulated a philosophy of history which placed man in competition with the divine creator: "For truly if the historian is so perfectly and completely aware of the conditions which shape and manufacture genius; if we grant, first of all, that these conditions which shape genius are external, may be grasped, can be known, and are known; that they shape not merely genius, but . . . talent, peoples, cultures and races. If we can really not hide anything from these historians. . . . [If] they hold in their hands the secret of genius itself," if it follows from this claim "that they can control the production and manufacture of genius," then the historian "is today usurping creation itself. He is encroaching on God the creator."[84] The ultimate implication of scientific history, as practiced by the epigones of Taine and Renan, was that "mankind has become God through the total infinity of its knowledge, the infinite fullness of its total memory."[85]

Such extreme pretensions appalled Péguy. They presumed a degree of human progress which events did not justify. Reality was not Promethean. On the contrary, it consisted of the Russo-Japanese War and the revival in France of civil and religious strife. The latter, in turn, revealed the inadequacy of the secular apostolate, which could not prevent the resurgence of friction precisely in those areas of human relations where open battle, according to Péguy, had been unknown since the Edict of Nantes.[86]

"Zangwill" did not entirely escape critical attention. Daniel Halévy, then a young disciple of Georges Sorel and of the recently deceased Nietzsche, had met Péguy during the brief period when the *Cahiers* shared an office with the ephemeral *Pages Libres.* Attracted to the idealistic editorial practices professed by the *Cahiers,* Halévy was now shocked by "Zangwill's" proclamation of the "joyful news that so many men are wrong and with them Taine and Renan, our own true masters." He

83 "Zangwill," lxxiii.
84 *Ibid.,* lxxiv–lxxv.
85 *Ibid.,* xxxvi.
86 *Ibid.,* xxxv.

recognized that behind Péguy's righteous indignation there lurked a nihilism which might at any moment deteriorate into a facile, indiscriminate iconoclasm. The creative promptings of Péguy's generous heart might be silenced once and for all if he abandoned the search for perfection in favor of the relentless persecution of evil.[87]

"Zangwill" was followed by the "Situations," essays on an intellectual scene dominated by the conflict between religion and secularism. Again Péguy concentrated his fire on the historians. In his estimation, the men who functioned as the national memory bore the chief responsibility for current national attitudes. If they were truthful, the course of the nation would run true; if they lied, they could lead it into an abyss. French historians, he found, were neither honest in their craft nor conscientious in the discharge of their duty to society. Devious as men and as scholars, they found themselves hopelessly entangled in a web of contradiction. Their calling forced them to search. Their profession—most of them taught at schools or universities—compelled them to assume postures of authority, the attitude of men who have found the truth. To make matters worse, most of them were employees of the state. Thus they were enslaved both by their profession and by their temporal master.[88]

As a result, Péguy concluded, the historian had become the servant of a new cult. Church and state had been separated, but metaphysics—Péguy's term for the worship of absolute, omnipotent man—and the state remained explicitly united.[89] The new secular priests, he warned, were dangerous and ambitious. They craved recognition and advancement to such a degree that their aspirations became an appalling force of corruption. Péguy found some slight consolation in the fact that the grasping henchmen of the laic dictatorship were at least convinced repub-

[87] Daniel Halévy, "Chad Gadya," *Pages Libres,* II (1904), 482–84.
[88] "De la situation faite à l'histoire et à la sociologie dans les temps modernes," 15–20.
[89] "De la situation faite au parti intellectuel dans le monde moderne devant les accidents de la gloire temporelle," 13–15.

licans; otherwise not even the constitution would be safe from them.[90]

Péguy closed his diatribe against the modern, secular state with this challenge: The modern commonwealth owed its power to two maneuvers, the systematic falsification of history, initiated by Taine's tendentious use of manuscript sources, and its monopoly of secondary and higher education, engineered, in his opinion, by Ferdinand Buisson, who had carried out the Ferry Laws in the 1880's and led the parliamentary fight for Separation in 1905. The new history, according to Péguy, substituted the year 1789 for the year one of the Christian era.[91] Its logical extension, secular education, suppressed classical and Christian learning in favor of the modernist faith in the perfectability of man.[92] These two pillars supported the modern world, which Péguy first castigated in "Zangwill" and with which he chose to remain at war for the rest of his life. "The modern world degrades. That is its specialty," he claimed. "I would almost say that is its craft, if it were not out of respect for the word 'craft.' Let us put it this way: when the modern world degrades, it is working in its own behalf." [93]

Until 1902, Péguy's life had been consecrated to the achievement of positive good. Man might be wicked, but "we must think of what he should be." During the next five years he turned to the fixed contemplation of man's darker side. There was evil in this world; there was delusion, corruption, ambition, and tyranny; and he was overcome by an apprehension that these vices were flourishing unrecognized. At the same time, his militancy on a new crusade increased his loneliness, because in the pursuit

[90] "De la situation faite au parti intellectuel dans le monde moderne," 7–14.

[91] Péguy failed to realize that history since the discipline's rebirth during the Renaissance had only rarely accorded Christ's coming the status of a seminal event. Cf. Theodore E. Mommsen, "Petrarch's Concept of the 'Dark Ages,'" *Medieval and Renaissance Studies* (Ithaca, N.Y., 1959), 113–15, 123–24.

[92] "De la situation faite au parti intellectuel dans le monde moderne devant les accidents de la gloire temporelle," 49–66.

[93] *Ibid.*, 98.

of the wicked, no less than in his earlier propagation of the *cité socialiste,* he trusted no one but himself. The contemporary world became his counter-utopia, which had to be destroyed before the march on the road to paradise could be resumed.

As Péguy's goals changed, so did the tone of his campaign. He substituted oratory for thought. His vision of laic hell was compelling, the thunder of his eloquence deafening as well as terrifying. A constant rumble of indignation replaced his earlier, calmer faith in eternal justice. Once his gaze had been lifted upward to a celestial horizon of infinite promise. Now he had himself fallen prey to those vices of which he accused the historian: overweening pride which, without encroaching on God, nevertheless claimed moral superiority over all men.

The orator also changed his style. "Zangwill" and the "Situations" were far more voluminous than the modest contributions to the *Revue Socialiste* and the *Revue Blanche.* Yet, it does not take long to summarize them. As a young man, Péguy said what he had to without circumlocution because the message burned in his heart. The convert to misanthropy, on the other hand, while no more complex or profound a thinker, was developing a self-conscious and smug virtuosity with words. Now his sentences covered pages with the froth of verbal themes and variations. After the reader had wrestled down this hydra-headed accumulation of clauses, allusions, similes, and subtleties, he might confront another verse—the word seems more appropriate than paragraph—exposing the author's ability to express one thought in an infinite number of ways. Péguy was not merely becoming a purveyor of self-righteous invective, he grew steadily more clever and more vain.

Both the grandeur and misery of Péguy's genius can be tested through his reactions to the two great warnings which the year 1905 offered a relatively complacent Europe—the first Moroccan crisis and the Russian revolution. The first acerbated the hostility of the two powers who fought the most decisive battles of the First World War; the second revealed the weakness of the thousand-year-old Russian monarchy and clearly posed the alternatives of gradual versus revolutionary reform.

Both events grew out of the Russo-Japanese War. Germany had attempted to use the Asian encounter to negotiate a new alliance with the harried czar. This failing, she turned her energies to Morocco, where France was threatening to establish a protectorate over an incompetent sultan. On March 31, the Kaiser called on the north African potentate and assured him that Germany would continue to support his independence. This step was designed to establish Germany's own position in the area and to drive a wedge into King Edward VII's and Théophile Delcassé's Entente Cordiale by convincing Britain of its risks and France of its uselessness.

The upshot was the proposal of an international conference, on whose call the Germans insisted even though French Foreign Minister Delcassé did not stint with offers of concessions, including exclusive use of specific Moroccan port facilities. The frustrated leader of French diplomacy finally sought the antidote of an alliance with Britain. But his fellow ministers, impressed by their Russian ally's defeat in Asia and concerned over the unsettling impact of the domestic struggle separating church from state, unanimously opposed a policy which in their view comprehended so high a risk of war. They saw no choice but to acquiesce in the conference proposal, and Delcassé resigned on June 6, 1905, after seven years at the Quai d'Orsay.

Péguy's response to these events, appearing in October under the title "Notre Patrie," might have been more appropriately called "The Moroccan Crisis and I." With "Zangwill" it had in common a title that was a clue or a point of departure instead of a heading. But whereas the preceding attack on the "modern world" and the later "Situations" reflected their author's ability to present the same idea in a multitude of forms, "Notre Patrie" was almost entirely descriptive. It has been pointed out above[94] that Péguy saw the Moroccan crisis as the prelude to war. His correspondence and his biographers disclose that he never troubled to unpack his officer's knapsack after the June days of 1905. However, none of this can be learned from "Notre Patrie."

[94] Pp. 19–21.

The essay begins where "Zangwill" ended: Péguy in his office on a late spring day in 1905, unaware of the gathering clouds in the Mediterranean, brooding over the degradation of the Dreyfus Affair and enumerating once again the dangers threatening France from a secular, civilian Caesarism. He speculates about the advisability of devoting a *Cahier* to Combism; the thought follows him after he has locked his office and walked from the narrow Rue de la Sorbonne to the Boulevard St. Michel, where the crowds are waiting to catch a glimpse of visiting King Alfonso XIII of Spain. Péguy threads his way through the surge of *"ce vieux peuple roi . . .* more royal, more prepared for its job than this young heir of a relatively young dynasty." [95] He smiles at the paradox of those republican masses flocking to see a king. As Péguy gains more walking room, he quickens his pace. The rhythm of his steps awakens echoes of Victor Hugo's verses "sounding like a fanfare, sounding like a call to action [from] the eternal drummer who will continue to beat ruffles and flourishes in our memories long after the regulation drummers will have ceased to advance before our regiments." [96] Hugo, Péguy reflects, was like the volatile, unpredictable masses he had just left behind. He loved peace, yet never extolled it in verse; they loved peace but needed an army for display and amusement. They want to live in peace, but dream of war; and Hugo, the apostle of pacifism, worshipped Napoleon I.

Without transition or explanation, Péguy leaps to the first day of June when another anarchist attempts to assassinate the Spanish monarch. This interruption, he adds, is not part of the program, but reality insisting on obtruding. It does not stay the festive glow for long. The guest emerges unscathed, the ceremonies continue. After Alfonso's departure on June 4 a happy afterglow suffuses the capital, to be brutally dissipated two days later.

So far Péguy has carried the reader from a review of his unchanging repertoire of editorial issues into the street, through a kaleidoscope of physical and visual impressions. He waits until

[95] *Notre Patrie* (Paris, 1915), 43–45.
[96] *Ibid.,* 59.

the last paragraph before revealing what really caused him to write this chronicle and why he called it "Notre Patrie."

"On June 6," Péguy finally discloses, "I had come to Paris at nine o'clock in the morning; as everyone else . . . I knew at twelve-thirty that within the space of two and one half hours a new period had begun: in my own life, in the history of this country, and assuredly in the history of the world." [97]

In view of "Notre Patrie's" publication date, its last paragraph must be accepted, not as hindsight, but as the spontaneous reaction of a prophetic mind. Historians can still agree that the first Moroccan crisis brought the world closer to a war that turned civilization on its axis. But whereas the young Péguy would have sounded the tocsin to call together peaceful citizens in an effort to thwart Armageddon, whereas the young Péguy confronted by predatory man would have responded by reminding his fellow citizens of what they should be, the Péguy of 1905 was morally neutral. This photographic chronicle, with its tangential and irrelevant embellishments lacked the visionary zest of Péguy's earlier honest if clumsy creations. Threats of war no longer aroused visions of peace, merely the mechanical response of self-defense.

The assault on the Russian monarchy broke out before the Moroccan crisis and was tied even more closely to the tragic battles fought in Manchuria and the China Sea. Labor unrest reached critical proportions after the destruction of Russia's Far Eastern Fleet in the Tsushima Straits on May 14. Mutiny infected the Black Sea squadrons during the week which decided Delcassé's fate. Signature of the Treaty of Portsmouth failed to allay tensions. A major strike enveloped Moscow on September 19, soon encompassing other cities and the railroads. Convinced that massive violence alone could not maintain his beleaguered autocracy, Nicholas II preferred to sign the October Manifesto which promised a number of basic civil liberties. He consented to the establishment of an assembly with limited legislative functions, elected indirectly by the adult male population.

[97] *Ibid.,* 117–18.

By that time Péguy's "Notre Patrie" was at the printer's and his attention was riveted on what he called, once more with insight and originality, "the resumption of the revolution in Russia."⁹⁸ The interest in Russia, discussed earlier as part of France's cultural transformation in the 1890's, had also left its mark in the pages of the *Cahiers de la Quinzaine*. In 1902 they had published Tolstoi's famous reply to a young Romain Rolland in search of a purpose in life.⁹⁹ This had been followed in the same series by Pierre Quillard's *Pour l'Arménie* (No. 19) and Jean Deck's *Pour la Finlande* (No. 21). By the time "Notre Patrie" approached publication, Péguy was undoubtedly hard at work editing the *Courrier de Russie* by Etienne Avenard, the Russian correspondent of *L'Humanité,* which appeared on November 19. In his editorial capacity, therefore, Péguy spent October reviewing a chronicle of events that began with the January strikes at the Putilov works. Through the correspondent's eyes he relived the horrors of Bloody Sunday, and it is in this connection that he must have read the text of that petition which the guns of police and army would not allow Father Gapon to deliver at the Winter Palace.

At last Péguy, too, spoke on the Russian Revolution in a strikingly clever and morally empty essay entited "Les suppliants parallèles." His *Cahier* began rather abruptly with two texts: Father Gapon's petition to Czar Nicholas II and the Priest's address to Oedipus from Sophocles' *Oedipus Rex*. Though they were printed in parallel columns Péguy did not at once proceed to compare them. Instead he allowed himself first to be side-tracked into an extensive discussion of the perplexities and pitfalls of translating Greek texts. Only then did the author return to the initial confrontation. He explained the parallel situations and helped the reader to understand how these similarities impressed themselves on two petitions separated by more than two thousand years. But *suppliants parallèles* were not matched by *suppliés parallèles;* Nicholas' and Oedipus' reactions

⁹⁸ *Oeuvres complètes,* II, 355.
⁹⁹ III, No. 2.

had little in common, and Péguy digressed again. He recalled the great actor Mounet-Sully whose Oedipus he had seen on the stage. He compared the tragedy in a variety of available translations. He tried his own hand at a number of passages, which provided more opportunities for a display of textual contrasts. At last he got to the nice, and seemingly barren, question of how to translate "Oedipus" from Greek into French. Leconte de Lisle transcribed Οιδιπους as Oidipous. Péguy preferred *Oedipe*, just as in the *Iliad* he preferred *Achille* to Akhilleus. The following representative passage from "Les suppliants parallèles" shows how much bloodletting this turnip had to endure:

As long as one translates, I ask myself in vain: "Why not translate everything?" As long as one translates all the other words, and common nouns in particular, is there no reason why one should not also translate proper nouns, which are part of the same language, and especially part of the same text. . . . If I translate ιερευς, βαμδι, τεχνα as priest, altar, children, why not translate equally and similarly Οιδιπους as Oedipus. If I translate to drink and to eat, to come and to go, why not also translate the name of him who drinks and eats, who sleeps, of him who comes and goes. Why this inequality, this imparity; why introduce into the translation this artificial disharmony, this lack, this breach of harmony, of symmetry, this breach of balance, this veneer, this corpse in a living organism [*sic!*], this dead fragment in a living sentence, this old splinter in a translation which is by its nature a new text, this fossil within an organism, this bone-splinter . . . this inert, solidified, motionless, and stiff component in a mobile, living and supple sentence. Why, finally, do you refuse to translate the same man, Oedipus, when he appears as Οιδιπους, while consenting to translate when he appears under the label τυραννος, which you translate neither as "tyrant" nor as "tyrannos," but quite simply and for historically sound reasons as "king." As a result, you have to be satisfied with this translation: "Oidipous-king." You are neither consistent nor orthodox. It should have been translated either Oidipous-Tyrannos or translated, as everybody does: Oedipus the King.[100]

This passage illustrated Péguy's style, his critical method and intent. It did not close the subject. He had more to say, and as he

[100] *Oeuvres complètes,* II, 411–12.

went on, he penetrated more deeply. He conceded that "Oedipus" was in no sense a translation of "Oidipous." But was "king" a translation of "tyrannos"? Was "priest" a translation of "iereus"? Péguy finally asked: Was translation possible at all? He concluded that it was not: "*Toute opération de traduction est essentiellement, irrévocablement, irrémissiblement une opération miséreuse, une opération misérable et vaine, une opération condamnée.*" [101]

Only after an exhausting exploitation of the pros and cons of this frustrating question did Péguy return to his subject of the parallel petitioners. Supplication, he explained, was the essence of the events of January 22, 1905. The march to the Winter Palace was not a gesture of revolution but "a tremendous act of petition." It was not, he went on, petitioning in the modern sense of seeking favors, offering debasement and humiliation for the sake of a palpable return. It was petitioning in the Greek sense of the word. Péguy held that the Ancients had a view of the relationship between the mighty and the suppliant that was totally at variance with modern practice. In Greek morality and religion, the powerful were marked by the envious fates, whose emissary the petitioner was. Through him the gods provided a warning, the chance to avoid their envious wrath by sharing with the humble the fruits of their extravagant good fortune.[102] Sophocles' Oedipus was the perfect illustration of this relationship. The unsympathetic recipient of the petition ultimately became the object of the tragedy. His eventual suffering far exceeded the discomforts from which the original suppliants sought redress. Péguy concluded with emphatic, aphoristic brevity, reminiscent of Nietzsche:

"He came on the scene like a king. He left, himself a suppliant. Mysterious (not to say mystic) elevation." [103]

At this point "Les suppliants parallèles" approached its cli-

---

[101] *Ibid.*, II, 413. The passage has been left untranslated to give the reader at least a taste of the later Péguy in the original. It also seemed particularly inappropriate to translate this statement.

[102] *Ibid.*, II, 426–32.

[103] *Ibid.*, II, 437.

max. One expected Péguy to carry the comparison to the final prophetic conclusion. One awaited the question: "Will Nicholas II, too, become the object of tragedy? Will the horror of his fate exceed the needs of his petitioners?" His critical insight had carried Péguy to the threshold of prophecy, but he appeared not to have been aware of it. The great disappointment of "Les suppliants parallèles" is that it contains no hint of the crime of Ekaterinburg where the entire imperial family was murdered in 1918. Péguy had been able to overcome his penchant for cleverness long enough to give a great, if uneven, performance as a critic, but when the prophet's greatness was within his reach the misanthrope took over once more.[104]

A younger Péguy would also have eulogized a tragedy that made January 22, 1905 a "bloody Sunday" for all mankind to remember. The reddening snow would earlier have prompted him to write a great sequel to *De Jean Coste*. As it is, "Les suppliants parallèles" has a shockingly negative significance: its author no longer cared about the misery of mankind. The essay collapsed into undisciplined carping. From a review of this Russian movement of supplication, Péguy meandered into a critical commentary on the activities of Russian exiles in Paris and concluded with an attack on their local sponsors, who included Jean Jaurès and Gustave Hervé.[105] Thence it was but a step to another attack on parliamentarism, and before the reader quite knows how, he is again treated to a sermon on the defects of the modern world, now appropriately illustrated by the rapid decline of the study of Greek in the public schools.

"Les suppliants parallèles" contains a number of peerless passages and one or two hints of awe-inspiring insight, but the

[104] Péguy's uncanny ability to see the essentials of the Russian revolution had been revealed earlier when he wrote in an otherwise rambling and undistinguished preface to Avenard's *Courrier de Russie* that the author exposed "this liberal constitutional movement puffing along its rut unaware of the subterranean vulcano" of popular discontent. *Ibid.*, 372–73. On French socialist reactions to the Revolution of 1905, see Encarnacion Alzona, *Some French Contemporary Opinions of the Russian Revolution of 1905* (New York, 1921), 10–17.

[105] *Oeuvres complètes*, II, 463–69.

gravity pull of cynicism and egotism turns out to be its main motivating force. It confirms Péguy's steep descent from the moralist to the amoral intellectual. The transformation seems to have gone largely undetected by the public. Contemporary critics probably did not notice the difference because they knew of Péguy only what they read in the *Cahiers*. They either identified him with the reactionary majority that currently dominated French criticism—the Swiss novelist Edouard Rod in 1907 broadly confirmed what Halévy had deplored in 1904[106]—or they continued surprisingly enough to think of him as a socialist.[107]

Under both labels Péguy emerged as a man of the opposition, sometimes as a kind of opposition's opposition even; and if his readers had until 1907 declined to label him emphatically, they were soon to find such a task all but impossible. Hatred of his surroundings turned out to be a limited theme. After the publication of the last of the "Situations" in October, 1907, Péguy ran out of things to say and fell silent except for an occasional *note du gérant* about the internal affairs of his editorial establishment. For two and a half years he only spoke once, at the end of the *Cahiers'* tenth year of publication. It was a characteristic valedictory to a decade that had changed his career and altered his position.

With bold perverseness the thirteenth *Cahier* of the tenth series, entitled "A nos amis, à nos abonnés," began with a brief page addressed to the latter, explaining some projected changes in the publication schedule. Then the editor turned to *"nos amis"* for an uninterrupted sermon of seventy pages. This reversal of the sequence may have been an act of deliberate cuteness, to show that an independent spirit was not even bound by the heading at the top of the first page. It may have been a subtle hint that he was not really sure which of his subscribers were also

---

[106] Edouard Rod, "Le mouvement des idées sur le rôle social des intellectuels," *Revue Hebdomadaire*, XVII, No. 11 (1907), 375.

[107] E.g. "Lettres Georges Sorel à Edouard Berth," *ACPFM*, No. 77 (1960), 26.

his friends or whether, in fact, a clear line of distinction could be drawn between the two.

As in "De la grippe," Péguy began by explaining the problems confronting him and his publication after his long illness. But this time he refused to take his readers to the sickroom, where, as we know today, he had revealed to Lotte his return to Catholicism. The world, France, and the *Cahiers* were viewed neither *sub specie aeternitatis* nor *mortalitatis,* but *sub mea specie.* The weeks of enforced idleness had convinced the editor that the *Cahiers* did not flourish as the public seemed to assume. "We live in such barbarous times that their neatness is being confused with luxury." It had taken a superhuman effort to survive, and he claimed that other editors had praised his accomplishment as being without parallel in publishing history.[108]

Péguy's second conclusion with which he emerged from his sickbed in the suburbs, was that despite the survival of the *Cahiers,* "we are defeated. The world is against us." [109] He had provided the only substantial refuge to men of culture, but had lost ground nevertheless. Defeat became the refrain of the remaining text: defeat of honesty and defeat of the Dreyfusard cause to which he had dedicated his youth. Leaving behind the condition of the *Cahiers,* Péguy discussed that catastrophe at length. In earlier reflections on this painful subject he had explained how the original idealistic quest for pure justice had been degraded through service in the cause of Separation. Now he went a step further. The Dreyfusard ideal had first been defiled and then forgotten. Like other combatants Péguy was discovering that no one cared any longer. In 1906 when the Court of Appeal set aside the verdict of Rennes, Drumont castigated General Mercier for his failure to demand a third conviction.[110] The Dreyfusards were all turning upon each

---

[108] "A nos amis à nos abonnés," *Cahiers,* X, No. 13 (1909), 8. For a confirmation of this claim, see Daniel Halévy, "Les 'cahiers' de Charles Péguy," *Le Temps,* December 12, 1909.

[109] "A nos amis, à nos abonnés," 11.

[110] Guy Chapman, *The Dreyfus Affair: A Reassessment* (London, 1955), 351.

other. Before becoming Clemenceau's minister of war, Picquart was venting his disgust in the pages of the *Gazette de Lausanne*. Daniel Halévy was preparing an apology for his Dreyfusard past. In 1908 an editorialist of *La Guerre sociale*, possibly Gustave Hervé himself, berated the bourgeoisie for abandoning the fight against injustice once its victims had become members of the proletariat.[111] Joseph Reinach's last volume of the monumental *Histoire de l'affaire Dreyfus* bespoke a shattering disillusionment. Péguy echoed the same sorrow, only his explanation varied: "We were born into a people of defeat. We were defeated in war. We were born shortly after the defeat [of 1871], after the disaster, after the invasion, into a people militarily crushed. We are by heredity and solidarity the victims of a disastrous war."[112] Next, his generation had been subjected to a disaster from within. It had collectively lost a war, then individually lost a cause. Péguy professed to be inconsolable by this succession of setbacks. But even that could have been borne if future generations understood the purpose of the struggle and the nature of his suffering. Unfortunately even such consolation was denied him. Péguy felt incurably alienated from the next generation. The young men of 1890 even pronounced the words "Dreyfus Affair" with a listless indifference that pierced his heart. The glow, the fervent inflection, the enunciation of commitment were gone. They were speaking of an event in history, not an event which had meaning in their lives.

Thus Péguy in "A nos amis, à nos abonnés" claimed spokesmanship for a lost, unique, and "sacrificed generation." "We threw our entire destiny into the affair. Without any historical return."[113] By his own admission it was not the defeat of justice but the oblivion that overtook its partisans which constituted the supreme tragedy. The frustrations of obscurity goaded him into the first spurt of eloquence in more than two years. Not only was

[111] Thalheimer, *Macht und Gerechtigkeit*, 765–69; Patrice Roussel, *L'Affaire Dreyfus et la presse* (Paris, 1960), 220.

[112] "A nos amis, à nos abonnés," 53.

[113] *Ibid.*, 26.

the battle lost—that could have been endured—but men had forgotten why it was ever fought. The Dreyfusard, according to Péguy, left no documents, no barricades, no heroes. No monuments would be erected in his honor, no holidays would command national remembrance. The movement had died slowly, undramatically, in a world that had more important matters to attend than following its casket to an unmarked grave in the cemetery of history.

Péguy had discovered a new hell: oblivion. After ten years of toil neither the causes for which he had labored nor his own work had gained fame for themselves or for him. It was ironical that the only significant instant of public recognition on record was an interview granted only a few months earlier, in August, 1909, by Maurice Barrès to Amédée Boyer of the *Echo de Paris,* in which the famous academician praised Péguy for "turning with disgust from the Dreyfus Party."[114] This was precisely what Péguy refused to do. In his opinion he *was* the Dreyfus party—which no one cared to credit with the salvation of France. In his opinion he and his comrades were the heroes of a great battle still waiting for their pensions and decorations. "A nos amis, à nos abonnés" revealed that the editor of the *Cahiers* had found his own way of degrading the Dreyfus Affair. He was admitting at last that his devotion, too, had not been disinterested. He had supported right, and he claimed to have risked all he possessed in a good cause. He had vainly waited for his reward. Now he called to task a world that had taken his services for granted.

Yet at the very end of this lachrymose *Cahier* brimming over as it was with self pity of every description, Péguy claimed in his review at least a partial reprieve from a lifelong sentence of failure. Before he let his readers go, he tempered the description of defeat by contrary assertions that all was not lost. Although the *Cahiers* presumably did not flourish, he described them as a "movement." What the socialists had denied him—leadership of a group directed and disciplined by his libertarian ideas—he now

[114] Maurice Barrès, *Mes Cahiers* (Paris, 1933), VII, 267–68.

claimed to have created on his own. "By and by, without binding anyone," he had founded "an organization of an unquestionably new *modus,* a kind of hearth . . . a kind of family of kindred spirits, precisely because I did not set about it deliberately; anything but a *group,* as they call it (this horror) but literally the finest there would be in the world: a fellowship, and a *Cité.*"[115]

Strangely enough this claim of victory was not entirely at odds with the cry, "we are the defeated." For many years Péguy had not spoken of the *cité harmonieuse.* Now he resurrected it on the spur of the moment, by suddenly claiming that it had become a reality. The *Cahiers,* though perhaps not *the cité,* were at least *a cité.*

Péguy submitted no evidence to support this claim. It was unmotivated and it was unreasonable. It was a false communique that could of itself not hide that his defeat was quite as complete as he had stated elsewhere in "A nos amis, à nos abonnés." The *Cahiers* were not a stable community. The life of their editor was too much shaken by continuous and successive feuds to become the center of a movement. Herr and Jaurès had long passed from the circles he frequented. Romain Rolland and the Tharaud brothers were disappearing from the table of contents of the *Cahiers.* The friendship with Jacques Maritain had soured because of their religious disagreements.[116] A year after the appearance of "A nos amis, à nos abonnés" Péguy had a serious difference with Daniel Halévy; and by 1911 Georges Sorel had been expelled from the Thursday afternoons at 8 Rue de la Sorbonne.[117] With him there departed from the imaginary spiritual commonwealth many young men who had never frequented it out of attachment to Péguy. Old friends were replaced by newcomers: Julien Benda and André Suarès, for instance. But Benda was an independent spirit who sought and found in Péguy

[115] "A nos amis, à nos abonnés," 16.

[116] R. Maritain, *Les grandes amitiés,* 209.

[117] M. Péguy, "La rupture de Charles Péguy et de Georges Sorel," 7–61; Variot, *Propos de Georges Sorel,* 250–68; Onimus, "Péguy et Sorel," 6–7, insists that Sorel's interest in Péguy was always a matter of principle and never a case of friendship.

a publisher, not a leader.[118] André Suarès was a lonely, neglected poet whom Péguy's interest encouraged. He never forgot the debt he owed to the man who had comforted him in obscurity,[119] but he never was and never could be a disciple. Péguy, to do him justice, did not demand the kind of allegiance which the master would exact from those who had come to sit at his feet. "Without asking anything of anyone," and without program or platform, as he accurately described his venture, he had made something of the *Cahiers.* They had lasted and they had value, but to invest them with the spiritual or physical appurtenance of a community was exaggerated. Was this claim the defiant response of the carpenter's son to failure in a world where fame and distinction seemed reserved for the sons of the bourgeoisie?[120]

Possibly Péguy had suddenly awakened to his surroundings and understood how far he was from the Faubourg Bourgogne and his mother's grocery store. Socially he was uprooted; intellectually he had entered a competition for the highest stakes among the most refined talents. The Paris of 1909 was far from passing through "barbarous times," although such novelties as Stravinsky's scores performed by the Russian Ballet and George Sorel's *Reflections on Violence* might appear to many as the barbarian's assault on a brilliant civilization. Péguy's spiritual mentor Bergson was the rage. His only hero among the Radicals, Clemenceau, was president of the council of ministers. As a fountain of thoughtful polemic and literary art, the *Cahiers* hardly stood out. The number of quality reviews, both *grandes* and *petites,* which offered working space to the large gathering of creative spirits and inspiration to an avid and sophisticated public, need not shirk comparison with any metropolis of modern times. The latest significant newcomer to the publishing scene, the *Nouvelle Revue Française,* appeared the very year in which Péguy bewailed the barbarity of the times; and its survival

[118] On Benda's profound philosophical differences with Péguy, see his autobiography *Un régulier dans le siècle* (Paris, 1937), 39–43, and Robert J. Niess, *Julien Benda* (Ann Arbor, Mich., 1956), 12, 80, 83.

[119] André Suarès, *Péguy* (Paris, 1915).

[120] Cf. Jacques Chastenet, *La France de M. Fallières* (Paris, n.d.), 171.

alone casts doubt upon the justice of his complaint. The years that brought into prominence Proust, Gide, Claudel, and Valéry; Debussy, Ravel, and Satie; Picasso and the *Fauves* has had few equals in the annals of French civilization. The barbarians whose destructive dogmas might threaten this surge, the coterie of a Sorel, and a Maurras, or Clemenceau's gendarmes and soldiers who in 1907 had re-enacted a miniature Bloody Sunday at Villeneuve-Saint-Georges, leaving four strikers dead and thirty wounded—these barbarians remained surprisingly immune from Péguy's strictures.

Péguy's judgment had been warped by the hard and bitter road he had traveled since 1900. In the course of his journey he had abandoned his search of the *cité harmonieuse,* and he had become silent about his quest for eternal salvation. He had withdrawn to new lines of defense, from which he attacked the modern world of anticlericalism and statism, whose defeat had to be consummated before he could once more set out on the road to utopia. But even that war seemed about to end in failure. He had resigned from idealism only to find the role of reactionary into which that resignation had pushed him, to be equally unrewarding.

From total failure there appeared only one exit: death. Péguy's prophetic intuition recognized it in a stark phrase that suddenly lit up the self-indulgent tergiversations of "A nos amis, à nos abonnés": "What I need is a death with a date." [121] His only entry into the pages of history, as he saw it, could be assured by a memorable end. Again, as in "Les suppliants parallèles," Péguy approached a mystic foreboding of the future. But the time to die had not yet come. The year 1910 began by suddenly and unexpectedly providing the fame he craved. Comatose hope was revitalized by a sudden outburst of poetic inspiration.

[121] "A nos amis, à nos abonnés," 39.

V

The Cahiers de la Quinzaine: Descent to Violence

BETWEEN 1897 and 1910, Péguy's life and work revealed a slow festering process which gradually transformed the idealistic humanitarian into a selfish reactionary. At the end of this period the editor of the *Cahiers de la Quinzaine* suddenly emerged as a poet whose first volume unveiled a talent that had matured thoroughly since the printing of *Jeanne d'Arc*. The poet, too, had abandoned the ambition to save mankind and became as, if not more, concerned than the prosaist with the welfare of his soul. From the "Mystère de la charité de Jeanne d'Arc," his first major offering in verse, to the alexandrines of "Ève," the confrontation with God became closer and more intense. The release of hitherto unsuspected creative energies neither diminished the vigor nor changed the course of Péguy's continuing polemical attacks on the modern world and its time servers. Only "Notre Jeunesse" in 1910 offered a last glimpse of the man willing to sacrifice for the good of others rather than the principles of his own choosing. Yet this classic confession of the unregenerate Dreyfusard signaled no resurrection of the secular saint; rather it stood as the bridge between years of near-barrenness and an impending harvest of monstrous and bitter fruits among which "L'Argent (suite)," published in 1913, became the most acidulous hybrid. It appeared as if Péguy were tirelessly preparing his acres for one last tremendous yield: a return that would either be so bountiful as to smother all weeds beneath its weight, or else fail so completely as to drive the tiller to an irrevocable foreclosure. Péguy was about to give all and risk all, driving his herds and his wagons along "the same straight road" which he claimed to have followed all his life.[1]

The tumultuous events of that last demi-decade seemed to touch Péguy but little. He was happily resigned to war; and the diplomatic maneuvers that appear to later generations as its prelude—Racconigi, the Haldane Mission, the second Moroccan crisis, Italy's war with the Turks, and the Balkan wars—seem not to have appeared significant in his eyes. It is not surprising that the only domestic issue treated in the *Cahiers* was the controversy over the extension of the term of military service from two to three years. Supported by Alexandre Millerand, no longer a socialist but an intermittent minister of war in several dead-center governments, and enacted under Louis Barthou on July 19, 1913, it became the subject of a bulky *Cahier* in November of the same year. The author of the discussion was Joseph Reinach, one of the law's sponsors who in Péguy's opinion was the only surviving Dreyfusard beside himself who had not defected and who now provided handsome proof that the true friends of the former prisoner at Devil's Island wanted only the best for France and her army.[2] Otherwise the *Cahiers* served as the outlet for Péguy's gigantic output and as publisher of interesting literary novelties, of the remaining volumes of Rolland's *Jean Christophe,* of Benda's *Ordination,* and of minor poets such as René Salomé and André Suarès. Finally Péguy took to editing memoirs. Theodore Naudy, his old elementary school principal, discoursed on the educational system after 1880;[3] Maxime Vuillaume and the Milliet family glorified in multivolumed monuments to the Paris Commune the violence which also indicated what aspects of the Third Republic's heritage most appealed to Péguy. In sum, the reader encountered again and again a world

---

[1] "Un nouveau théologien, M. Fernand Laudet," 237–38.

[2] J. Reinach, "La loi militaire," *Cahiers* XV, No. 3 (1913), 299.

[3] Theodore Naudy, "Depuis 1880—l'enseignement primaire et ce qu'il devait être," *Cahiers,* XIV, No. 7 (1913).

composed of somber dreams, a future steeped in the blood of war, and a glorious past, the 1870's, long since degraded by the betrayals of laic Radicalism. Against this composite background of a constricted editorial horizon and withdrawal from the issues of the present, one must finally see the epic outpourings of the frantic artist struggling with time running out, the compulsive frenzy of a man who on the one hand seeks death and who yet admits the need to complete a vast and ambitious labor before his wish is granted.

II

The "Mystère de la charité," published in January, 1910, confirmed the quest for spiritual salvation as Péguy's most abiding and absorbing concern. In a text which expanded the first two acts of *Jeanne d'Arc* into an epic of some 160 pages, he resumed the interrupted investigation of the circumstances that preceded Joan's acceptance of her divine mandate. He recreated her once more as she might have been before she had understood her mission: the innocent shepherd girl, seized by an inexplicable unrest, goaded into doubt and despair by an otherworldly force within her whose nature and intent she could not fathom.

At the outset, the "Mystère" repeated the Sophoclean confrontation of Joan and Hauviette which opened the original. It became immediately evident, however, that Hauviette had changed. The insensitive defeatist of *Jeanne d'Arc* was transformed from a mere "straight man" into an antagonist. The hungry children, whom Joan fed but could not save from tomorrow's hunger, elicited no tears from Hauviette. She had seen them sated and content after the unexpected feast. She thought that they and Joan should be satisfied with their temporary surcease from hunger. Hauviette urged Joan to accept the temporal and spiritual uncertainties of man's fate. She scorned Joan's intention of seeking solace in the counsel of the saintly nun, Madame Gervaise. Wearing the veil, she asserted, conferred upon that pious lady no unusual powers, for baptism and communion had equally blessed and uplifted all believers. "Prayer is the same for everyone," Hauviette insisted. "The sacraments are the same for everybody." [4] Those who abandoned their daily duties to run after God, either by taking holy orders or by committing themselves to some mission of national or human salvation, misinterpreted the divine will. In time of war, Hauviette went on, it was easy to become a soldier, but it took courage to cultivate fields which one might never live to harvest. Passing the day on one's knees was easier than working, and it did not reflect greater devotion. "Everything one does in a day is pleasing to God, as long as it is done as it should be. Everything is God's, everything concerns God, everything is accomplished under God; the whole day belongs to God. All prayer is God's, and all work is His also." [5] Hauviette believed that all men must remain at their post and satisfy the demands imposed by their calling. She pictured herself at her household chores, ready to take off her apron and lay down her utensils only when God called. When that moment came she would go wherever he beckoned. [6] Joan's inquietude baffled her. "She must be suffering deeply to dare demand an accounting from the good Lord"; but suffering could be healed if Joan understood the sole human duty: humility and obedience. [7]

Hauviette of the "Mystère" became more complex and substantial than she had appeared in *Jeanne d'Arc*. As far as her image was concerned, the new work was more than a repetition of the old. The changed portrait conformed to a changed drama. *Jeanne d'Arc* had contained a message of universal salvation from *all* ills. "Le Mystère de la charité de Jeanne d'Arc" only retained the heroine's pursuit of spiritual salvation. Under these circumstances, Hauviette's indifference to the English invasion became unimportant. The new dialogue ended before specific mention of the war was made. If appeasement was no longer an issue, then Hauviette's religious beliefs had to be brought into meaningful conflict with Joan's, unless she was to be dropped from the *dramatis personae* altogether.

[4] Péguy, *OPC*, 26–27.
[5] *Ibid.,* 33.
[6] *Ibid.,* 34.
[7] *Ibid.,* 36.

The Joan to whom this new Hauviette addressed herself remained the same God-ridden visionary; and although the dialogue following Hauviette's departure, and the powerful argument with Madame Gervaise on the life of Christ and virtue of
the Saints transcended the original framework of *Jeanne d'Arc*
more frequently and elaborately, one seeks in vain for a new or
transformed heroine.

Joan's vision of the "little town of Bethlehem," elevated in
history above all other towns as the Savior's birthplace,[8] linked
the discourse with Hauviette and the dialogue with Madame
Gervaise that was to ensue. At first, action and presentation
once more followed the original until Joan confessed that the
existence of damnation had burdened her soul with an agony so
unendurable that she was willing to undergo any suffering to lift
it from mankind. In *Jeanne d'Arc* Madame Gervaise reproved
her by recalling Christ's death cry on the cross, the sign of
ultimate alienation of the Son of God, who had himself become
irredeemable man.

> "The Son of God knew that the suffering
> of the son of man cannot save the damned,
> and maddened more than they by his despair,
> dying Jesus wept over their lost souls." [9]

Thus the awful vision of a Christ who in his own death agony
shed tears for an abandoned humanity was firmly and clearly
part of the original drama. But in the "Mystère" Péguy interjected at this point a majestic recital of Christ's life. A weeping
Jesus was portrayed but not explained until Péguy flashed back
across the entire sacred life, seeking in Christ's own past the
answer to this frightening and unbelievable spectacle. Yet, after
this unique *tour de force*, Péguy admitted that the effort merely
confirmed what he had known since 1897. A new approach had

---

[8] *Ibid.*, 38–51.

[9] One may compare this vision with Luther's interpretation of Christ's
last words on the cross as an expression of the supreme sacrifice. After
sin had alienated man from God, Jesus in his effort of redemption was
also partaking of that alienation. Cf. Roland Bainton, *Here I Stand, A
Life of Martin Luther* (New York, 1950), 62.

provided no new answers. Again Madame Gervaise rebukes Joan for aspiring to greater powers of salvation than the Savior himself had possessed.[10] In both versions the nun admonishes the heroine to walk in humility.

This return to the anterior script, however brief, is of fundamental importance. The point of departure for the third digression is the restatement of Joan's original question: "How must we save?" Péguy's retelling of the gospels neither answered nor invalidated it. Madame Gervaise's answer begins by repeating *Jeanne d'Arc:* "By imitating Jesus, by listening to Jesus."[11] Christ did not want us to attempt salvation of the damned because He knew of no exit from hell. According to the nun, his life symbolized the futility of sowing plentifully, since He was able to feed thousands with a few loaves. Above all, He ordered St. Peter to sheathe his sword, for "one must not make war."[12] That the Joan of 1897 refused to accept the last of these commands became clear from her subsequent actions; but the heroine of the "Mystère" was confined to a static drama. She could merely protest, and did so at once, against the disciples' abandonment of their master. They had swords, but did not use them. "I believe if I had been there, I should not have deserted Him," she exclaims.[13] The dialogue on salvation at this point explodes into a bitter and angry exchange between the nun, protesting this insult to the community of the Saints, and the peasant patriot who feels that war is the only expedient which can preserve that which we hold dearest.[14] Madame Gervaise wins the argument by pointing to the martyrdom of the Apostles and of the many saints after them. They have proved to be above the charge of desertion. The nun offers a variation of the theme earlier intoned by Hauviette: man must remain at his designated place and respond to his calling to please God, recognizing that there can be no higher duty.

[10] Péguy, *OPC,* 126.
[11] *Ibid.,* 71–123.
[12] *Ibid.,* 960–61 for the old version, p. 128 for the new.
[13] *Ibid.,* 129.
[14] *Ibid.,* 127–57.

Salvation, Madame Gervaise continued, derives from the infinite treasury of grace, of suffering, and of prayer filled to overflowing by the passion of Jesus Christ. He has provided grace of which we have none, suffered anguish the like of which we could not endure, and offered prayers "of which ours are mere echoes." Once more her conclusion was lifted straight out of *Jeanne d'Arc:* "We are fortunate when the good Lord in His infinite mercy, deigns to accept our works, our prayers, and our sufferings to save with them one soul." [15] Man can only save with God's help. The epic embellishments of the "Mystère," in other words, could not conceal that the questions and the answers remained identical with those of *Jeanne d'Arc.*

One might wish to justify this repetition and textual expansion of an earlier message by pointing to the superior literary quality of the "Mystère." *Jeanne d'Arc* was an unperformable oddity. The "Mystère," on the other hand, has been acclaimed as one of the brightest treasures of modern French literature. But this study is not concerned with esthetic judgments. What it must point to are the changed conditions under which the later work was written. Joan's resurrection as a national heroine had produced a veritable flood of obscure works throughout the nineteenth century, a great number of which were plays and tales of uplift written by members of the clergy for the female inmates of Catholic finishing schools. After the turn of the century, however, popularity and quality were added to quantity. As early as 1889 the great Sarah Bernhardt discovered Joan of Arc when she revived Jules Barbier's *Jeanne d'Arc* with incidental music by Charles Gounod. On November 25, 1909, only weeks before Péguy's "Mystère" went to the printer, the aging first lady of the French theater once more displayed her inexhaustible talents at the Châtelet in Émile Moreau's *Le procès de Jeanne d'Arc.*[16] Quality was contributed first by Maurice Pottecher's *Passion de Jeanne d'Arc* in 1904 and far more impressively and lastingly by Anatole France's *Vie de Jeanne d'Arc* in a careful, subtle, and

[15] *Ibid.,* 159 for the new, p. 961 for the original context of this statement.

[16] Jan J. Soons, *Jeanne d'Arc au théâtre* (Purmerend, 1929), 230–33.

convincing fusion of historical scholarship and literary imagination in the tradition established by Ernest Renan's *Vie de Jesus.*[17]
Like his scholarly forerunner, France aroused controversy[18]
and contradiction[19] and elicited other notable essays by historians who wrote in a more respectful vein.[20] Meanwhile,
Barrès, Maurras, and other nationalists were waging their own
campaign to revitalize the myths of Joan of Arc. The *Action
Française* in 1908 chose her to help attract members from
among the conservatives. When Professor François Thalamas of
the Lycée Condorcet, a notorious debunker of the Maid of Orléans, was invited to lecture at the Sorbonne, the *Camelots du
Roi* broke up the gathering and at a subsequent lecture thrashed
the hapless pedagogue.[21]

Péguy's Joan stood above these battles. But an aroused public
nevertheless responded with surprising intensity to the unexpected epic from the maverick editor of the *Cahiers*. The topic
was anything but novel, but the treatment in the "Mystère" was
sufficiently original to be of intrinsic interest and to cause indignation and surprise among Péguy's secular friends and wonder
and suspicion among his clerical readers. Of both there was a
sufficient number to warrant several reprintings of the original
Cahier so that a work of his was for the first time widely bought
and widely reviewed. The "Mystère" generated a flood of praise,
criticism, and publicity for which Péguy's past had not prepared
him.[22]

[17] Carter Jefferson, *Anatole France: The Politics of Scepticism* (New
Brunswick, N.J., 1965), 66–67.

[18] Cf. Michel Arnauld, "Jeanne d'Arc et les Pingouins," *Nouvelle Revue
Française,* I No. 1 (1908), 3–13, the first article in the first issue of that
important review.

[19] E.g. Andrew Lang, *La Jeanne d'Arc de M. Anatole France* (Paris,
1909).

[20] Such as Gabriel Hanotaux, *Jeanne d'Arc* (Paris, 1911).

[21] Cf. Edward R. Tannenbaum, "The Myth of Counterrevolution in
France, 1870–1914," in Harold Parker (ed.), *Ideas in History* (Durham,
N.C., 1965), 277–28; Tannenbaum, *The Action Française,* 96–97; Eugen
Weber, *Action Française: Royalism and Reaction in Twentieth-Century
France* (Stanford, Calif., 1962), 53–54. See also Barrès' preface to Jules
Baudot, *La vocation de Jeanne d'Arc* (Bar-le-Duc, 1912).

[22] Apart from the incidental or obscure references indicated so far,

Despite the mixed reception Péguy reveled unashamedly in the fact that a work of his should be reviewed in more than twenty different publications. He bore up well under the reserved praise and the undisguised mistrust of clerical critics, one of whom openly denied him a place among the faithful as long as his heroine spoke of the damned as "suffering in vain." [23] He manfully concealed his disappointment over Barrès' snide references to his style which the academician considered to be in greater need of improvement than his morals.[24] He reacted with vigor and indignation only to strictures from the anticlerical camp.[25] Péguy also obviously delighted in a host of new and equally ill-assorted admirers which the "Mystère" had made him. These included Edouard Drumont, rejoicing over the reclamation of a soul from socialism,[26] Georges Sorel who identified Péguy as a representative of the current patriotic revival,[27] Paul Acker whose best-selling novel *Le soldat Bernard* had become a kind of *réponse du soldat* to Barrès' equally popular *appel*,[28] and Maurice Reclus, the biographer of Jules Favre, who warned these nationalists that Péguy had changed far less than they wishfully anticipated.[29]

It was not altogether surprising, and certainly no source of discomfiture to Péguy, that the "Mystère" aroused interest primarily as a new *prise de position*. Only two reviewers discussed it as a work of art. One of these was André Gide who confessed to

Michel Arnauld (pseud. Marcel Drouin), the brother-in-law of André Gide had published a fairly detailed appreciation of Péguy in "Les Cahiers de Péguy," *Nouvelle Revue Française*, II (1909), 258–59, which concentrated on him as a writer at a time when his slender fame still rested in his editorial achievements.

[23] Georges Dumesnil, writing in the *Cahiers de l'Amitié de France,* quoted in Tharaud, *Pour les fidèles de Péguy*, 109–110.

[24] *Echo de Paris,* February 21, 1910.

[25] Such as Georges Guy-Grand's "Le Mystère de la charité de Jeanne d'Arc," *Les Annales de la jeunesse laïque*, VIII (1910), 376–77, whom Péguy attacked in "Les amis des Cahiers," *Cahiers*, XII, No. 2 (1910), 69–70.

[26] *La Libre Parole,* March 10, 1910.

[27] *Action Française,* April 14, 1910.

[28] *Gil Blas,* May 27, 1910.

[29] Reclus, *Le Péguy que j'ai connu*, 95–98.

the readers of the *Nouvelle Revue Française* that the "Mystère" was a poetic revelation of blinding intensity, intoxicating as a source of ideas as well as of beauty. He urged his readers and their friends abroad in particular, to discover Péguy for themselves because no other contemporary writer, he insisted, would present the foreign reader with a more impressive case for the wealth and subtlety of the French language.[30] Gide took his own advice. He sent a copy of the famous *Cahier* to Paul Claudel, then French consul in Prague. A second was addressed to the Belgian poet Emile Verhaeren.[31] An even more prestigious discoverer of Péguy's genius at the time was Paul Souday, acclaimed by some contemporaries as *the* French critic since Sainte-Beuve.[32] Souday praised both the spirit of the writer, whom he described rather inaccurately as the "Don Quixote and the Alcestis of humanitarianism," as well as his spontaneous protean talent.[33]

Thus the changing reactions to the national heroine and Péguy's peculiar version of her struggle suddenly changed his own position. Since 1897 some of his opinions had been superficially altered. His life had become stabilized around the *Cahiers*. He had acquired and met the social and personal responsibilities that fall on the shoulders of most men. Now he had also become famous. How would he respond to this revolution in his own life? Would the assault on the modern world continue, or would fame soften the harshness of his judgments?

The enthusiastic clamor aroused by the "Mystère de la charité de Jeanne d'Arc" was still intense when the appearance of "Notre Jeunesse" silenced the hopes to which it had given rise. While finishing the "Mystère," Péguy's friend Daniel Halévy was completing his own act of penance, the anti-Dreyfusard essay

---

[30] "Journal sans date," *Nouvelle Revue Française*, III (1910), 399–405.

[31] Albert Saffrey, "Correspondance André Gide–Péguy," *ACPFM*, No. 65 (1958), 10–13; *The Correspondence (1899–1926) between Paul Claudel and André Gide* (New York, 1952), 108, 111–14.

[32] John Charpentier, "Paul Souday," *Mercure de France*, CCXIII (1929), 669.

[33] "Charles Péguy," *L'Opinion*, III (1910), 468–70.

"Apologie pour notre passé," which was subsequently submitted to the *Cahiers de la Quinzaine* for publication. The arrival of these pages placed an unbearable strain on Péguy's principles of editorial objectivity. Here was a manuscript whose quality called for publication. At the same time, the editor of the *Cahiers* perused with mounting consternation Halévy's attack upon their Dreyfusard past. Péguy could not accept a *mea culpa* which described the supporters of the Jewish captain as unpatriotic men who had left France divided and leaderless. He boggled at Halévy's conclusion that the veterans of this struggle must abandon their past allies and allegiances.[34]

Whatever Péguy's literary plans after January, 1910, originally might have been, his editorial integrity and his attachment to the memories of the Dreyfus Affair imposed upon him two obligations: first, he decided with a heavy heart to print Halévy's work, though it went deeply against his grain; next, he countered with a stinging reply.[35] Before his mind passed the illusions of a victory which he had hailed in 1900[36] and the continuing obligation to the Dreyfusard heritage which he had accepted as a lifetime commitment.[37] He as well as anyone knew that men like himself who had manned the trenches for a blameless and unpopular cause had not been unpatriotic. The service of virtue could not be incompatible with service to France. If France had been weakened, the cause for her decline had to be sought elsewhere.

[34] Daniel Halévy, "Apologie pour notre passé," *Cahiers*, XI, No. 10 (1910), 53–54, 100–15.

[35] Nelly Jussem-Wilson, "L'Affaire Jeanne d'Arc et l'Affaire Dreyfus: Péguy et 'Notre Jeunesse,'" *Revue d'histoire littéraire de la France*, LXII (1962), 400, postulates that "Notre Jeunesse" was more than a reply to Halévy and points to its defense of men like Bernard-Lazare whom the "Apologie pour notre passé" had not specifically attacked. In addition, she insists that "Notre Jeunesse" was a riposte to Sorel's *La révolution Dreyfusienne*, whose second edition (Paris, 1911), 3–7, explicitly defended Halévy against Péguy's criticism. See also, Pierre Andreu, "Un article ignoré de Georges Sorel sur 'Notre Jeunesse,'" *ACPFM* No. 6 (1949), 7–13.

[36] "Lettre du provincial," 16.

[37] "Préparation du congres," 69.

How then, Péguy asked, had Halévy reached the conclusions which forced him to write "Apologie pour notre passé"? His answer was that his friend had allowed the disillusionment of the years since 1899 to cloud his memory. It was true, Péguy admitted, that the *élan* of republican idealism had been stifled by political compromise.[38] But in his own select circle, at the *Cahiers de la Quinzaine,* the pure spirit of the Dreyfusard movement had been preserved, and the survival of that *mystique* bore witness to its original nobility. Péguy challenged Halévy to judge the past by the actions of those who had remained faithful, not by the maneuvers of its betrayers. At No. 8 Rue de la Sorbonne, he proudly concluded, no one apologized for his past.[39] The constancy with which the republican ideology had been protected by the *Cahiers,* the fidelity with which *"nos amis et . . . nos abonnés"* supported their editor constituted the true measure of the *Affaire.* The heroism which the Dreyfusard had once displayed in his successful effort to save France from committing an injustice refuted the aspersions cast on his patriotism by Halévy. Even the fact that the partisans of Dreyfus had been an "army of lions led by asses" had been in the best French tradition.[40] In other words, Péguy decided that nothing in the history of the Dreyfus Affair justified putting the true Dreyfusard on trial.[41]

Péguy did more than plead for a cause which, in his opinion, had been unjustly attacked. "Notre Jeunesse" accomplished more than a defense of the past. To be sure, it belabored the heroism of the author's own generation, much as "A nos amis, à nos abonnés" had; but these latest Dreyfusard confessions also documented a stoutness of character that remains impressive. Péguy courageously warned his contemporaries that he was not

---

[38] "Notre Jeunesse," *Cahiers,* X, No. 12 (1910), 13.

[39] *Ibid.,* 90–91.

[40] *Ibid.,* 205–12.

[41] *Ibid.,* 92. Chapman, in *The Dreyfus Affair: A Reassessment,* distinguishes between the Dreyfusard, who joined the fray for personal and political gain, and the Dreyfusist whose pure devotion to justice was above question. Péguy obviously would have counted himself among the latter had he accepted such a distinction.

another Paul Acker or another Tharaud, who, attracted by the success of the best-selling Maurice Barrès or the cynical master essayist Charles Maurras, had turned to nationalism as one would turn to a new and promising field of business in times of economic expansion. Neither the *Action Française,* nor *La Croix,* certainly not *La Libre Parole,* had gained a subscriber or adherent.[42]

Péguy avowed that he would oppose anti-semitism as long as he combatted treason. The Jew-haters had advocated injustice in the 1890's and had brought France to the edge of perdition. Unregenerate, they continued to depict the Jew as the source of French weakness and corruption. In reality, Péguy asserted, French Jews were patriotic, loyal, and faithful. He knew only one prominent Dreyfusard who had not sought to profit from victory: the Jew, Salomon Reinach.[43] The anti-semites, Péguy stressed, encouraged Frenchmen to expend their strength against imaginary foes. While they tilted with windmills, they were shielding the real traitors, Jaurès and Hervé, and condemning France to further disaster. Events since 1905 should have opened their eyes, but their commitment to the betrayals of 1898 was too complete. Péguy had for them only one answer: "You remain the defenders of treason, and I shall remain its foe. In no event shall I break with my past devotion to the defense of France, undertaken side by side with her loyal Jewish citizens."[44]

Péguy insisted with equal tenacity that he was and remained a *French* socialist. Socialism was the gospel of temporal salvation. Its heaven on earth was open to all men and not reserved for socialists. For this reason he had decided to leave a socialist party which, in his opinion, restricted the *cité* to the faithful. He believed, no less, that the perfection of society would be rewarded eternally in heaven.[45] Eternal salvation followed temporal perfection. But Paradise too, was not reserved for the elect, except in the eyes of a Church which forever catered to the

---

[42] Cf. Jussem-Wilson, "L'Affaire Jeanne d'Arc," 403–407.
[43] "Notre Jeunesse," 187–94.
[44] *Ibid.,* 134–35.
[45] *Ibid.,* 116, 136–40.

wealthy by diluting divine justice with its notions of exclusiveness. Hence, Péguy felt that he must remain an anticlerical Christian. Party and Church, mutually incompatible, were equally repugnant to him. But Socialism and Christianity harmonized and complemented each other. Perfection on earth and in heaven were inseparable aspirations.

"Notre Jeunesse" was another vigorous restatement of Péguy's earlier views. Like the "Mystère de la charité" it confirmed the growth of his creative powers, for it is from these pages that the present-day reader becomes acquainted with Péguy, not from *Jeanne d'Arc, Marcel,* or "De la grippe." But it proved once more that his views had remained constant. He remained a socialist whom nothing could reconcile with the Socialist party. He admitted that he was a Christian, but now, as before, on terms that remained strictly between him and his maker. To the editor of the *Cahiers,* as to the author of *Marcel,* salvation was the destiny of all men, believers and heathen alike. The unbelieving Péguy had first said it; the believing Péguy reaffirmed it. One can understand why the reviewers of the "Mystère" questioned his conversion.

Thus Péguy took up once more the theme of salvation last considered in the first series of the *Cahiers,* this time in the unaccustomed company of success. Acclaim was unexpected, and there are some indications that its resultant temptations disturbed him.[46] At the same time recognition made Péguy less skeptical of the world's virtue. A civilization that had at last recognized him could not be entirely devoid of redeeming features. In obscurity he had doggedly clung to an unpopular position; in the limelight of success he was at least ready to soften the dissonances of disillusionment and to acknowledge the children of his past. "Notre Jeunesse" appears to be a gesture of renewed devotion toward the humanitarian values of his youth. Yet it turned out to be both more and less than a sentimental rediscovery of past idols. The mature, successful writer was also flinging a challenge into the face of his new admirers in clerical

[46] See above, p. 29.

and national circles. He was saying to them, "If you like what I am now, you must also accept what I once was." He was exacting fealty as well as homage. How else can one explain the passages in which Péguy enumerated the conditions under which he would agree to consider himself a Catholic? How else make plausible the posture of a man who even in "Notre Jeunesse" called himself a socialist, although he damned again and again the policies of the party which had been organized only a few years earlier to represent him and his views?

Alas, regardless of how one interprets "Notre Jeunesse," it soon appears that Péguy's fame was too new and too fragile to bear the multiple burdens under which this bridge of ideas between his past and his successful present was soon to buckle. If "Notre Jeunesse" had ever in his mind constituted an effort to turn away from the sour reflections on his corrupt contemporaries, the critical reaction to this *Cahier* or rather its absence must soon have convinced him that he could not keep his new friends while worshipping his old gods. Again the first edition of his Dreyfusard autobiography was quickly sold out and a second printing was provided by the Librairie Ollendorff. Public curiosity had not abated and the unanimous silence of the reviewers may have been motivated by confusion rather than disapproval. A few reactionary voices, the only responses on record, confirm that supposition. Henri Massis and Alfred de Tarde paused long enough in *their* war on the French academic tradition to pay a kind of stupefied tribute to the infectious fervor and the lucidity with which Péguy had resurrected his republican creed.[47] Henri Vaugeois, the editor of the *Action Française,* on the other hand, objected to the contention that everything began *en mystique* and ended *en politique.* If Péguy's professed devotion to Jeanne d'Arc was genuine, observed this prominent advocate of *politique d'abord,* he must view her achievement as "the apotheosis of the true *politique* of Lorraine and of France, a *politique* which was both sound and heroic."[48] But Péguy, who had castigated

---

[47] *L'Esprit de la nouvelle Sorbonne* (Paris, 1911), 144.
[48] *Action Française,* June 12, 1911.

the followers of Charles Maurras in "Notre Jeunesse" as apostles of disorder whom one must not mistake for servants of tradition, paid no attention to this advice.[49] Once, his mother had made a living mending chairs, but he never proposed to safeguard his livelihood by mending fences. And so he lost his new following almost as quickly as he had gained it. Some of his ephemeral admirers had never ceased to suspect him; others whose curiosity he had aroused no less fleetingly turned their backs in irritation; others yet saw in his behavior merely confirmation of the belief that he was an irresponsible and unpredictable crank. Péguy's own response to the fickleness of fame soon became all too clear: his reawakened concern for the ideals of the past turned out to be equally superficial. To the extent that he soon experienced anew neglect and hostility, his bilious polemic spirit reappeared. Only now the vocation of the poet offered a refuge which he had not sought heretofore.

III

The three last years of Péguy's life—years of unbelievable productivity—constituted a kind of final battle. The poet narrowed his purpose to a quest for eternal salvation, not of mankind, but of himself and his family. The essayist abandoned the pursuit of utopia as his pen sought pretext after pretext for a fight, invariably with success. This hunger for battle spawned a whole series of argumentative essays: "Victor-Marie, Comte Hugo"; "Un nouveau théologien, M. Fernand Laudet"; "L'Argent," and "L'Argent (suite)." Different titles concealed one recurring sermon, Péguy's private war on corruption. Volume after volume replenished the arsenal with which he maintained a continuous barrage against the ramparts of the modern world.

Incapable of living in peace with his fellow men, Péguy the poet sought to come to terms with God. The resumption of *Jeanne d'Arc*, so gloriously begun in the "Mystère," was abandoned. Péguy's second epic poem, "Le porche du mystère de la deuxième vertu" pursued Joan's anxieties without disguising any

[49] "Notre Jeunesse," 215.

longer that they were his own. If the "Mystère" had once more concluded that man could not achieve salvation either for himself or others without the aid of divine mercy, "Le porche" considered just how tangible a role God appeared willing to assume in the unfolding human tragedy of doubt. What Péguy seemed to be asking was, will God save me and my children?

In order to possess the courage to ask that question and to endure the agonizing suspense while awaiting the answer, the poet called upon the virtue of Hope to sustain him. He pictured her as a child, because "children are not yet defeated by life." [50] Like a child, she pointed to growth, maturity, and achievement that was yet to be. Hope symbolized the unfinished, that which was unattained but appeared attainable. She constituted the challenge and the comfort which man, especially in moments of setback and frustration, found in his children. To Péguy, resigned to failure, his own children now exemplified the hopes which he had had to bury:

> His oldest, his boy who will be twelve next September
> His daughter who will be nine years in September
> And his youngest who will be seven in June.[51]

These little "Frenchmen and Lorrainers," *"de bonne race"* and *"de bonne maison,"* would take his place on earth one day, his place in the parish, in the Church, in town, and "in Christendom."

Tenderly he looks forward to the day when they shall no longer need him
Tenderly he looks forward to the time when he will be no longer. . . .

They will do better than he, in a better world, and he wished them well, even though his hope for them was a measure of his own disappointed expectations.[52]

Péguy committed these children to the care of the Holy Virgin. When they had been ill, he tells his readers, their suffering had become more than he could bear, and so he had laid

[50] "Le porche du mystère de la deuxième vertu," 6.
[51] *Ibid.,* 37.
[52] *Ibid.,* 38–44.

their souls at her feet. He had bypassed their patron saints, who were indadequate in this emergency, and had "stepped right up to the Lord God and the Holy Virgin." Boldly he did what seemed direct and obvious, and "since that time everything has gone well. Naturally." [53]

"Le porche" announced that Péguy's search for salvation had been partially successful. For his children, whose very nature exemplified hope, timely commitment to the care of God and the Virgin assured health and the rewards of heaven. Temporally and spiritually they had been rescued from their mother's help-lessness and their father's failure. This boon, however, had not brought the poet nearer to his goal. He stood between the Church, whose exclusiveness he rejected, and his unbelieving wife whose agnosticism he no longer shared. "Le porche du mystère de la deuxième vertu" went on to tell the parable of the lost sheep which exacted from the Savior more concern and effort than the remaining herd which had never strayed. Why this seemingly twofold injustice, Péguy asked, of valuing one above all others, and the sinner more than the virtuous? The answer, he thought, lay in God's own preference for the "astonishing" virtue of Hope. "He knows that the virtuous will be saved, but he must hope that we [sinners] will save ourselves." [54]

This divine anxiety for the sinner's ability to rise above his own imperfection was also the subject of the "Mystère des saints innocents." His supreme concern for those souls who remained in jeopardy explained His predilection for the French nation: "Everything they do," Péguy's God explained, "they do as free-men. They are less slavish and freer even in sin." [55] Above all, God insisted:

> I am their judge. My son has told them that.
> I am also their father.
> I am in particular their father.[56]

---

[53] *Ibid.,* 58–62.
[54] *Ibid.,* 114–17.
[55] "Le mystère des saints innocents," *Cahiers,* XIII, No. 12 (1912), 74.
[56] *Ibid.,* 44.

To this father Péguy continued to concede every power; from Him he expected every benefaction. But now, at last, he also claimed from Him the knowledge of personal salvation. In a blinding flash of revelation he recognized

> If there is justice, who shall be saved;
> If there is mercy, who shall be lost. . . .[57]

Again Péguy confirmed what he had known when he wrote *Jeanne d'Arc*. Everything, from the consciousness of sin to the certitude of boundless compassion, emanated from God. His will was absolute, His power was irresistible, and His pity knew no limits. Péguy merely repeated, perhaps as the result of some mystic, mysterious contact with the Almighty, what he had always surmised.

Yet Péguy had not exhausted his creative powers in the *mystères*. The unsurpassed goodness of God, furthermore, had not persuaded him to make his peace with men. This dichotomy reminds one of an earlier outcry in his "Chanson du roi Dagobert": "I have been truly divided." Then, in 1903, he had been torn between militarism and pacifism, which was understandable enough. Now he stood between the peace that should come from the sure knowledge of spiritual salvation, and the anger that nevertheless continued to boil in his heart when he contemplated the corruption of man. God's love for the sinner, to which Péguy attributed his salvation, inspired no corresponding tolerance in him. Those who entered heavenly eternity, thanks to divine concern, had been cleansed by the blood of Christ; but on earth the sinners had gathered at the gates of the *cité*, not penitently prepared to leave behind them expediency and ambition, but in order to conquer and to corrupt the precincts of purity. They had even been so bold as to enter and defile the shrine. They had introduced temporal hell into temporal heaven, and for them there could be neither forgiveness nor salvation. Péguy consigned them to damnation in these uncompromising terms:

[57] *Ibid.*, 53.

I want to know nothing of a Christian charity which would mean perpetual capitulation to the powers of this world. I want to know nothing of a Christian charity which means constant capitulation before temporal power. I want to know nothing of a Christian charity which means constant capitulation to princes, millionaires, and the powers of mammon. I want to know nothing of a Christian charity which forever abandons the poor and the oppressed.[58]

In Péguy's opinion Christian charity was concern for the unfortunate, not necessarily the poor, but for those who had been denied their just rewards. When he addressed himself to the powerful and the wealthy, therefore, he remained the cruel and unforgiving polemicist. It was an intensely personal feud that he was waging. The cause of the deprived was also his cause, his enemies were also theirs. Romain Rolland might believe that Péguy's continuing wars indicated a spiritual evolution not yet completed.[59] In reality there was little indication that Péguy's habitual positions were changing and no sign at all that he was developing toward the saintly ideal which Rolland hoped would be the goal and purpose of his lifelong travail.

This rigidity is continually substantiated by Péguy's last polemics, which constitute a lengthy monologue on old themes joined to an uninterrupted diatribe against his enemies. "Le Mystère de la charité de Jeanne d'Arc" had been the overture to his conversations with God; "Notre Jeunesse," a debate with Halévy, was continued in the pages of "Victor-Marie, Comte Hugo." Each successive *Cahier,* regardless of its title, took up where the previous one had left off, or at least repeated and reconsidered openly and explicitly what had been treated before. "L'Argent (suite)," published in the spring of 1913, formed the last act of this drama in which Péguy assumed the role of Joan while the powers of government and university were cast in the unprepossessing guise of an invading enemy.

Péguy talked about his youth, his work at the *Cahiers,* his

[58] "L'Argent (suite)," *Cahiers,* XIV, No. 9 (1913), 60–61.
[59] *Chère Sofia, choix de lettres de Romain Rolland à Sofia Bertolini-Guerrini-Gonzaga* (Cahiers Romain Rolland, No. 10–11) (Paris, 1959–1960), II, 121.

religion, and his honor. The shadow of Dreyfus continued to flit across the scene. The author introduced no new questions, but he abandoned some previous restraints. In domestic and international affairs he increasingly opted for action regardless of its consequences. An analysis of French attitudes toward Germany from 1911 to 1914, for instance, which distinguishes between a "nationalist Right," a "nationalist Center," and a "pacifist Left," identifies Péguy and Barrès as the major literary figures in sympathy with the views of the first category. His growing belligerence added a new dimension to his war against the Sorbonne. The "professors" now stood accused not only of disloyalty to their calling, but also toward their country because they refused to accept the inevitability of war with Germany.[60] Thus Péguy made his contribution to the continuing "armed peace" which threatened ruin and eventual war because neither Frenchman nor German truly wanted to understand the cultural peculiarities of the other.[61] The editor of the *Cahiers* who never traveled, who read little and only within the compass of a narrow range of interests, certainly knew nothing and cared nothing about Germany. His uncompromising attitudes would hardly have been possible otherwise, for he did not understand many of his countrymen either. Much as he hated Germany, he did not hate Germans alone. Activism and brutality became increasingly paramount also in his treatment of domestic foes. Whatever else his last essays might lack or exhibit, they revealed the editor of the *Cahiers* as reaching new heights in the art of vituperation.

To be sure, Péguy remained his own favorite topic of conversation. The name of Victor Hugo reminded him that he was even at the time of the great bard's death in 1883 a "poor and serious lad," and a "fanatic fool." [62] In "Fernand Laudet," written in 1911, a substantial digression exposed his mother's inability to understand his youthful aspirations.[63] Much of "L'Argent" was

---

[60] Gilbert Ziebura, *Die deutsche Frage in der oeffentlichen Meinung Frankreichs von 1911–1914* (Berlin-Dahlem, 1955), 12–13, 55–56.

[61] *Ibid.*, 128–29.

[62] "Victor-Marie, Comte Hugo," 130.

[63] "Un nouveau théologien, M. Fernand Laudet," 141.

autobiography pure and simple. The author reviewed his scholastic career, the fateful discovery of his intellectual gifts by Maître Naudy, the stalwart qualities of his secular and clerical teachers.[64] The exciting friendships of the Lycée Ste. Barbe lived again in the pages of "Fernand Laudet"—"those two or three miraculous years of our youth, those eager years. Everything was still pure, everything was still young." [65]

In "Victor-Marie, Comte Hugo" Péguy again appealed to Halévy for recognition of the Dreyfus Affair as the great battle on behalf of French civilization. "Without us it would have been lost."[66] The worn *Leitmotiv* of a heroic defeat emerged once again in "L'Argent": "We were quite courageous, we anti-antisemitic and dreyfusist partisans. We were well led (for we led ourselves), and we conducted a powerful offensive, commensurate with the principles of modern warfare. In those days only the Radicals were cowards. But those days are gone." [67]

The struggle to keep alive the *Cahiers de la Quinzaine* constituted another component of Péguy's intermittently serialized autobiography. He claimed to have courted ruin the first time when he founded his review; he continued to risk financial disaster in his desperate effort to keep it alive.[68] To succeed he added to his tasks of founder and editor those of secretary and contributor.[69] The number of subscribers never rose above a precarious minimum. "Every year on the first of September we begin with 900 subscriptions. Every year our effort and unbelievable devotion raises [this figure] to eleven or twelve hundred. And every succeeding first of September we are back to 900." Pride in this accomplishment was tempered by his concern for his livelihood.[70] "When I look back on my life," he cried out, "I find that I have been badly used and exploited. If a man is

---

[64] "L'Argent," *Cahiers*, XIV, No. 6 (1913), 9–33.
[65] "Un nouveau théologien, M. Fernand Laudet," 224.
[66] "Victor-Marie, Comte Hugo," 225.
[67] "L'Argent," 104.
[68] *Ibid.*, 159–61, 217.
[69] "Les amis des Cahiers," *Cahiers*, XII, No. 2 (1910), 71.
[70] *Ibid.*, 65–66.

worth what I am worth he is used badly as long as he must exhaust himself in care and in anguish." [71]

Péguy charged this exploitation of his talents and energies to the account of that formidable *parti intellectuel* with whom he had been feuding openly since the publication of "Zangwill." Their own declaration of war on him, he believed, dated from the first issue of the *Cahiers*. It has been argued that much of this conflict existed chiefly in Péguy's imagination. Whether it did or not, the mention of it in print invariably arrested his rhapsodies of self-pity. If public indifference to his efforts was a cause for despair, then the hostility of the academic hierarchy seemed the indispensable counterstimulant. "They can hurt us greatly," Péguy wrote. "We have seen that. They can make us suffer greatly. We have seen that. We see it now. But they shall not keep us from bringing forth. The race of creators contains forces that will vanquish all." [72] Péguy bolstered his flagging morale with the thought that his *Cahiers* were the fortress most frequently attacked because they posed the greatest threat to the vested interests of educational officialdom. "To be the butt of violence, perfidy, insults, conspiracies, plots, and humiliations" was a great distinction of which he must continue to be worthy.[73] It was an irrefutable testimony to his strength. Péguy never possessed the necessary detachment to admit that in order to keep his creative *élan* alive, he would have had to invent the *parti intellectuel,* had it not existed.

Péguy's autobiographical recitals were not confined to what he had done and experienced. With equal persistence and intensity he described what he thought he had been and what he believed he had become.

Looking backward, Péguy discovered his roots in a French tradition which, he claimed, had died with the laic laws of the 1880's. His birthplace was *"l'ancienne France,"* his nation *"le peuple de l'ancienne France."* "It was a world . . . which used that grand word 'people' in its straight-forward, time-honored

---

[71] *Ibid.,* 74.
[72] "Un nouveau théologien, M. Fernand Laudet," 170.
[73] *Ibid.,* 186–87.

meaning." Today, he complained, "there is no people. Everybody is middle-class." [74] In remaining true to himself, Péguy thought that he had remained a part of this *"France peuple."* At the same time he clung to certain pretensions of humbleness and humility. He preserved the illusion of solidarity with the plain men and women of factory and farm which he had first expressed in the articles for the *Revue Blanche.* Although he complained that his mother did not understand him, he proudly claimed that he owed "everything" to a grandmother who could neither read nor write. [75] In 1911 Péguy added a new page to his repertory when in "Victor-Marie, Comte Hugo" he described himself as a peasant, ill at ease in the drawing room, preferring a hard chair without sides to a comfortable chaise longue. He reminded the grand bourgeois Daniel Halévy: "When you call on me, you enter the house of a peasant, you are on a farm of the *Beauce* country." [76]

The earlier populist pretensions of the young intellectual who could not decide whether the chatter of the third-class railway carriage on the Paris-Orléans train or Bergson's lectures at the Collège de France constituted the repository of ultimate wisdom have been questioned in the preceding chapter. The image of Péguy in peasant garb was likewise a phantom. The author himself confirmed it when he transported the reader back to his Faubourg Bourgogne in Orléans on the very next page of "Victor-Marie, Comte Hugo." [77] He could not conceal for long that he was born and bred in town. The editor of the *Cahiers* never lived on a farm; he had never tended the animals of the courtyard; he had never guided a plow. His short apprenticeship as a printer and the resultant respect for that craft might have established a tenuous tie with those who survived exclusively by manual labor, but the Péguy of 1910 was no more a farmer than was Halévy.

Nor was Péguy the great fisher of men he repeatedly claimed

---

[74] "L'Argent," 11–12.
[75] "Victor-Marie, Comte Hugo," 19–20.
[76] *Ibid.,* 40.
[77] *Ibid.,* 41.

to be. Without doubt, he inspired many ardent friendships. But they were not lasting. In fact, he had no lifelong friends, and this rankled in his bosom. At the time of his debate with Halévy, which concluded in "Victor-Marie, Comte Hugo," the place of earlier close associates, in his own mind at least, had been taken by Julien Benda. With him Péguy claimed to have gained the conviction that he would one day become powerful, that he would organize his own party.[78] But these were futile gestures of resistance against loneliness, no less than the earlier description of the *Cahiers* as a unique dynamic nucleus," a kind of free city, a free aggregation (*faisceau*)."[79] In reality Péguy could not decide where he stood in relation to his fellow men, even those who approached him with sympathy and some understanding. Twenty pages earlier in the same volume he had announced with equal dogmatic harshness: "For twenty years I have been walking alone. It agrees with me."[80] Worker and peasant, leader of an intellectual phalanx, defender of a great past, founder of future political movement, and solitary prophet of honor; Péguy claimed to be all of these, with the same disregard for facts and the same cavalier contempt for consistency that had characterized his earlier self-appraisals.

Oddly enough, Péguy never wrote his artistic autobiography. His polemics revealed little of his creative *modus operandi*. Only occasionally did a chance phrase cast light on the poet and writer, such as when he wrote in "Victor-Marie, Comte Hugo": "A given word does not emerge with the same significance from different writers. One tears it from his belly; the other pulls it out of the pocket of his overcoat."[81] Creation was agony, and the author of the *mystères* disclosed that he never began a new work without fear and trembling. These fears, he confessed, increased with every page. The more deeply Péguy burrowed into a topic, the more forbidding its magnitude appeared to him. Writing was like climbing a mountain whose peak receded with every upward

---

[78] *Ibid.*, 248–65.
[79] "Un nouveau théologien, M. Fernand Laudet," 220–21.
[80] *Ibid.*, 195.
[81] "Victor-Marie, Comte Hugo," 167.

step. But none of these difficulties compared to the supreme trial haunting every artist: the brevity of life. At the completion of every work Péguy was overcome by the consciousness of having accomplished far less than he had intended. Time was short, and yet he seemed to be wasting what little he had.[82]

This facet of Péguy's confessions stands isolated because it treats a subject on which he was ordinarily silent. It is unusual because it breathes a spirit of uncertainty and self-criticism which he ordinarily managed to conceal. Although he never wearied of impressing the readers of the *Cahiers* with his virtues as an editor and his integrity as a citizen, Péguy, the writer, was willing to let his work rest on its own merit. Only at the very end of his life, in 1914, following the appearance of *Ève,* did Péguy, in desperation, appeal for recognition of his poetic genius. In the *Bulletin des Professeurs Catholiques de l'Université,* he hailed himself as the greatest epic talent since Dante,[83] but carefully hid his identity behind the pseudonym of "J. Durel."

One must add furthermore that this camouflaged advertisement of the grandeur and authenticity of "Ève" stressed moral rather than esthetic qualities. "The entire work reflects, so to speak, the human position confronting Judgment Day," Péguy-Durel wrote.[84] He was actually reviewing the great successful unfolding of his spiritual quest: man facing God the judge and the father. Although the "Mystère des saints innocents" testified that the search had been rewarded, Péguy's essay on "Ève" exhibited his abiding desire to remind the world how gracious God had been to him.

This bold assurance of salvation entered every discussion of religious problems which Péguy essayed during the last years of his life. "Fernand Laudet" was his stubborn defense as Catholic and Christian. If the *mystères* had been anxious prayer, the polemic was confident challenge to those who questioned them as

---

[82] *Ibid.,* 61–65.
[83] Béguin, *L'Ève de Péguy,* 208–13. Compare Péguy's critique of Dante at this point with an earlier one of Zola, which was almost word for word the same: "De Jean Coste," 45.
[84] Béguin, *L'Ève de Péguy,* 213.

art when they should have been understood as sacrifice. Like the Dreyfusard whose incorruptibility cast an unblemished light over his political past, Péguy the sinner who had found grace saw no need to deny past errors of faith.[85] The magnitude of his imperfections emphasized the extent of divine forgiveness. God's special concern for the stray lamb remained his theme in prose as in poetry. The sinner "made" Christianity, although the smug clerical might refuse to sit down with him at the same table.[86] The sinner who was conscious of the boon of salvation was the dynamic force within the Church. In return for his salvation he became the "soldier of Christ," the zealous devotee ready to commit himself to a holy war. The "good folk" might make up the bulk of each congregation, but it took a converted sinner to start a crusade.[87]

The mystic experience (or illusion?) of salvation encouraged in Péguy a pride more unshakable than the placidity of the habitual Catholic who presumably counted his standing in heaven by the number of masses he attended each week. Péguy affirmed that his spiritual suffering sufficed to make him a superior Christian, as he wrote Lotte in 1912: "I am the instrument of a Catholic revival." [88] With that conviction he was ready to assume the leadership of all true Christians. Christ, like Dreyfus, had been appropriated by vested interests. The Radical secular opportunists in the chamber and in the Sorbonne found their counterparts in the frigid theological *fonctionnaires* of the hierarchy. Though at war with metaphysicians of the secular state, Péguy added the *metaphysique des curés* to his lengthening list of abominations. "L'Argent" claimed for the first time that the *Cahiers* were not only the meeting place of honest citizens, but also a refuge of idealistic young priests.[89]

As the leader of a pure Christianity, unhampered by the restraints of clerical opportunism, Péguy came to the defense of

[85] "Un nouveau théologien, M. Fernand Laudet," 237.
[86] *Ibid.*, 280.
[87] *Ibid.*, 110–14.
[88] Pacary, *Un compagnon de Péguy, Joseph Lotte*, p. xxi.
[89] "L'Argent," 38–39.

Bergson, after that master's work had been placed on the Index. He maintained that Bergson had freed the human mind from the artificial constructs of Cartesianism. Bergson was the philosopher of reality, pure and simple.[90] His liberating insights had led Péguy on his Christian search. Without comprehension of reality the path of God had been blocked. Bergson had cleared it for him.[91] He had enabled Péguy to become first a free man, then a free Christian. Was it right, Péguy asked, to place this guide on the Index? Was it right, he went on, to stultify the freedom of Christians through the constraints of the Index? A free mind, illuminated by the philosopher's understanding of the nature of things, was immune to error. Péguy had discovered through experience that free men found their way to salvation without benefit of signposts. Only clerics needed them, their brains being so crippled by the conventions of their estate that they had become incapable of finding their way without assistance.[92]

These words in defense of Bergson, the last Péguy was to write, confirmed that the universalist humanitarian had become satisfied merely with finding his own way. The young idealist intent upon rescuing mankind had become the arrogant leader of a party without benefit of members and of a Church without benefit of clergy. Perched behind his desk at No. 8 Rue de la Sorbonne, he damned the world for being what he thought it should not be. If he claimed that the role of leader without followers "agreed with him," and if that claim were true, it could only mean that he found in his phantom movements and programs what had become his goal and consolation: certitude of salvation.

For this clearly had become his only possible reward. The public acclaim that had greeted the advent of "Le Mystère de la charité de Jeanne d'Arc" remained without sequel. "Notre Jeu-

[90] "Note sur M. Bergson et la philosophie bergsonienne," *Cahiers*, XV, No. 8 (1914), 26.

[91] *Ibid.*, 73.

[92] *Note conjointe sur M. Descartes et la philosophie cartesienne* (Paris, 1935), 302–18.

nesse" raised new suspicions without healing old wounds. "Fernand Laudet" antagonized powerful segments of the Catholic world and discouraged critics as such from exposing themselves to these destructive verbal canonades. Bernard Grasset's publication of an anthology of Péguy's *Oeuvres choisies: 1900–1910* in 1911 still elicited a number of very mixed reactions,[93] and Maurice Barrès pressed his candidacy for the French Academy's Grand Prix Littéraire with partial success.[94] Then there was silence. Only Joseph Lotte reviewed "Le Mystère des saints innocents" in his obscure *Bulletin des Professeurs Catholiques de l'Université,*[95] and the only other persistent member of the dwindling group of admirers was Paul Souday, whose accolade in the autumn of 1912 came too late to lift Péguy's sinking spirits.[96] The year 1913 was no less dismal. A sonnet sequence, "La tapisserie de Sainte Geneviève," was nowhere reviewed. A few weeks later, "La tapisserie de Notre-Dame" fared little better, although the longest poem of that cycle, the *Présentation de la Beauce à Notre Dame de Chartres,* has since become a fixture in most anthologies of modern French verse.[97] "L'Argent" and "L'Argent (suite)" merely elicited an angry rebuttal in the oldest laic newspaper *Le Siècle,*[98] while the only French review of "Ève," by Guillaume Apollinaire, described Péguy's last epic as a "mixture of humility and ridiculous sadism." [99]

[93] *L'Aurore,* May 8, 1911; *Le Temps,* June 9, 1911; *La Revue du mois,* XIII (1911), 512; *Études,* CXXVIII (1911), 368–71; *L'Opinion,* IV (1911), 720–22; *Mercure de France,* XCIII (1911), 827–28; *Revue critique des livres nouveaux,* VI (1911), 123–25.

[94] In the voting Péguy became deadlocked with Romain Rolland and received the Prix Estrade-Delcros: Auguste Martin, "Péguy, lettres à Romain Rolland (suite et fin)," *ACPFM,* No. 27 (1952), 8–9; *Gil Blas,* June 10, 1911; *Le Temps,* December 8, 1911.

[95] March 20, 1912.

[96] *Le Temps,* September 25, 1912, for Péguy's reaction, see "Quelques lettres à Pierre Marcel," *ACPFM,* No. 69 (1959), 9.

[97] For its only review, see *Nouvelle Revue Française,* X (1913), 282–85.

[98] Robert-Pimienta, "Les idées de Charles Péguy sur la préparation et le charactère des instituteurs," *Le Siècle,* June 5, 1913.

[99] Quote in Béguin, *L'Ève de Péguy,* 256.

At the same time various critics, both illustrious and obscure, derived visible pleasure from gratuitous attacks upon Péguy's "cattle merchant's style," encumbered with "useless epithets." [100] Obviously he was a good subject for parody. In a mock announcement patterned after the *modus operandi* of the *Cahiers,* the authors of a volume of literary imitations published in 1913 explained that one subscription to Péguy's semimonthly entitled the recipient to a military salute (*salut militaire*), whereas the reward for two subscriptions was "eternal salvation" (*salut eternel*).[101] Early in 1914 the young Bergsonian, Gilbert Maire, who had just left the *Action Française* in order to keep faith with his philosophical mentor, contrasted the decline of Péguy's fame with the ascent of two other "mystics," Francis Jammes and Paul Claudel. Why, he asked, were the stars of these three men moving in opposite directions? He blamed Péguy's unreasonable dogmatism and his impossible style. A promising talent had turned into a complete failure.[102] Or, as Georges Sorel had early put it with scathing succinctness: "Péguy lives in a world of illusion. He is miserable because his dreams conflict forever with reality." [103]

It is true that a careful sifting of all evidence leads even in these closing years to the discovery of a few scattered voices of praise.[104] In 1914 there appeared the first slender brochures on Péguy's work.[105] Young François Mauriac acclaimed Péguy, Claudel, and Jammes as the poetic heralds of the current clerical

---

[100] Lucien Martin-Mamy, *Les nouveaux païens* (Paris, n.d.), 173–77; Alexandre Mercereau, *La littérature et les idées nouvelles* (Paris, 1912), 269.

[101] Paul Reboux and Charles Muller, *À la manière de . . .* (Paris, 1913), 135.

[102] "Trois poètes mystiques," *La Revue,* CIX (1914), 145–49.

[103] Pierre Andreu, "Georges Sorel, lettres à Joseph Lotte," *ACPFM,* No. 33 (1953), 14.

[104] Cf. Francis Vincent, *Ames d'aujourd'hui* (Paris, 1914), quoted in Delaporte, *Connaissance de Péguy,* II, 336; Paul Sabatier, *L'Orientation religieuse de la France actuelle* (Paris, 1912), 144–45.

[105] Johannet, *Vie et mort de Péguy;* François Porché, *Charles Péguy et ses Cahiers* (Paris, 1914).

and national revival.[106] Ernest Psichari dedicated his *L'Appel des armes* (1913) to the editor of the *Cahiers*. Nevertheless, after many battles and many defeats, after great and recurring expectations and repeated disasters, Péguy retreated into a private universe, leaving in ruin many exalted and now abandoned positions. Whether this total withdrawal was justified or not, he chose to execute it and to end his days in a solitude which both depressed and brutalized his mind. His wars of the pen engendered a fondness for all wars: "I would donate my complete works, past, present, and future, and my four members to march into Weimar at the head of my platoon," he wrote to another famous ex-socialist, Alexandre Millerand, in 1912.[107] In that mood, Péguy likewise could not forgive his immediate forebears for having made peace in 1871: "I favor the National Convention over the Bordeaux assembly; Paris over the rural areas. I am for the Commune . . . and against peace and against surrender. I am a partisan of Proudhon and Blanqui against that awful little Thiers."[108] In that mood, Péguy's socialism re-emerged as the national-socialism of Barrès and Sorel; and if Marcel Péguy began in the late 1920's a fascist cult in his father's name, he was not without bona fide scriptural authority. More immediately, Péguy reconstructed a socialist program based on the collectivism of the regiment, where he found the "ideal French existence" free from the responsibilities of civilian life and the servilities of society.[109] Within the protecting warmth of that primitive organism he was willing to abandon everything for which he had ever fought. Unthinkable though it might appear, the man who indulged in feud after feud over details of political or religious principle asserted in "L'Argent (suite)" that it did not matter what a man believed as long as he did not surrender, which in this instance was synonymous with changing his mind. War

---

[106] In Jean Muller and Gaston Picard, *Les tendances présentes de la littérature française* (Paris, 1913), 200.

[107] Auguste Martin, "Péguy et Millerand (suite et fin)," *ACPFM*, No. 79 (1960), 20.

[108] "L'Argent (suite)," 128.

[109] *Ibid.*, 142–43.

fought to the bitter end made all Frenchmen second cousins to Joan of Arc.[110] How such an aggregation of individuals, holding uncompromisingly firm to conflicting opinions, could emerge as an orderly society or a disciplined regiment was left by Péguy to his reader's stupefied imagination. This dilemma concerned him no longer as he stood with ordered arms, waiting for the cloudy future to bring forth resumption of the war which Danton had begun and which the leaders of France's provisional government had interrupted in 1871 with their cowardly surrender.

While waiting for Armageddon, Péguy kept in mental trim by engaging in one vendetta after another. To the many accomplishments of his last years was added his growing mastery of invective. His battle against the intellectuals and the institutions that harbored them continued. "We distrust everything intellectual," he asserted in "Laudet." Intellectualism was the antithesis of truth; the intellectual had lost his instinct for reality. Worse, he had explicitly forsaken both because he valued success more highly.[111] These were familiar tunes, harkening back to the days of "Zangwill" and Péguy's debut as a critic. Now he often went further and took upon himself the additional role of judge and executioner. He sought revenge against those who had opposed him and who had withheld the honors and distinctions he claimed as his due. He pursued his critics doggedly and systematically. Sorel had taught him to strike at the head of the hate-object; and he broadened that rule into the principle: only attack the powerful.[112] When a critic disparaged him in the columns of the *Revue Hebdomadaire*, Péguy retaliated with an attack on the editor. His denigration of academe resulted in an unceasing barrage of vituperation against the Sorbonne. Its professors, he insisted, were unworthy of respect. The literary historian Gustave Lanson lacked integrity. The historian Ernest Lavisse was the syringe through which poisonous treason filtered into an unsuspecting student body.[113] Charles Langlois, the medievalist, who had subjected Péguy's *Oeuvres choisies* to a

[110] *Ibid.*, 135.
[111] "L'Argent," 61–63.
[112] "Un nouveau théologien, M. Fernand Laudet," 171–72, 198.
[113] "L'Argent," 79.

harsh and unfair attack, was charged with marrying for money and with drunkenness. Péguy claimed that the offending essay had been written on July 15 while its author was recovering from a hangover due to excessive celebration of the national holiday.[114] Lucien Herr, the librarian of the École Normale, was a traitor and a coward. In the days of the Dreyfus Affair, Péguy recalled, he had led his friends when there was fighting to be done, while Herr had taken charge whenever all was quiet.[115]

Péguy's foulest blows were reserved for Jean Jaurès. The socialist leader, he averred, was the spearhead of German imperialism in France.[116] Other socialists, like Gustave Hervé and François de Pressensé, might be capable of folly and of crime, but Jaurès ranked below them on the human ladder. Jaurès was dishonest. At this point Péguy's yearning for the good old days of the Terror became irresistible. Revival of the forces that had brought about the execution of Louis XVI would lead to the liquidation of "that other fat man," Jean Jaurès.[117] "I am a good republican," he thundered. "I am an old revolutionary. In times of war there is but one policy, the policy of the National Convention. And let no one conceal that this . . . will mean Jaurès on the way to the scaffold, and rolling drums to drown out that powerful voice."[118] What had begun as a great friendship in the days of the Dreyfus Affair ended, on Péguy's side, in clear incitement to murder. On the subject of Jaurès, Péguy, the avowed Christian, spoke with the same venomous viciousness as the atheist, Charles Maurras.

Jaurès "ignored this hatred." He remained among the faithful who never allowed their subscriptions to the *Cahiers* to lapse. Shortly before his death he read Péguy's defense of Bergson and expressed his admiration for the author's grasp of the subject.[119]

[114] *Ibid.*, 75–76, 84.
[115] "L'Argent (suite)," 108.
[116] "L'Argent," 25–26.
[117] "L'Argent (suite)," 141.
[118] *Ibid.*, 127.
[119] For a well documented and thorough exposé of this relationship, see Henri Guillemin, "Péguy et Jaurès," *Les Temps modernes*, No. 194 (1962), 78–108.

Péguy's treatment of Jaurès exposed the extent of his moral decline. But a mere comparison of the two men and their characters does not constitute the last word on this episode. On July 31, 1914, Raoul Villain became the protagonist of that spirit of the National Convention invoked by Péguy when he fired the bullet that stilled the "powerful voice" from Tarn. On the stand in 1919, the assassin confessed to having planned this deed for fifteen months, indicating that he had first thought of it in late April of 1913. "L'Argent (suite)" which had demanded the death sentence for the socialist tribune, appeared on April 27, 1913.[120] The weight of this circumstantial evidence prompted Georges Sorel to write Edouard Berth on May 9, 1919: "I am strongly inclined to believe that the *Cahiers* may have imparted to Villain not the thought of the crime perhaps, but at least the energy to commit it." And he added, "Péguy, unlike the *Action Française*, would not have rejected this moral complicity."[121] It was a perceptive judgment by a man who himself had been a powerful inspirer of thoughts of violence. The Péguy of 1914 valued constancy over morality. In his eyes even a murderer had become a good man when he killed for the sake of principle. How much more mischief and tragedy might Péguy have inspired in the years to come had not war and death ended his existence five weeks after the assassination of Jaurès?

Equally disturbing was Péguy's failure to include among his targets men who were not notably chaste in their political activities. Why was Clemenceau passed over in silence when the secularization of French society was under discussion? After all, the Separation Law had been passed after Combes' fall, and much of its important implementing legislation was guided through parliament by Aristide Briand under Clemenceau's premiership in 1907 and 1908.[122] Had not Alexandre Mil-

---

[120] Georges Tétard, *Essais sur Jean Jaurès* (Colombes, 1959), 147–52.

[121] A[guste] M[artin], "Georges Sorel à Edouard Berth (extraits)," *ACPFM*, No. 77 (1960), 33; see also, Alexandre Zevaès, *Jean Jaurès* (Paris, 1951), 304–309.

[122] Joan Marie Gallagher, "Implementation and Modification of the Separation Law in France, 1905–1909" (M.A. Thesis, Tulane University, 1963), 46–85.

lerand changed his spots often enough to call forth doubts as to his disinterestedness both during and after the Dreyfus Affair? What was the secret of Péguy's devotion to this eminently political politician?[123] Was Maurice Barrès the exponent of a *mystique* that refused to be degraded into *politique?* And why was he permitted to criticize Péguy's work with impunity? Obviously Péguy's standards were not nearly as absolute and inflexible as he would have his readers believe. There were exemptions, though the reasons for these remain obscure or unknown. But if it was possible for a Clemenceau, a Millerand, and a Barrès to gain absolution with such apparent ease, how much less defensible was the excommunication hurled at Jaurès and the professorial guild, particularly the historians, of the Sorbonne?

From 1910 to 1914, Péguy strode inexorably toward an inferno of arbitrary violence and capricious disorder. He got "right with God," which added another fillip to his burgeoning arrogance. Before the bar of public opinion, he continued to press his case against the betrayers of the Dreyfusard *cité* and the *mystique* of the Republic, with the stipulation that he was to be the sole judge of who these culprits were. The darkness of this anarchic spirit was not only capable of brutal injustice, it seemed to explain that Péguy had lost confidence in his fellow men, had become disillusioned about the prospects of social salvation, and no longer expected anything from the future.

Toward the end of the long and thunderous proceedings that described this tragic evolution, Péguy the prosecuting attorney lost patience with an indifferent jury and the dilatory judges of public opinion. He began to summon the executioner; and if the law was not ready to pass sentence as he wished, then he stood ready to entrust the guardianship of justice to the lawless.

---

[123] Millerand's support of the three-year law, according to Eugen J. Weber, *The Nationalist Revival in France, 1905–1914* (Berkeley, 1959), 122.

VI

Conclusion:
Death, Rebirth, and Meaning
of Charles Péguy

CHARLES PÉGUY began his career as a reformer and died a destructive iconoclast. In a short life he moved from one extreme to another, and yet he claimed never to have changed. He spoke not without reason. In the course of years riven with controversy, his sights never strayed from two central problems of existence: man's position in society and man's relation to God. From the days of his first faltering steps as a writer to those turbulent years during which his pen never rested, Péguy preached a gospel of duty, integrity, and faith.

Péguy discovered duty in the steadfastness with which Joan of Arc persevered in the task laid upon her by God's command. He adapted that example to his own time when he embraced socialism whose disciples "must stand for every just cause which has not yet triumphed." Subsequent alienation from socialism did not provide him with the excuse to lay down his burden. Instead, he submitted to the discipline of launching and maintaining his own apostolate through the *Cahiers de la Quinzaine.*

Integrity in the context of Péguy's life meant that duty could not be compromised. It was easy to know what man must do. It was far harder to do it. Following the categorical imperative from day to day could result in certain failure or entail grinding solitude. Despite these cheerless alternatives, Péguy insisted that the exacting demands of his conscience could not be softened by compromise.

Added to duty "from man" was Péguy's faith in "mercy from God." Even the most punctilious fulfillment of one's assigned function in society could not assure a reward in heaven. Only God could save. But would he? On that score Péguy's *Jeanne d'Arc* had ended in a dissonance of doubt. The young editor of the fledgling *Cahiers* next confessed that to die before obtaining certitude about the hereafter was a terrifying prospect. Not until he had completed the "Mystère des saints innocents" did Péguy profess to comprehend that a boundless divine compassion was in effect sufficient to save all if it was enough to save one.

Had Péguy been content to plough his furrow on this large but clearly circumscribed field of duty, integrity, and religious faith, and had his unswerving commitment to these three qualities been as simple and as unequivocal as he believed it to be, there would have been nothing left to future generations but to do him just homage and to let the process of canonization take its course. But he was no saint. He did not possess the childlike simplicity which prompted a Saint Francis to seek the company of animals while escaping the contamination of humanity. As Péguy recognized what man should do, so he discovered that human performance fell short of the moral imperative. Society was not governed by those who chose right over wrong, but by leaders who preferred expediency to probity. While Christianity extolled faith, the Church was ruled by theologians who were themselves the servants of reason and compromise. Faced by these contradictions, Péguy became convinced that doing right was not enough. His responsibility, on the contrary, must encompass the additional effort of leading others unto righteousness. The guides of his generation must be disabused of their errors and the masses prevented from following the errant. Péguy cast himself in the role of the community conscience and the guardian of the national soul.

The veneer of universality which overlay some of Péguy's early writings could not conceal that the world to whose perfection and salvation Péguy devoted a life, was always French. The temporal duty which brought Joan of Arc from the valley of the Meuse to the Champagne, thence to the gates of Paris and finally to her dungeon in Normandy was the liberation and salvation of France. The just causes which socialism was bound to defend involved without exception French interests, French honor, and French prestige. The God whose mercy Péguy extolled in his *mystères* was a French Jupiter hovering over the Beauce, that heartland where dwelt the finest offspring in his temporal preserves. The enemies of France were likewise French. Joan of Arc had been martyred by the sinister theologians of the Kingdom of France, by men who betrayed their country and their religion. The French clerics were the villains, the English merely intruders. Péguy hoped to lead his platoon through the streets of Weimar, and no specter of German resistance clouded that dream. But traitors were abroad in his own country, intent upon frustrating this triumphal progress. Whether Péguy viewed the past or explored the present, the ubiquity of treason in France became his trial and his obsession.

Marcel, it is true, spoke of a haven for all civilizations and all religions; but if one attempts to relate it to his other work, one cannot take these assertions at face value. Either *Marcel* was an isolated lapse without roots in history and without visible relation to the contemporary world, or its writing was prompted by specific events in Péguy's own time—the problem of Dreyfus and the irritating exigencies of socialist discipline. If the former was true it remains a mystery to be solved by future research. In the latter case its emphasis on a spiritual rather than material socialism and its vigorous eulogy of intellectual freedom bespeak an attempt of ridding the social movement from the mortmain of Marx. In either case, the *cité harmonieuse* became a city of dreams forgotten amidst the tribulations of reality.

Soon after the launching of the *Cahiers* even Péguy's patriotism lost its collectivist tolerance. The purported villainies of false socialists and false Dreyfusards alienated him from large segments of the intellectual community. As a force among the rising university generation of 1890 his major targets were his professors and his former fellow students. The historical anti-intellectualism of *Jeanne d'Arc* first assumed sporadic reality in the articles for the *Revue Blanche;* it did not reach the stature of an article of faith until Péguy met Sorel. Once he chose to follow this pied piper of violence he entered hell, pure and simple. He foreswore faith in mankind and declared perpetual war on the modern world, a deceptively general term used to describe the power elite that governed France's political and intellectual institutions. To that "world" and its representatives he ascribed every vice and every defect that crossed his rambling path.

Péguy did not recognize his own transformation. He continued to claim that the *Cahiers* were a pilot *cité,* overlooking that the exclusiveness of his own microscopic and changing coterie contrasted irreconcilably with the universality of his earlier harmonious commonwealth portrayed in *Marcel.* He continued to profess love for France, but could he really esteem a country whose citizens, by their own choice, were governed by a coalition of socialist traitors and Radical charlatans?

One can only agree with Sorel that illusion abounded at every stage of Péguy's intellectual evolution. At the outset it appeared as if he entertained the expectation of remaking mankind in his own image. With every successive disappointment he withdrew farther into an inner sanctuary of prejudice and conceit until he was utterly alone. At the end of his life he had love only for his children and himself.

One single comfort remained to Péguy in this purgatory of his own devising: the prospect of an eventual ascent to heaven. In 1912 he claimed to have obtained from God the promise of salvation. The historian can only record that claim. The "Mystère des saints innocents" is his only source and his only evidence. God may have spoken to Péguy; He did not speak to his biographers.

Under these circumstances death became the only meaningful purpose in Péguy's existence. The final passage in "A nos amis, à nos abonnés" was in this regard doubly revealing. He sought death to enter heaven, but he also craved a conspicuous death which would reveal to France that she had sinned in failing to take this prophet to her bosom. If Péguy died a proper death, his fellow citizens would then not merely mourn the passing of a poet, but they would have to accept the duty of penance for their failure to follow a unique apostle of virtue.

II

Péguy's wish was granted. He died heroically in a decisive battle of history, in 1914 the first major French writer to give his life for his country. But the results of that death were again as warped and as compromised as had been the results of the Dreyfusard victories or the winning of the Prix Estrade-Delcros. The martyr was immediately pressed into the service of that republic which he had so often denounced.

Maurice Barrès and Charles Maurras at once enlisted Péguy in their work of national propaganda.[1] In the changed circumstances it was now safe to appropriate him. Death on the battlefield in 1914 was not recognized as the supreme sacrifice of a man who had gone out to defy the modern world, but as an isolated option of bravery overshadowing everything else Péguy had accomplished.[2] The Catholic writer, Victor Poucel, addressing the French colony of Alexandria in the winter of 1914, shunted aside discussion of Péguy's merit as a writer. Only his death on the battlefield mattered.[3] These sentiments reverberated through the contemporary press.[4] Lavisse's *Revue de Paris* settled accounts in its own way. It closed its books on Péguy by expressing satisfaction that he had finally charged an enemy deserving of his hate.[5] Even foreign observers saw him in a martial light. The Swiss Protestant pastor Paul Seippel compared the France of 1914 to the resurgent Prussia of 1813 and Charles

[1] Maurice Barrès, "Charles Péguy mort au champ d'honneur," *Echo de Paris*, September 17, 1914; Charles Maurras, "Charles Péguy," *Action Française*, September 18, 1914.

[2] Charles Silvestre, *Charles Péguy* (Paris, 1915), 55.

[3] Victor Poucel, "Charles Péguy et la thèse d'espérance," *Études*, CXLIII (1915), 5–6.

[4] "Comment la presse parisienne accueillit la mort de Péguy," *ACPFM*, No. 15 (1950), 11–14.

[5] Harlor, "Charles Péguy," *Revue de Paris*, XXII, No. 2 (1915), 647.

Péguy to Germany's most illustrious literary casualty of the Napoleonic wars, Theodor Körner.[6]

The dead Péguy was neither accepted nor rejected: he was simply used. Barrès encouraged a member of the 276th Infantry Regiment to write his recollections of the Battle of Villeroy so that Péguy's example might continue to inspire the many who must continue to fight an invader whom the reverse at the Marne had not dislodged from France.[7] In 1916, the year of Verdun and of the slaughter at the Somme, René Doumic, Brunetière's successor as editor of the *Revue des deux Mondes,* reminded the youth of France that Péguy had volunteered for frontline duty.[8] The first major French writer to die in the holocaust of the First World War became an effective recruiting symbol.[9]

The Church also sought to profit from Péguy's heroism. Buoyed and rejuvenated by a number of conspicuous conversions since 1905 and by the rapid increase of the number of practising Catholics among students in lycées and universities, restored by numerous examples of bravery on the part of chaplains and monks serving in the ranks, uplifted at last by the conspicuous piety of such military leaders as Castelnau and Pétain, it was bound to reconsider Péguy's case after death had silenced that dissonant voice. In 1915, the editor-in-chief of *La Croix,* France's most widely distributed clerical newspaper, paid homage also to Péguy as a Catholic hero. The question of whether or not he could or did find salvation while formally remaining outside the Church seemed to have become moot. The

[6] Charles Seippel, *Un poète français tombé au champ d'honneur: Charles Péguy* (Paris, 1915), 34.

[7] Lately expanded into a more pretentious but not superior volume Cf. Victor Boudon, *Mon lieutenant Charles Péguy* (Paris, 1964).

[8] *Reception de Bergson à l'Académie Française,* quoted in C. L. Turquet-Milnes, *Some Modern French Writers, a Study in Bergsonism* (New York, 1921), 212 n.

[9] Cf. Paul Flat, "La leçon de Charles Péguy," *Revue Bleue,* LIII (1915), 496–97; Adolphe Brisson, "Les étoiles éteintes: Charles Péguy," *Les Annales Politiques et Littéraires,* XXXIII (1915), 624–25; Henri Massis, "Le témoignage de Péguy," *L'Opinion,* IX (1916), 385–86.

war, as one Catholic propagandist explained, had identified anew Church and nation. Péguy's death, therefore, in the service of a country which stood forth as "Christ's missionary to the world" was of itself sufficient to lift him into the arms of God.[10] By this ingenious line of reasoning, Péguy's fangs were pulled; and his startling religious opinions, though not forgotten, were rendered harmless.

Acceptance of the maverick convert was facilitated by the publication in 1916 of a letter which Péguy had written to Jeanne Maritain on August 20, 1914, and which promised: "Some day I shall perhaps tell you in which parish I heard mass on Assumption Day." [11] This announcement removed the most serious formal barrier that had hitherto separated Péguy from other practicing Catholics: his refusal to attend Mass as long as the Church would not recognize his marriage to an agnostic. It reached a far wider public than had the technical, theological controversies of "Fernand Laudet." In a few simple words it erased hundreds of angry pages, leaving only the memory of the volunteer officer, simply and devoutly standing before the altar of God, Virgin, and country with his platoon of weary and heroic men. It opened the way for an even more indulgent interpretation set forth by Julien Laurec, one third of whose *Renouveau catholique dans les lettres* dealt with Péguy. Published at the end of 1917, the year of crisis, mutiny, and revolution, this book identified Péguy as a plain and steady Catholic whose pure life and whose heroic death entitled him to a privileged place among the faithful.[12] As the war drew to a close, the Catholic literary historian, Fortunat Strowski, both a professor at the Sorbonne and a member of the Institute, declared: "Péguy's Catholicism, his patriotism and the principles to which he showed such great devotion, were not ideas, which

---

[10] Julien Laurec, "Le catholicisme de Péguy," *Revue du Clergé Français,* LXXXVIII (1916), 92.

[11] First printed in Victor Boudon, *Avec Charles Péguy, de la Lorraine à la Marne* (Paris, 1916), 170.

[12] Julien Laurec, *Le renouveau catholique dans les lettres* (Paris, 1917), 108–110.

once acquired might again be discarded at any moment. They were part of him, once and for all, and he would sooner have given up his life than his faith." [13] No student of the *mystères* could have reached this conclusion. The question of dying for his faith had never arisen in Péguy's life. He had sought God in the expectation that the gift of His mercy would make the inevitability of death more bearable. Sound or not, however, Strowski's comments appeared in a general volume on the state of Catholicism in France, edited by the Vicar-General of Paris, Cardinal Baudrillart. They may be assumed to reflect the final official hierarchical assessment of this erratic hero of the Republic.

Writing and editing had obviously been the basis of Péguy's fame. His literary labors had made him a center of controversy. But in a France at war, the nation's secular and clerical publicists concentrated their searchlights on the most acceptable act he had ever performed: dying in defense of his homeland. This sacrifice confirmed him as a sterling citizen. The events preceding it redeemed him as an exemplary Christian. The habitual outsider was transformed into a defender of institutions which he had continually assailed and often explicitly rejected in his lifetime.

Peace reduced the importance of Péguy's posthumous career as a national hero. It revived within narrow limits the herald of conflict. Some of his surviving contemporaries may even have been spurred by the distorted adoration of the war years to remind themselves and their readers that death on the battlefield could not validate ideas which they had rejected before the war. The critic Pierre Lasserre revived these lingering doubts about Péguy's religious soundness. He attacked the shallowness of Péguy's anti-intellectualism.[14] Georges Guy-Grand, a confirmed Radical, lumped together Péguy and Maurras as victims of their own spectacular inconsistencies. Maurras was the representative of an atrophied rationalism whose professed penchant for action

[13] In Alfred, Cardinal Baudrillart (ed.), *La vie catholique dans la France contemporaine* (Paris, 1918), 483.

[14] *Les chapelles littéraires* (Paris, 1920), 232–46.

remained forever bound to the printed page. Péguy had been the activist without a positive program of action.[15]

Péguy's literary reputation grew but slowly. The publication of his collected works in limited edition, begun in 1916 and terminated in 1944, was almost completely disregarded by the critics. An infrequent reminiscence by a former contributor to the *Cahiers* or a rare article by a specialist in contemporary literature reminded the public of him from time to time. The most important gift to Péguy's fame between the wars was the charming two-volume memoir by the Tharaud brothers, published in 1926.[16] This work, *Notre cher Péguy,* opened with a roseate recollection of his days at Ste. Barbe. The rest was the work of imagination rather than history. The Tharauds had not been close to Péguy during the last decade of his life and could only reconstruct these years through hearsay and on the basis of his own exhaustive and often misleading testimony. They perpetuated the myth of the mature man who alone in his generation had kept faith with the ideals of his youth.[17]

Notre cher Péguy succeeded with a public that knew next to nothing about the subject but which enjoyed the authors' gift to entertain. The bitterness of war and the disappointments of peace combined to perpetuate a futile yearning for the halcyon days "d'avant guerre." It was this frame of mind which the Tharauds exploited. Their book minimized conflict and anger while idealizing the causes of Péguy's isolation. Rather than shed light on a controversial subject, the authors suffused it in the glow of countless Japanese lanterns.

Even so, *Notre cher Péguy* began a Péguy revival. The late 1920's saw the reprinting of several of his more popular works. In 1929, *Le bien public,* a small Parisian newspaper catering primarily to small business men and rentiers, devoted an entire page of its September 11 issue to the observance of the fifteenth anniversary of Péguy's death. This homage to a heroic figure

[15] George Guy-Grand, *Le conflit des idées dans la France d'aujourd'hui* (Paris, 1921), 72–73.
[16] *Notre cher Péguy.*
[17] *Ibid.,* II, 248.

before an audience whose mores and values were not Péguy's and whose members certainly had not read him continued in two commemorative volumes appearing in 1930.[18] The content of one of these in particular, published under the auspices of the *Nouvelle Revue Française,* was largely biographical. Little was said about the editor and writer. Péguy remained a world war memorial. The man did not emerge from the shadows except to those who had known him personally.

That the crises of the Hitlerian era revived the heroic cult of 1914–18 was not surprising. Now Péguy had new admirers, younger men who sought to save France not only from a resurgent enemy but from a new wave of scandal of which the Stavisky affair in 1934 became the most notorious. Daniel-Rops,[19] the advocate of an orthodox Catholic return to religion, and Emmanuel Mounier,[20] who propounded Christianity in a morally pure, noncapitalist society, became spokesmen of a generation born in the shadow of one war and destined to die in the night of a great defeat. They hungered for and found in the diffuse writings of Péguy religious and social values which sustained them in their lives of uninterrupted tribulation. They discovered not the true, historical Péguy but a spur in combat and a consolation in individual and national captivity. They read "L'Argent (suite)" not because it advocated the assassination of Jaurès but because it exhorted:

Whoever defends France defends the Kingdom of France.
Whosoever stands his grounds may be as republican as he wishes or as anti-clerical as he chooses. . . .

The man who surrenders, on the other hand, will always be a scoundrel, even if he be the pillar of his parish.[21]

To a nation perplexed and demoralized, these words provided assurance of an indestructible unity. Rather than remind France

---

[18] *Homage à Péguy* (Paris, 1930); *Porche à l'oeuvre de Péguy* (Orléans, 1930).
[19] *Péguy* (Paris, 1933).
[20] *La pensée de Charles Péguy* (Paris, 1931).
[21] "L'Argent (suite)," 135.

of Péguy's sterile feud with Jaurèsian socialism or with the hierarchy of the Sorbonne, they provided a text for many patriots who burned with shame at the thought of Pétain's surrender to Germany.

Throughout the Second World War Péguy's patriotic and religious scriptures reappeared openly and clandestinely. They provided answers to the questions posed during France's darkest hour. Editors on both sides of the civil war begun by the occupation extracted from Péguy's rambling and undisciplined discourses anthologies for specific topical and tendentious purposes. A collection of excerpts entitled *La France* appeared in 1939 in Paris and was subsequently reprinted in Montreal (1942) and in Algiers (1943). *Saints de France* followed in 1941. *Paroles aux educateurs de France* made an appearance in unoccupied France a year later. *Notre Seigneur,* a collection of excerpts on religious subjects was printed publicly in 1943; *Capitulation et Résistance* emanated from the underground presses of the Éditions de Minuit in 1944, the year of liberation. *La République, notre royaume de France,* a collection of political texts, appeared on the book stalls in the birth year of the Fourth Republic. At the same time, purposeful biographies of Péguy the "prophet," the "soldier of freedom," and the "soldier of truth" recounted his life, suitably camouflaged by the clerical or resistance bias of the respective authors.[22]

The pattern of recognition became set. It was easy to exploit Péguy the polemicist, the man of many opinions, of many predilections, and of many antipathies by stringing together out of context any number of specific passages addressed to one particular cause or directed against one certain foe. Given the "heavenly length" of many of his works in verse and prose, the public never clamored to read all. Expurgated, fragmentary selections became the only way of winning him a devoted public. The Péguy of one particular attitude could now win a like segment of public opinion and hold it, since such a procedure permitted the convenient omission of every dissonance. As a

[22] Cf. Auguste Martin, "Bilan bibliographique," *Cahiers de l'Amitié Charles Péguy,* I (1948), 68–69.

result the fractious debater whose crusty intractability had succeeded in alienating most of his contemporaries, now began to exercise, through skillful editorial separation, an equally universal attraction. The man who had written more than an ordinary mortal could be expected to read and absorb, was now pursued—as he once predicted—by several parties, each one of which chose to hear what suited its purpose, while treating everything else as insignificant, irrelevant, or nonexistent. Posterity had discovered ways of accepting Péguy. In need of specific insights and consolations, it had responded to those parts of his work which provided them.

III

One may consider Péguy noble or craven, saintly or corrupt, consistent or capricious. His work may have accurately reflected a time and its struggles or distorted it. Subsequent generations may have been and continue to be rational or arbitrary in the way they have used and interpreted his message. The controversy surrounding these questions will continue and perhaps it will in due time contribute to a complete and reasonably satisfying assessment of the man and his work. But one question remains: was Péguy an isolated phenomenon, or did he reflect together with other tortured men the perplexities of an age that produced change more rapidly and more abundantly than men could absorb? Was he a spokesman of that rare quality, independence, or a symptom of that common human reflex, fear?

The physical discoveries and the religious reforms of the sixteenth century had undermined a stable world that was evolving so slowly as to appear unchanging. The shock of seeing world trade tear apart the fabric of local agriculture and provincial commerce, the stunning impact of controversy over the presumably unchallengeable truths of divine revelation never had a chance to wear off before the scientific discoveries and pseudo-discoveries of the Newtonian age produced another ominous shift under the groundwork of human consciousness. John Locke called the resultant human frame of mind "uneasiness" and praised it as the great prod that saved man from standing still. But the truth is that many men liked standing still and would have preferred to rejoice in the certitude that the world of their old age should resemble the environment of their youth.

When the revolutionary penchant for innovation produced for the first time a mass of victims at the end of the eighteenth century, some of these—the émigrés of the French Revolution—expressed an uneasiness of their own over the everpresence of change, the perpetuity of progress, and the rejection of tradition. They began to preach "the bad tidings of the wicked modern age brought to pass by Jacobins, democrats, and apostles of progress." [23] Reaction was born, and its birthplace was France.

Until 1875 French reaction was a normal political movement with normal political outlets; but once monarchism—a movement to restore monarchy in the person of a concrete, legitimate pretender—became royalism—an abstract hankering for a system which in the absence of such a pretender could not be restored—reaction became neurotic vacillation between conservative and revolutionary theories. Fear of change might emerge either as opposition to change or as a frantic effort to outrun it in an orgy of nihilism. Reaction ceased to be exclusively monarchist. It ceased to be stable and predictable. Edward R. Tannenbaum's study of the *Action Française* as a movement of "die-hard reactionaries" presents the dichotomy in a host of ways. In the evolution of Léon Daudet, revolutionary socialism and royalism succeeded one another.[24] Maurras presented his version of the new society in a corporate setting which proposed the restoration of traditional privilege and peace between contending interests and which promised to prevent "finance" from gaining control of the state. Like Péguy, whose description of the hated modern world revealed a society in which everything was for sale, Maurras had had a vision of a golden age in which he and his friends would no longer be forced to appeal to and depend on a callous mercenary public.[25] Like Péguy, too, they

[23] Friedrich Heer, "Der Konservative und die Reaktion," *Die neue Rundschau*, LXIX (1953), 495.
[24] Tannenbaum, *The Action Française*, 54.
[25] *Ibid.*, 60–87.

found that golden age in the past rather than in the future. The only difference was that Maurras' glorious past ended in 1789, whereas Péguy's terminated in 1881.

Hence Péguy's reactionary utopia was not necessarily monarchist, and its galaxy of heroes included the leaders and luminaries of the *grand siècle* as well as such revolutionary figures as Robespierre, Proudhon, Victor Hugo, and the leaders of the Paris Commune. He rejected, therefore, the *Action Française* as a movement of royalist restoration, but his own views were still not far removed from a national socialism which Maurras described in his *Dictionnaire politique et critique* as having been "freed of democratic and cosmopolitan elements." [26]

This socialist component of French reaction furthermore drew support from men and orders among whom Péguy had spent his childhood. It was not until 1896 that Barrès coined the word "national socialism," and only two years later the facile Lorrainer stood for the Chamber of Deputies from Nancy under the auspices of a "Republican Socialist Nationalist Committee" advocating the trinity of "nationalism, protectionism, and socialism." But reaction had existed since Robespierre. In due time it was to spawn republican leaders like Millerand, Viviani, Albert Thomas, France's socialist secretary of state for munitions during World War I, and lastly the passionate anti-patriot Gustave Hervé who ended his days as the discredited prophet of the unsuccessful savior Philippe Pétain. It is well known that not every socialist in the 1890's was a Marxist. It deserves emphasis that a good many of them were former Boulangists.[27] One must remember that Péguy's fatherly friend Boitier was a socialist chauvinist whose political beliefs were inspired by Hugo's *Châtiments*. In short, the line between social reformers and die-hard

---

[26] Quoted in Eugen Weber, "Nationalism, socialism and national socialism in France," *French Historical Studies,* II (1962), 277. The soundness of Péguy's political instincts is further attested to by the attraction which the *Action Française* held for some latter-day disciples of Auguste Comte; cf. W. M. Simon, "Comte's orthodox disciples: the rise and fall of a cénacle," *Ibid.,* IV (1965), 59.

[27] Ligou, *Histoire du socialisme en France,* 124; Goguel, *La politique des partis sous la IIIe république,* 67–68.

reactionaries became invisible amidst these crosscurrents; and Péguy, who in a short life managed to be both, remains one of the best representatives of a French ideology that attracted all by its appeal to an instinctive distrust of strangers and a universal discontent with democracy and with capitalism. No wonder that French national socialism found supporters, for different reasons, in every stratum of society and in every segment of the political spectrum.

This malaise of chauvinistic and social discontent for which Péguy spoke so volubly was not an exclusively French movement. Nietzsche has been viewed both as anarchist and classicist and his work as the juncture of a nostalgic return to past esthetic ideals joined to a brutal call to arms against a materialistic present which had desecrated them.[28] Fritz Stern in his *Politics of Cultural Despair* describes the ideas of Paul de Lagarde, Julius Langbehn, and Möller van den Bruck (Péguy's German contemporaries) whose collective hatred of "bourgeois life, manchesterism, materialism, and the parties" capsules equally well some of the Frenchman's more striking prejudices.[29] These men constituted part of a general revolt prompted by the spiritual and material dissatisfactions engendered by "our liberal and industrial society," and Stern has labeled their reaction as "the ideology of . . . conservative revolution." All three, like Péguy, attacked their own national culture as too cosmopolitan; all three in various ways were troubled by the loss of religion; and all three everlastingly scored the commercialized city and its press.[30] The youngest of them, Möller van den Bruck, greeted war with the same relieved exultation as the editor of the *Cahiers de la Quinzaine*.[31] As a postwar epilogue one might add the book *Nationaler Sozialismus* by the Austrian Rudolf Jung which also attacked the "disintegrative forces of modern civilization," among which it listed haphazardly "wage labor on farms and in

[28] Reino Virtanen, "Nietzsche and the Action Française," *Journal of the History of Ideas,* XI (1950), 194.

[29] (Berkeley, 1961), xii.

[30] *Ibid.,* xv-xviii, 40–41, 130, 148–49.

[31] *Ibid.,* 206, although he had the misfortune of surviving it.

factories, interest, credit, liberal democracy and marxist socialism." The sum of these factors was viewed as a triumph of
materialism against which Jung pitted the saving promise of
national socialism as a last resort.[32]

In a different vein the specter of a nihilistic national socialism
raised its head in Italy during those very years that bred the
hatred of "L'Argent" and "L'Argent (suite)." In one respect the
Italian situation differed from the French in that the activists—
having likewise the choice between European grievances (Italia
Irredenta) and overseas conquest—opted for the latter at the
expense of Turkey's crumbling African empire. In the elections
of 1913 the propagandistic work of Enrico Corradini's *Associa-
zione nazionalista italiana* bore fruit by making deep inroads in
Catholic circles, a far more significant achievement than in
France, considering that he had to overcome a feud far more
acrimonious than that provided by Separation and had no Joan
of Arc myth to aid him. Equally important was the divisive
impact of the Libyan war on the Socialist party. Leaders like
Arturo Labriola and Paolo Orano, to whom Corradini's *Asso-
ciazione* was anathema, nevertheless adopted its tone and its
thought when justifying the African adventure. "A rapport de-
veloped between syndicalism and nationalism, reinforced by the
growing acceptance on the part of the Nationalists of a syndical
organization of the economic life of the nation." [33]

The examples could be multiplied elsewhere. National socialism, a mixture of literary and ideological myths about the past,
of troubled responses to economic and technological change, and
of adaptations of national-revolutionary doctrines of the nineteenth century to the needs of a new age and to societies whose
national identities had been formally recognized, was becoming
a pervasive western ideology. Although its purveyors in the
1930's and 1940's infused the word with a horror of which

[32] Rudolf Jung, *Nationaler Sozialismus,* (3rd ed.; Munich, 1922),
quoted in Andrew Whiteside, "Nationaler Sozialismus in Oesterreich vor
1918," *Vierteljahreshefte für Zeitgeschichte,* IX (1961), 550.

[33] Ronald S. Cunsolo, "Libya, Italian Nationalism and the Revolt
Against Giolitti," *Journal of Modern History,* XXXVII (1965), 199–200.

Péguy's time had no inkling, one must not shrink from associating this valiant, brilliant, and fiery Frenchman with Hitler's nominal precursors, hastening to add that when carried to that extreme the similarity is only verbal.

Whether Péguy is viewed as a unique or as a typical product of his time, the conclusion remains inescapable that his spiritual path began on a peak of idealism and descended into a valley of anger. In his youth he tried to love mankind; on the threshold of death he placed himself above man, arrogating to himself a special seat at the foot of the throne of God. Once he felt secure, he embraced a cult of violence which, by implication, rejected all hope of human progress.

Our generation cannot accept Péguy's breathless pursuit of battle. The last fifty years, which themselves have given the word "change" so many new and ominous connotations, have transformed the volunteer defender of France into an advocate of human destruction. Today his polemics serve to inspire only those who reject the Western heritage of rebirth, enlightenment, and science. His example stands as a terrible warning: Do not judge man, lest you abandon man. It poses an agonizing question: Must we hate ourselves to find peace with God?

Péguy the political thinker and ideological fighter was both more and less than he and his disciples have claimed. Less in that much of his work was directed by self-interest rather than human concern. More in that his existence, despite the lasting residue of poetic inspiration, constitutes a terrifying preview of man's ability to embrace and rationalize a doctrine of self-destruction.

Bibliography

A. The works of Charles Péguy.
Original editions in chronological order of their appearance.

a. Before 1900.

Jeanne d'Arc. Drame en trois pièces par Marcel et Pierre Baudouin (Paris, 1897).
"Un économiste socialiste, M. Léon Walras," *La Revue Socialiste,* XXV (1897), 174–86.
"A propos des affaires d'Orient," *ibid.,* 258–61.
Marcel. Premier dialogue de la cité harmonieuse par Pierre Baudouin (Paris, 1898).
"De la cité socialiste," *La Revue Socialiste,* XXVI (1898), 186–90.
"Durkheim's 'Le suicide,' étude de sociologie," *ibid.,* 635–36.
"Service militaire," *La Revue Blanche,* XVIII (1899), 217–19.
"Quelques égarés," *ibid.,* 382–84.
"Désaisissement," *ibid.,* 449–50.
"L'Opinion publique," *ibid.,* 539–41.
"L'Enquête publiée," *ibid.,* 623.
"Enseignements," *ibid.,* XIX (1899), 211–13.
"La crise et le parti socialiste," *ibid.,* 462–68.
"La crise du parti socialiste et l'Affaire Dreyfus," *ibid.,* 626–32.
"L'Affaire Dreyfus et la crise du parti socialiste," *ibid.,* XX (1899), 127–39.
"Le ravage et la réparation," *ibid.,* 417–32.
"Les récentes oeuvres de Zola," *Le Mouvement Socialiste,* I (1899), 537–52, 600–615.

b. Works published in the Cahiers de la Quinzaine, *1900–14.*

"Le triomphe de la république," I, No. 1 (1900).

"De la grippe," I, No. 4 (1900).

"Encore de la grippe," I, No. 6 (1900).

"Toujours de la grippe," I, No. 7 (1900).

"Entre deux trains," I, No. 9 (1900).

"Pour ma maison," II, No. 3 (1900).

"Pour moi," II, No. 5 (1901).

"Casse-cou," II, No. 7 (1901).

"De Jean Coste," IV, No. 3 (1902).

"La chanson du roi Dagobert," IV, No. 15 (1903).

"Zangwill," VI, No. 3 (1904).

"Notre Patrie," VII, No. 3 (1905). Republished in 1915 by Gallimard.

"Les suppliants parallèles," VII, No. 7 (1905).

"Louis de Gonzague," VII, No. 8 (1905).

"De la situation faite à l'histoire et à la sociologie dans les temps
modernes," VIII, No. 3 (1906).

"De la situation faite au parti intellectuel dans le monde moderne,"
VIII, No. 5 (1906).

"De la situation faite à l'histoire et à la sociologie et de la situation
faite au parti intellectuel dans le monde moderne," VIII, No. 11
(1907).

"De la situation faite au parti intellectuel dans le monde moderne devant les accidents de la gloire temporelle," IX, No. 1 (1907).

"A nos amis, à nos abonnés," X, No. 13 (1909).

"Le Mystère de la charité de Jeanne d'Arc," XI, No. 6 (1910). A
second printing in 1910 issued by Plon.

"Notre Jeunesse," XI, No. 12 (1910). Second printing in 1910 by
Ollendorff.

"Victor-Marie, Comte Hugo," XII, No. 1 (1910).

"Un nouveau théologien, M. Fernand Laudet," XIII, No. 2 (1911).

"Le Porche du mystère de la deuxième vertu," XIII, No. 4 (1911).

"Le Mystère des saints innocents," XIII, No. 12 (1912). This and the
preceding work were reissued in 1912 by Emile-Paul.

"La tapisserie de Sainte Geneviève et de Jeanne d'Arc," XIV, No. 5
(1912).

"L'Argent," XIV, No. 6 (1913).

"L'Argent (suite)," XIV, No. 9 (1913).

"La tapisserie de Notre-Dame," XIV, No. 10 (1913).

"Ève," XV, No. 4 (1913).

"Note sur M. Bergson et la philosophie bergsonienne," XV, No. 8 (1914).

c. Posthumous publications.

"Note conjointe sur M. Descartes et la philosophie cartésienne," *Nouvelle Revue Française,* No. 70 and No. 71 (1919). The *Note* on Bergson and the *Note conjointe* were reissued in one volume by Gallimard in 1935.

"Le Mystère de la charité de Jeanne d'Arc (suite inédite)," XVI, No. 11 (1926). In 1925 the publication of the *Cahiers,* interrupted by Péguy's departure for the front, was resumed by his oldest son Marcel.

"L'Épreuve," XX, No. 7 (1930).

"Pierre, commencement d'une vie bourgeoise," XXI, No. 7 (1931).

"Ébauche d'une étude sur Alfred de Vigny," XXI, No. 7 (1931).

Clio. Paris: Gallimard, 1932.

Par ce demi-clair matin. Paris: Gallimard, 1952. According to his son Pierre, Péguy published "Les suppliants parallèles" in the *Cahier* for which this sequel to "Notre Patrie" was originally intended. No one appears to know the reason for the switch.

L'Ésprit de système. Paris: Gallimard, 1953. Like "Zangwill" in 1904 and the first of the "Situations" in 1906, this essay was intended for the first *Cahier* following the academic summer holidays of 1905. It was displaced above all by the events which prompted Péguy to write and publish "Notre Patrie."

Un poète l'a dit. Paris: Gallimard, 1953.

Deuxième élégie XXX (suivi de Clio). Paris: Gallimard, 1955

La thèse. Paris: Gallimard, 1955. This title conceals the fifth *Situation*—"De la situation faite à l'histoire dans la philosophie générale du monde moderne"—which Péguy first thought of in terms of an academic thesis and which he subsequently abandoned altogether.

d. Other major editions.

Notes politiques et sociales. With introduction by André Boisserie (Cahiers de l'Amitié Charles Péguy, No. 11). Paris, 1957.

Oeuvres complètes. 20 vols. Paris: Gallimard, 1917–55. A fine printing of all of Péguy's known texts without any critical apparatus.

The introduction to the first volume was written by Alexandre Millerand; the last five contain the posthumous essays, published between 1952 and 1955 and listed above.

Oeuvres en prose, 1898–1908. With introduction and notes by Marcel Péguy. Paris, 1959.

Oeuvres en prose, 1909–1914. With introduction and notes by Marcel Péguy. Paris, 1957.

Oeuvres poétiques complètes. Introduction by François Porché, notes by Marcel Péguy. Paris, 1957.

B. Printed sources, memoirs, and major contemporary commentaries.

Arnauld, Mich. (Pseud. Drouin, Marcel). "Les cahiers de Charles Péguy," *Nouvelle Revue Française,* I (1909).

Barrès, Maurice. *Mes Cahiers,* Vol. VII. Paris, 1923.

Benda, Julien. *Un régulier dans le siècle.* Paris, 1939. More critical of Péguy than any of his associates, but for that reason particularly valuable.

Boudon, Victor. *Avec Charles Péguy de la Lorraine à la Marne.* Paris, 1916. Reminiscences of a member of Péguy's infantry company.

Brémond, Henri. "Joseph Lotte et les Entretiens de Péguy," *Le Correspondant,* CCLXIII (1916).

Challaye, Félicien. *Péguy socialiste.* Paris, 1954. Not what the title implies, but another memoir-biography by one of the last surviving contributors to the *Cahiers.*

The Correspondence (1899–1926) between Paul Claudel and André Gide. New York, 1952.

Doumic, René. "Charles Péguy," *Revue des Deux Mondes,* Ser. VI, Vol. 23 (1914).

Fautras, Gustave. "L'Enfance de Péguy," *Réforme Sociale,* LXX (1915). Recollections by one of Péguy's teachers in Orléans.

Favre, Geneviève. "Souvenirs sur Péguy," *Europe,* XLVI (1938).

Halévy, Daniel. *Charles Péguy et les Cahiers de la Quinzaine.* Paris, 1919.

Isaac, Jules. *Expériences de ma vie.* Vol. I: *Péguy.* Paris, 1959. A careful and conscientious reconstruction of the past by a French educator. Especially useful on the period 1895–1900.

Johannet, René. *Charles Péguy et ses Cahiers.* Paris, 1914.

————. "Projets littéraires et propos familiers de Péguy," *Le Correspondant,* CCCXXI (1919).

The Journals of André Gide. Translated by Justin O'Brien. 3 vols. New York, 1948.

Laudet, Fernand. "Un disciple de Charles Péguy," *Revue Hebdomadaire,* VII, No. 8 (1911). Fernand Laudet's modest revenge.

Laurec, Julien. "Le catholicisme de Péguy," *Revue du Clergé Français,* LXXXVIII (1916).

————. *Le renouveau catholique dans les lettres.* Paris, 1917.

LeGrix, François. "Charles Péguy," *Revue Hebdomadaire,* VII, No. 6 (1911).

Luchaire, Jean. *Confessions d'un Français moyen, 1876–1914.* Marseille, 1943.

Maire, Gilbert. "Trois poètes mystiques," *La Revue,* CIX (1914). Claudel, Jammes, and Péguy.

Maritain, Raïssa. *Les grandes amitiés.* Paris, 1948.

Massis, Henri. "Le témoignage de Péguy," *L'Opinion,* IX (1916).

Méjan, Louise V. (ed.). *La séparation des églises et de l'état, l'oeuvre de Louis Méjan. . . .* Paris, 1959.

Pacary, Pierre. *Un compagnon de Péguy: Joseph Lotte, 1875–1914.* Paris, 1917.

Paul-Boncour, Joseph. *Entre deux guerres; souvenirs sur la Troisième République.* 3 vols. New York, 1946–47.

Péguy, Charles. *Lettre ouverte à Franklin-Bouillon.* Introduction by Daniel Halévy. Paris, 1948.

————. *Lettres à Alain-Fournier.* Bordeaux, 1946.

————. *Lettres à André Bourgeois.* Paris, 1947.

Péguy, Marcel (ed.). *Lettres et entretiens de Charles Péguy.* Paris, 1926.

Porché, François. *Charles Péguy et ses cahiers.* Paris, 1914. Porché was author of the last *Cahier* published under Péguy's editorship.

Psichari, Henriette. *Ernest Psichari, mon frère.* Paris, 1933.

Reclus, Maurice. *Le Péguy que j'ai connu.* Paris, 1951. By the biographer of Jules Favre whom Péguy frequently met at Geneviève Favre's home.

Rivière, Jacques and Alain-Fournier. *Correspondance, 1905–1914.* 3 vols. Paris, 1926–28.

Roberty, J. E. "Charles Péguy," *Revue Chrêtienne,* LXIII (1916).

Rolland, Romain. *Choix de lettres à Malwida von Meysenbug* (Cahiers Romain Rolland, No. 1). Paris, 1948.

————. *Correspondance entre Louis Gillet et Romain Rolland* (Cahiers Romain Rolland, No. 2). Paris, 1949.

————. *De Jean Christophe à Colas Breugnon, pages de journal.* Paris, 1946.

————. *Péguy.* 2 vols. Paris, 1944. The last major work of an author whom Péguy was the first to publish.

Saffrey, Alfred (ed.). *Une amitié française, correspondance entre Charles Péguy et Romain Rolland* (Cahiers Romain Rolland, No. 7). Paris, 1955.

Salome, René. "Péguy chez les protestants," *Revue des Jeunes,* XIII (1916).

Seippel, Paul. *Un poète français tombé au champ d'honneur: Charles Péguy.* Paris, 1915.

Silvestre, Charles. *Charles Péguy.* Paris, 1916.

Suarès, André. *Péguy.* Paris, 1915.

Tharaud, Jérôme and Jean. *Notre cher Péguy.* 2 vols. Paris, 1926.

Vincent, Francis. "Charles Péguy," *Revue Pratique d'Apologétique,* XIX (1914).

NOTE: The above list does not include newspaper articles cited in footnotes, and it excludes the numerous references to documents published in the *Feuillets Mensuels* of the *Amitié Charles Péguy* (Paris, 1948————). Edited by the devoted and indefatigable Auguste Martin, they appear about six to eight times per year and constitute an absolutely indispensable *corpus* of evidence and information on Péguy.

C. Secondary works and articles.

a. On Péguy and his work.

Abraham, Marcel, "Charles Péguy au lycée," *Revue Hebdomadaire,* XXXV, No. 9 (1926).

Ageorges, J. "Charles Péguy, berger de son troupeau," *Le Correspondant,* CCCIII (1926).

Archambault, Paul. *Charles Péguy, images d'une vie héroique.* Paris, 1939.

Aubenque, Jacques. *Images de Péguy.* Paris, 1942.

Auriant, Georges. "Georges Sorel, Charles Péguy et les Cahiers de la Quinzaine," *Mercure de France,* CCXC and CCXCI (1939).

Avice, Robert. *Péguy, pélerin d'espérance.* Bruges, 1947.

Barbier, J. *Le vocabulaire, la syntaxe et le style des poèmes reguliers de Charles Péguy.* Paris, 1957.

————. *L'Ève de Charles Péguy.* Paris, 1963.

Béguin, Albert. *La prière de Péguy.* Neuchâtel, 1944.

————. *L'Ève de Péguy* (Cahiers de l'Amitié Charles Péguy, Nos. 3 and 4). Paris, 1948.

Bellerose, Leo M. "Le républicanisme de Péguy," *Georgetown University French Review,* VI (1938).

Boudon, Victor. *Mon lieutenant Charles Péguy.* Paris, 1964. The author has expanded his 1916 memoir into a biography of sorts, without increasing his contribution to our knowledge of Péguy.

Brunet, Frantz. *La morale de Charles Péguy.* Moulins, 1962.

Cattui, G. *Péguy témoin du temporel chrétien.* Paris, 1964.

Chabanon, Albert. *La poétique de Charles Péguy.* Paris, 1947.

Christophe, Lucien. *Le jeune homme Péguy: de la source au fleuve (1897–1905).* Paris, 1964.

————. *Les grandes heures de Charles Péguy: de la fleuve au mer (1905–1914).* Paris, 1914.

Comiti, Paulette. *Le Dieu de Péguy.* Aix-en-Provence, 1956.

David, Maurice. *Initiation à Charles Péguy.* Paris, 1945. The best introduction to the subject.

Delaporte, Jean. *Connaissance de Péguy.* 2 vols. Paris, 1944. A thorough analysis of Péguy's work.

Dru, Alexander. *Péguy.* New York, 1956.

Dubois-Dumée, J. P. *Solitude de Péguy.* Paris, 1946.

Duployé, P. *La religion de Péguy.* Paris, 1965.

Dupey, J. R. *Un utopiste du passé. Péguy penseur politique.* Aix-en-Provence, 1957.

Fonségrive, George. *L'Évolution des idées dans la France contemporaine: De Taine à Péguy.* Paris, 1920. A pioneering synthesis whose vintage makes it particularly valuable.

Fossier, Andrée. *Tables analytiques des oeuvres de Péguy.* Paris, 1948. Covers only major works published in the *Cahiers.*

Fowlie, Wallace. *De Villon à Péguy, grandeur de la pensée française.* Montreal, 1944.

Gallie, W. B. "Péguy the Moralist," *French Studies,* II (1948).

Garric, R. "Charles Péguy et Jeanne d'Arc," *Nouvelle Revue des Jeunes,* I (1929).

Goldie, Rose-Mary. *Vers un héroisme intégral dans la lignée de*

Péguy. With a preface by Albert Béguin (Cahiers de l'Amitié Charles Péguy, No. 5). Paris, 1951.

Greminger, Elisabeth. *Charles Péguy. Vom Sozialismus zur Christlichen Weltschau*. Olten, 1949. A Swiss dissertation, directed by Albert Béguin. Impressively competent and thorough.

Guillemin, Henri. "Péguy et Jaurès," *Les Temps Modernes,* No. 194 (1962).

Guyon, Bernard. *L'Art de Péguy* (Cahiers de l'Amitié Charles Péguy, No. 1). Paris, 1948.

———. *Itinéraire spirituel de Charles Péguy*. Aix-en-Provence, 1954.

———. *Péguy, l'homme et l'oeuvre*. Paris, 1960. The best biography.

Guyot, Charly. *Péguy pamphlétaire*. Neuchâtel, 1950.

Hardré, Jacques. "Charles Péguy et la mystique française," in *Romance Studies, Presented to William Morton Day*. Chapel Hill, N.C., 1950.

Henry, André. *Bergson, maître de Péguy*. Moulins, 1945.

Izard, Georges. "A la source de la pensée religieuse de Péguy," *Le Correspondant,* CCCXI (1930).

Johannet, René. *Vie et mort de Péguy*. Paris, 1950.

Jussem-Wilson, Nelly. "L'Affaire Jeanne d'Arc et l'Affaire Dreyfus," *Revue d'Histoire Littéraire de la France,* LXII (1962).

Lasserre Pierre. *Les chapelles littéraires: Claudel-Jammes-Péguy*. Paris, 1920.

Mallard, H. V. *La morale de Péguy*. With a preface by François Hertel. Paris, 1952.

Margenburg, Edith. *Charles Péguy, ein Beitrag zur Geschichtsphilosophie, Kulturkritik und Gesellschaftslehre im gegenwärtigen Frankreich*. Berlin, 1937.

Massis, Henri. *Aux sources de Charles Péguy*. Liège, 1964.

Maxence, Jean and N. Gorodetzkaya. *Charles Péguy*. Paris, 1931.

Nelson, Roy Jay. *Péguy, poète du sacré, essai sur la poétique de Péguy* (Cahiers de l'Amitié Charles Péguy, No. 13. Paris, 1960.

Onimus, Jean. *L'Image dans l'Ève de Péguy. Essai sur la symbolique et l'art de Péguy* (Cahiers de l'Amitié Charles Péguy, No. 7). Paris, 1952.

———. *Incarnation. Essai sur la pensée de Péguy* (Cahiers de l'Amitié Charles Péguy, No. 6). Paris, 1952.

———. *Introduction aux quatrains de Péguy* (Cahiers de l'Amitié Charles Péguy, No. 9). Paris, 1954.

———. *Introduction aux 'trois mystères' de Péguy* (Cahiers de l'Amitié Charles Péguy, No. 15). Paris, 1960.

————. *Péguy et le mystère de l'histoire* (Cahiers de l'Amitié Charles Péguy, No. 12). Paris, 1958.

————. *La route de Charles Péguy.* Paris, 1962.

Péguy, Marcel. *Le destin de Charles Péguy.* Paris, 1941. The son claiming the father for Pétain's national republic.

————. *Pourquoi Péguy fonda les Cahiers.* Paris, 1949. A recapitulation of the well-known circumstances attending the founding of the *Cahiers* on the eve of the fiftieth anniversary of that event.

————. "Les prophéties de Charles Péguy, essais sur la valeur prophétique du premier dialogue de la cité harmonieuse," *Le Journal Vrai, Organe des Amis de Charles Péguy,* I, 1 (1929).

————. *La rupture de Charles Péguy et de Georges Sorel.* Paris, 1930.

Péguy, Pierre. *Péguy présenté aux jeunes.* Paris, 1941. A discreet presentation by Péguy's second son, who worked for the Resistance.

Poncheville, Mabille de. *Jeunesse de Péguy.* Paris, 1943.

————. *Vie de Péguy.* Paris, 1945.

Puy, Michel. "Charles Péguy," *Les Marges,* XIX (1920).

Quoniam, Theodore. *De la sainteté de Péguy.* Paris, 1929. The most eloquent and most moving case for Péguy's catholicism.

Rousseaux, André. *Le prophète Péguy.* 2 vols. Neuchâtel, 1946.

Roussel, Jean. *Mesure de Péguy.* Paris, 1946.

Sargent, Daniel. *Four Independents: Péguy-Claudel-Hopkins-Brownson.* New York, 1935.

Secrétain, Roger. *Péguy, soldat de la liberté.* New York, Montreal, 1944.

Servais, Yvonne. *Charles Péguy: The Pursuit of Salvation.* Cork, 1953.

Suire, P. *Le tourment de Péguy.* Paris, 1956.

Truc, Gonzague. "Charles Péguy," *Grande Revue,* LXXXI (1931).

Vade, Yves. *Péguy et le monde moderne.* Paris, 1965.

Villiers, Marjorie. *Charles Péguy. A Study in Integrity.* New York, 1965.

b. On related topics.

Ahting, Georg. *Henri Alain-Fournier 1886–1914.* Barssel, 1932.

Alzona, Encarnacion. *Some French Contemporary Opinions of the Russian Revolution of 1905.* New York, 1921.

Andler, Charles. *Vie de Lucien Herr, 1864–1926.* Paris, 1932.

Arbour, Roméo. *Henri Bergson et les lettres françaises.* Paris, 1955.

Baudrillart, Cardinal Alfred (ed.). *La vie catholique dans la France contemporaine.* Paris, 1918.

Bernanos, Georges. "Jeanne relapse et sainte," *Revue Hebdomadaire,* XXXVIII, No. 7 (1929).

Boisdeffre, Pierre. *Maurice Barrès.* Paris, 1962.

Bonnerot, Jean. *Jérôme et Jean Tharaud, leur oeuvre.* Paris, 1927.

Bougeat, Jacques. *Proudhon, père du socialisme français.* Paris, 1943.

Bourgin, Hubert. *De Jaurès à Léon Blum: L'École Normale et la politique.* Paris, 1938.

Bouvier, Jean. *Le krach de l'Union Générale, 1878–1885.* Paris, 1958.

Brunetière, Ferdinand. "La mensonge du pacifisme," *Revue des Deux Mondes,* V, No. 28 (1905).

Bucaille, Victor. *La jeunesse catholique d'aujourd'hui.* Paris, 1924.

Byrnes, Robert F. *Anti-Semitism in France.* New Brunswick, N.J., 1950.

Calvet, Jean. *Le renouveau catholique dans la littérature contemporaine.* Paris, 1927.

Carré, J. M. *Les écrivains français devant le mirage allemand.* Paris, 1947.

Chapman, Guy. *The Dreyfus Affair: A Reassessment.* London, 1955.

Charpentier, John. "Paul Souday," *Mercure de France,* CCXIII (1929).

Chastenet, Jacques. *La France de M. Fallières.* Paris, 1949.

———. *La république triomphante, 1893–1906.* Paris, 1958.

Clouard, Henri. *Les disciplines.* Paris, 1913.

———. *Histoire de la littérature française, 1885–1914.* Paris, 1947.

———. *La poésie française moderne.* Paris, 1924.

Cole, G. D. H. *A History of Social Thought.* 5 vols. London, 1953–61.

Cornuz, Jean. *Jules Michelet: Un aspect de la pensée religieuse au XIXᵉ siècle.* Geneva, 1955.

Cornilleau, Robert. *De Waldeck-Rousseau à Poincaré.* Paris, 1927.

Cunsolo, Ronald S. "Libya, Italian nationalism and the revolt against Giolitti," *Journal of Modern History,* XXXVII (1965).

Curtius, Ernst T. *Maurice Barrès.* Bonn, 1921.

———. *Der Syndikalismus der Geistesarbeiter in Frankreich.* Bonn, 1921.

Daniel-Rops, Henri. *Notre Inquiétude.* Paris, 1927.

Davy, Georges. "Émile Durkheim," *Revue Française de Sociologie,* I (1960).

DeLubac, Henri. *The Un-Marxian Socialist: A Study of Proudhon.* New York, 1948.

Digeon, Claude. *La crise allemande de la pensée française, 1870–1914.* Paris, 1959.

Dominique, Pierre (pseud. Pierre Lucchini). *Les polémistes français depuis 1789.* Paris, 1962.

Drain, Henri. *Frédéric Nietzsche et André Gide.* Paris, 1932.

Fowlie, Wallace. *Ernest Psichari, A Study in Religious Conversion.* New York, 1939.

Freedman, Charles E. *The Conseil d'État in Modern France.* New York, 1961.

Freund, Michael. *Georges Sorel, der revolutionäre Konservatismus.* Frankfurt-am-Main, 1932.

Frohock, Wilbur M. *Pierre Lasserre, the Evolution of his Critical Doctrines.* Ann Arbor, Mich., 1937.

Goguel, François. *La politique des partis sous la IIIe république.* Paris, n.d.

Goldberg, Harvey. *The Life of Jean Jaurès.* Madison, Wis., 1962.

Grave, Jean. *La société mourante et l'anarchie.* With a preface by Octave Mirbeau. Paris, 1893.

Grenzmann, Wilhelm. *Die Jungfrau von Orleans in der Dichtung.* Berlin, 1929.

Grieve, J. W. *L'Oeuvre dramatique d'Edmond Rostand.* Paris, 1931.

Guy-Grand, Georges. *Le conflit des idées dans la France d'aujourd'hui.* Paris, 1921.

———. *La renaissance religieuse.* Paris, 1928.

Haac, Oscar H. *Les principes inspirateurs de Michelet.* New Haven, Paris, 1951.

Hanotaux, Gabriel. *Jeanne d'Arc.* Paris, 1911.

Hayes, Carlton J. H. *France, a Nation of Patriots.* New York, 1930.

Hughes, H. Stuart. *Consciousness and Society, 1890–1930.* New York, 1961.

Jackson, A. B. *La Revue Blanche, 1899–1903.* Paris, 1960.

Jeanné, Égide. *L'Image de la Pucelle d'Orléans dans la littérature historique française depuis Voltaire.* Liège, 1935.

Jefferson, Carter. *Anatole France: The Politics of Scepticism.* New Brunswick, N.J., 1965.

Johnson, Mary-Elizabeth. *Michelet et le christianisme.* Paris, 1951.

Jones, P. M. "Whitman in France," *Modern Language Review,* X (1915).

Kaegi, Werner. *Michelet und Deutschland*. Basel, 1938.

Koerner, Karl Wilhelm. *Jacques Rivière und die franzoesische Literatur von 1905 bis 1925*. Frankfurt-am-Main, 1929.

Kumar, Shiv K. *Bergson and the Stream of Consciousness Novel*. London and Glasgow, 1962.

Lang, Andrew. *La Jeanne d'Arc de M. Anatole France*. Paris, 1909.

Latreille, A., et al. *Histoire du catholicisme en France*. Paris, 1962.

Ligou, Daniel. *Histoire du socialisme en France, 1871–1961*. Paris, 1962.

Maitron, Jean. *Histoire du mouvement anarchiste en France (1880–1914)*. Paris, 1951.

Malon, Benoît. *Le socialisme intégral*. 2 vols. Paris, 1891.

Mesnard, Pierre. "Autour de l'École Normale avec Lucien Herr et Édouard Herriot," *La Vie Intellectuelle,* IV, No. 17 (1932).

Michon, Georges. *The Franco-Russian Alliance, 1891–1917*. Translated by Norman Thomas. London, 1929.

Morand, Paul. *1900*. Paris, 1931.

Niess, Robert J. *Julien Benda*. Ann Arbor, Mich., 1956.

Noland, Aaron. *The Founding of the French Socialist Party, 1893–1905*. Cambridge, Mass., 1956.

Roth, Jack J. "Revolution and morale in modern French thought: Sorel and the Sorelians," *French Historical Studies,* III (1963).

Roussel, Patrice. *L'Affaire Dreyfus et la presse*. Paris, 1960.

Simon, Walter H. "Comte's orthodox disciples: the rise and fall of a cénacle," *French Historical Studies,* IV (1965).

Tannenbaum, Edward R. *The Action Française: Die-Hard Reactionaries in Twentieth-Century France*. New York, 1962.

———. "The Myth of Counterrevolution in France, 1870–1914," in Harold Parker (ed.). *Ideas in History*. Durham, N.C., 1965.

Thalheimer, Siegfried. *Macht und Gerechtigkeit. Ein Beitrag zur Geschichte des Falles Dreyfus*. Munich, 1955.

Tétard, Georges. *Essais sur Jean Jaurès*. Colombes, 1959.

Van der Esch, Patricia. *La deuxième Internationale (1889–1923)*. Paris, 1957.

Virtanen, Reino. "Nietzsche and the Action Française," *Journal of the History of Ideas,* XI (1950).

Weber, Eugen. *Action Française: Royalism and Reaction in Twentieth Century France*. Stanford, Calif., 1962.

———. "Nationalism, socialism, and national socialism in France," *French Historical Studies,* II (1962).

Whiteside, Andrew. "Nationaler Sozialismus in Oesterreich vor 1918," *Vierteljahrshefte für Zeitgeschichte,* IX (1961).

Zevaès, Alexandre. *Histoire du socialisme et du communisme en France de 1871 à 1947.* Paris, 1947.

———. *Jean Jaurès.* Paris, 1951.

Ziebura, Gilbert. *Die deutsche Frage in der öffentlichen Meinung Frankreichs von 1911–1914.* Berlin, 1955.

Index